Sweeps Servants Slaves

Sweeps Servants Slaves: child labour past & present

First edition

Published by
Carnegie Publishing Ltd
Chatsworth Road,
Lancaster LA1 4SL
www.carnegiepublishing.com

British Library Cataloguing-in-Publication data
A catalogue record for this book is available from the British Library

ISBN 978–1–85936-235-8

Designed, typeset and originated by Carnegie Publishing
Printed and bound by Jellyfish Solutions

Sweeps Servants
SLAVES

child labour past & present

JENNIFER TANN

For Felicity
in gratitude, with love
Jenny

For
Isabella, Gabriel, Orla,
Rory, Connor

Contents

Acknowledgments

I AM GRATEFUL TO EVERYONE who has suggested lines of enquiry, given me references, told me stories, pointed out omissions and errors. A glance at the Bibliography will show my huge indebtedness to a number of authors on the subject of working children; in particular: Hugh Cunningham, Michael Winstanley, Michael Lavalette, Peter Kirby, Martin Woodhead, Jane Humphries, Pamela Horn, Katrina Honeyman. I thank John Loosley, Malcolm Nixon, Lorna Parker, Maureen Anderson, who have all given me original material; Angela Lamond read and helpfully commented on the final chapter; Tony Preece has been hugely helpful when the text on my computer seemed to have a mind of its own. I am grateful to Anna Goddard, Director of Carnegie Publishing, for her encouragement, and to Penny Hayashi for her scrupulous copy editing. Roger Tann has discussed issues, commented on the text and, as always, has been unfailingly helpful, I thank them all. Most of the illustrations are my own personal copies. If I have failed to acknowledge any others I apologise. All remaining errors are my own.

Illustrations

Preface

For parents and teachers of children aged between five and eight, it takes a stretch of the imagination to realise that these children's counterparts, 200 years ago, were pushed up chimneys, worked in mills standing for twelve or more hours a day, were engaged in all sorts of domestic trades, and worked underground in mines. From the ages of eight to thirteen they were expected to work longer hours; by thirteen, many were expected to earn their own keep, being treated in this respect, as adults. And, while voices were raised against child exploitation, sometimes likening it to slave labour, it took most of the nineteenth century for controlling legislation to be introduced and to be effective.

Children were employed in agriculture and craft industries from medieval times. In the Industrial Revolution they were employed in a vast range of occupations. In this book I address some of the major ones – I allude to others, but by no means all.

I have consulted a great number of sources; those contemporary to child labour, including Government Commissions, as well as recent academic and more popular writings. The main sources are listed in the Bibliography. I have quoted from quite a few contemporary accounts which record wages in sterling; all these have been converted to metric currency. I very much hope that this book will be read by those who reflect on changing conditions for working children in their own lifetimes in the West, as well as on contemporary child labour in Developing Countries.

The scene is set in the Introduction; what follows is a series of chapters, of varying length, which focus on child labour in different sectors in Britain, largely from the Industrial Revolution. The penultimate chapter considers the attempts to legislate on child labour and education in Britain, while the final chapter sets twentieth- and twenty-first-century British child labour in a world context. From this it emerges that to legislate fairly on working children is not, perhaps, as straightforward as it might, at first, appear.

Introduction

THE EMPLOYMENT OF CHILDREN was the focus of Royal Commissions in the 1840s and the 1860s. In both, Commissioners visited mining and industrial areas in Great Britain, collecting evidence from employers, teachers, local clergy and the children themselves, some of whose evidence was printed verbatim in the reports. Complemented by a range of other sources, much of the evidence from the Commissions informs this book.

The nineteenth century is characterised by piecemeal legislation governing children's employment between the first Factory Act of 1802 and the 1894 Act to license child street traders, the intentions of which were to control the worst excesses of child workplace exploitation. This meant that, while some industries were subject to legislation controlling the minimum age of employment and maximum hours of work at any one time, there were other industries and occupations without such controls, where exploitation continued. The 1844 Factory Act, for example, applied only to textile mills, limiting the work of children aged between eight and thirteen to 6.5 hours a day, instituting the concept of half-timing, a practice which was not abolished until 1918 and which could be subject to abuse, interfering with education. The definitions of a factory and a workshop became both more specific and inclusive from the second half of the nineteenth century. It was not until 1867 that workshops were covered by legislation specifying the minimum age and number of hours a child could work, while working in the home was not effectively addressed until investigated by a Parliamentary Committee in 1907. Employers and, to an even greater extent it seems, parents, were adept at turning a blind eye to legislative requirements. Until a factory inspectorate was created and given authority, with a sufficient number of inspectors, regulations were difficult to enforce.

While it was acknowledged that all children should have an education, and the Commissioners investigating children's employment in 1841/2 sought evidence on literacy and numeracy, there was not a sufficient number of school places available until the end of the nineteenth century and, until school attendance was made compulsory and education was free of charge, many parents would prioritise a child's earning potential over education. Compulsory universal education provision and child labour regulation needed to be introduced hand-in-hand. The Education Act of 1870 created the concept of compulsory education, while not insisting on it initially; it made provision for board schools for five- to ten-year-olds; these were fee-paying but the parents of poor children could be exempt. The 1876 Education Act stated that it was the duty of all parents to ensure that their children had a working knowledge of the 'three Rs', and it prohibited child employment under the age of ten.

In 1880 school attendance for five- to ten-year-olds was made compulsory, the school leaving age, thereafter, being raised to thirteen. A child under thirteen years of age could be employed but had to have a certificate to show that he/she had reached a required standard and there is evidence of a degree of collusion between some powerful local employers who sought child labour and the degree of difficulty of the locally set tests. The 1883 Elementary Education Act was followed by the radical 1902 Balfour Act in which school boards were disbanded, the divide between church and state schools abolished and Local Education Authorities established.

Child labour did not end with the 1902 Education Act; girls continued to be expected to undertake the minding of siblings and to contribute to cleaning, washing and sometimes cooking in the home; both boys and girls continued to work on milk and paper rounds, in cafés and shops, as well as having out-of-school-hours and holiday paid work. And, towards the end of the twentieth and in the twenty-first centuries, perhaps a third of young people in their mid-teens have a part-time job, besides the work-experiences sought for career advancement.

Children's work in Britain embraced a vast range of industries and activities over time, only some of which can be considered in this book.

The main focus will be on the period from the Industrial Revolution to the present day, a period that included child sweeps, children in coal mines, children who worked in furnace industries, children who were employed in outwork, often by their parents; the term 'slaves' was applied in a number of these contexts. The final chapter considers child labour in the world economy to which, once more, the term 'slaves' is sometimes applied.

Child labour was prevalent in medieval times; as soon as a young person could perform a useful task for the working family, they would have been required to do so. A statute of 1388, with reference to labour scarcity after the great plague, ordained that any boy or girl 'which used to labour at the Plough or Cart, or other Labour or Service or Husbandry till they be of Age of Twelve Years, that from thenceforth they shall abide by the same Labour, without being put to any ... Handicraft.' This must have been almost impossible to enforce and may suggest that there were other trades to which children were being put at the time.

Children of the aristocracy and gentry – the 'well-born' – often left home from the age of seven or upwards to become servants in another rich person's household. There was a large body of literature telling them how to behave: 'Keep from picking your nose, your teeth, your nails at meal-time' and 'at table beware of cleaning thy teeth with thy knife ...'

From the early sixteenth century inequality in living standards increased: the relative cost of a high-income life declined, whereas the price of staple foods for the poor rose. Society was stratified: the higher ranks had private tutors and governesses for their children; the middle-ranks could afford to keep their children at school, while the poor had difficulty in feeding and clothing their children and the child's contribution to family income, however small, was deemed more important than education. In Elizabethan times legislation expressly encouraged child labour, while the idleness of children was a cause for concern. Christ's Hospital opened in 1552 to address this. In the first year there were 340 children, all wearing blue uniforms (hence the name Blue Coat School), who were employed in spinning yarn for canvas to be used in clothing and sheets. A number of initiatives were short-lived, when it was found that the income from the children's labour did not meet the cost of provisions for them.

The 1562 Statute of Artificers set out two forms of apprenticeship: one enabled a boy to become first a journeyman and then a master at a trade which was, in London and a number of other towns, rigorously controlled by guilds; the other addressed child poverty and idleness through the activities of Guardians of the Poor. The guilds and London livery companies enforced regulations to control specific trades such as weaving, dyeing, bootmaking and many others, until the 1750s. In many towns with guilds a young person, having served their formal apprenticeship was entitled to the freedom of the town – and this included young women in sixteenth-century Bristol. These apprentices were masters-in-the-making and would not have considered themselves to be servants. Youths usually entered this kind of apprenticeship at the age of fourteen, although boys as young as ten were sometimes taken on. Premiums paid by the parents or family members ranged from about £13 to £30 and even £400 in exceptional cases. Other forms of apprenticeship were artisanal and not connected with town guilds. But, with advances in mechanisation, formal apprenticeships became less and less necessary or desirable, despite rearguard action in some threatened trades such as handloom weaving. The Statute of Artificers was repealed in 1814. Working people, nevertheless, continued to see apprenticeship to a trade as a key to economic security.

Child poverty and idleness was linked with the persistent concern that there were not enough jobs for children in the sixteenth century. A 1536 Act allowed parishes to allocate healthy children aged five to fourteen found begging, to masters in various crafts or husbandry. Idle children were regarded as potentially dangerous, but there was also concern for the child. In 1597 an Act for the Relief of the Poor was passed, being re-enacted in 1601 with slight modification and remaining on the statute book (and popularly known as The Old Poor Law) until 1834. Under this law, not only destitute and vagrant children, but all whose parents were thought to be unable to keep them, were apprenticed, the premium being paid for out of the Poor Rate. By the seventeenth century almost all indentured females, whether they were privately apprenticed or were parish apprentices, were apprenticed as 'servant maids', or in a combination of domestic and craft work such as clothing or textiles. In the seventeenth and eighteenth centuries a fifth of female parish apprentices in the southern counties of England were apprenticed in agriculture, others being apprenticed in clothing, food or drink. While many poor children probably endured a life of drudgery as apprentices, there are occasional stories of enlightened training. Tom Grenville was a blind boy at the London Foundling Hospital. In 1753, when he was seven years old, the governors agreed that he could receive harpsichord lessons. He was a quick and enthusiastic learner and two years later the governors agreed that he could be taught to play the organ. He left the Hospital at the age of 21 and, thereafter, supported himself as an organist until, in later years, he fell into poverty and was granted a pension.

The Foundling Hospital was opened in 1741, the result of what, in the eighteenth century was called 'associated philanthropy' – a group of people coming together to form an organisation for a specific cause. It took nearly twenty years to become a reality – Thomas Coram having decided, in 1722, to do something about babies he saw abandoned in the streets. A house was secured in Hatton Garden, London, in 1741; the house was opened at 8 p.m. on the first day and the doors were closed by midnight – it was full. Babies, if healthy, were sent out to be nursed and then returned to London or to one of six provincial branch hospitals where, from the age of three upwards, they were educated and trained, the boys mainly going to sea and the girls to domestic service. It was the governors' policy that children should learn to accept the 'most Servile and laborious offices', and not to have the expectation of jobs which children raised by their parents might expect. That would be to compare abandoned babies with children of the middling classes, rather than children who, while raised by their families, lived in poverty and, at least in London, worked on the streets in the eighteenth and

The purpose-built Foundling Hospital, London; founded by Thomas Coram, a philanthropic sea captain. This building, originally a single wing, was begun in 1745, a second wing being added in 1752, to separate boys from girls.

nineteenth centuries. William Blake, in his *Songs of Experience* wrote that 'their ways are fill'd with thorns; It is eternal winter there.' There was little pretence about these children acquiring skills. After the payment of an indenture fee, the poorhouse child was dispatched to work for no wage but their keep, and the system was open to abuse. And abuse, in many cases, it was. The child was bound to the age of 21, notwithstanding the early age at which some were apprenticed. Some received minimum pay towards the end of their apprenticeship; some did not.

Poor Law authorities not only dispatched children to distant mills but also to the army and navy. In 1797 three regiments were formed with the aim, partly of relieving parishes of pauper boys. There were 1000 boys in each regiment. In 1756 poor boys were taken from the streets of London and clothed by Lord Harry Powlett, to add to his crew. This, it is alleged, inspired Jonas Hanway (a champion of London child sweeps) to found the Marine Society to take destitute boys, clothe them and, after some basic training, send them to sea in either the Royal or the merchant navy. 10,625 boys and men were sent by the Society into the Navy during the Seven Years' War. While the scheme was admired by many, others alleged that: 'all the sweepings of the unions ... and the troublesome boys of the Neighbourhood' were being recruited. In the mid-nineteenth century thousands of workhouse boys were still being recruited. During the age of sailing warships, boys were recruited as powder monkeys, whose task was to take gunpowder from the ship's hold to the guns on deck – a highly dangerous task for which they were given a patronising nickname. Many boys were kidnapped for the task which they usually did between the ages of twelve and fourteen. And pauper boys were still recruited for ships, early in the twentieth century; for Grimsby fishing vessels.

Boy soldiers, often called 'drummer boys', had been employed in the British army in times of war over the centuries; 4000 were involved in the 1815 Battle of Waterloo, for instance. They were in the Crimean War and, in 1900 Robert Baden Powell recruited twelve-year-old boys to deliver messages under fire in the Siege of Mafeking during the Boer War, the team being led by thirteen-year-old Warner Goodyear. The American Civil War of 1861–65 has sometimes been called the Boys' War on account of the high proportion of children in the armies on both sides; boys from the age of eight upwards. Between one tenth and one third of all troops were said to have been under-age in the First World War; approximately 250,000

British under-age boys signed up for the army. They lied about their age; they were required to be eighteen years old before they could join up and nineteen before going overseas; some changing their names so that they could not be traced by parents. In the Second World War many child soldiers fought in Eastern Europe in, for example, the Warsaw Uprising and the Jewish Resistance.

The economic value of young children to outworking parents was admired by some eighteenth-century commentators, such as Daniel Defoe. As winders, stitchers, menders, bellows blowers, bird scarers, they performed tedious tasks hour upon hour. During the 1820s and '30s there was an increase in child work and children were engaged at a younger age. If a child began work at a younger age, schooling was likely to suffer and, on growing older and reaching adulthood, he/she could possibly be less able to earn a decent living wage to support their own children, thus perpetuating the cycle. One boy began punching cards for jacquard looms before he was seven and became a half-time piecer at his eighth birthday. At the legal minimum age he was taken on for full-time work but was subsequently turned down by an examining surgeon, whereupon he obtained work in an unregulated sector. Some children knowingly broke the law by working overtime, aged thirteen, if they believed that their home circumstances required it – living with a disabled widowed mother, for example.

As the price paid for domestic labour such as handloom weaving fell, fathers worked longer hours but were unable to support a family and children began work at a younger age. Other domestic industries suffered too, for example boot and shoemaking. A London bootmaker visited Northampton, a provincial centre of the industry, in the 1820s and was appalled to see equipment redesigned to enable women and children to be employed. This led to a reduction in the price paid for closing shoes in Northampton. The choice was stark; either the man worked for sixteen hours a day to scrape a living for his family, or his work was assisted by women and children whose labour had led to the reduction in wages in the first place.

Not even compulsory schooling and more effective workshop inspection eradicated child employment in outwork, for children could still be expected to work in the evenings and on Sundays. A report of 1899 estimated that more than 200,000 children were still employed at home part-time and in 1907 a woman giving evidence to the Select Committee on Homework described children being at work before and after school in the Somerset gloving industry, in lace finishing in Nottingham and in box making, button-carding and other workshop trades in Birmingham.

Whatever the causes for the reduction in the number of children employed in a wide range of industries – and various explanations have been put forward – it is clear that, by the 1880s, the proportion of children aged five to nine that worked was a very small percentage of the total number in the age group – less than 1 per cent is a figure that has been put forward. Some have suggested that changes in technology e.g. in mining during the 1830s, and in many of the so-called outwork industries in the 1870s, making outwork too low-paid, led to less demand for child labour; others argue that compulsory education gave the state a key role and, although half-timing was permitted into the twentieth century, the pattern of regular school attendance was gradually enforced. Still others write of 'the new childhood' – a different way of thinking about childhood, promoted by the 'socially conscious well connected' who argued that child labour was a social evil, since it did not conform to the idea of a proper childhood. But there is also the argument that child labour should not only be seen as an issue of supply, but also of demand, for technological change, particularly in the textile industries, increased child employment not only as helpers to adults, but also as substitutes.

The early Industrial Revolution saw younger children starting factory work, particularly orphans or those from fatherless families. Did child work enable family living standards to rise? Did parents, besides employers, exploit children? Was children's work essential to the course of the Industrial Revolution? Was there an inevitable knock-on effect from child labour – namely that the children of parents who had worked early in their lives were expected to work too? Was schooling inevitably crowded-out? Were there any benefits to the child? Why did child labour begin to decline in Britain? And why does it continue in the developing world, despite resolutions of the United Nations and the International Labour Office to ban it? Answers to these questions are not straightforward, but it is important that they are explored.

ONE

Agriculture

Children had worked on the land from well before the Industrial Revolution. In rural areas there was often little alternative employment. They could be put to a wide range of activities depending on their age and the time of year. William Stout (1665–1757), a Quaker from a small-scale landowning family in Lancashire, described how, from the age of ten he was frequently taken out of school in the spring and summer to help with ploughing, hay-making and harvest, besides attending to sheep and shearing. Not surprisingly, when he returned to school in the autumn, he could not remember much of what he had been taught the previous spring. But he was fortunate in coming from a sufficiently well-to-do family to stay at school until he was ten. Many children from poorer families received little or no education and were required to work in all weathers from a very young age.

This practice continued in the eighteenth and nineteenth centuries, schooling being a low priority when large families needed to be fed. The rector of a Nottingham parish, writing in 1814, regretted that his efforts to extend schooling were hindered by 'the objections of the farmers to losing the labour of a boy who is capable of work, and the inability of the parents to forgo the price of that labour.' And seasonal tasks, when put together, could become year-round work. Like many boys, William Arnold first worked as a crow-scarer in fields newly sown with wheat and barley during late February and early March, after which, when the barley had grown sufficiently, he was sent to mind a flock of 100 sheep. He then had to help his mother and father in reaping with a sickle, after which he worked with the waggon team, carrying the harvest. Later in the year he was sent to mind pigs (reflecting that he much preferred the sheep.) At the conclusion of the acorn harvest he was put to driving the plough. And all this before he was seven years old.[1]

In the late eighteenth/early nineteenth centuries, a number of measures for relieving poverty were publicised by The Society for Bettering the Condition and Increasing the Comfort of the Poor, whose four-volumes of Reports were published in 1801/2. One of the most frequently reported-on examples was a House of Industry. These were built in both rural and urban locations and accommodated several hundred men, women and children at any one time; sometimes taking in children on their own from very large families. Around half the inmates of one House of Industry in Norfolk were under the age of fourteen. At that age they were distributed to local farmers or tradespersons for a year, but many were returned at the end of the year 'being found too delicate to perform that service which the farmer gets from those he hires out of cottages'. The author of the Norfolk account was adamant that:

> children brought up in cottages, half naked, and indifferently fed, make hardier and better labourers than those in parish workhouses ... tho' the latter generally look healthy, yet they become so delicate as to be unfit for husbandry labour in a farmer's service.[2]

The apprenticing of pauper children to farms seems to have been routine in the eighteenth century, but farmers were not necessarily willing to take them and considerable pressure was exerted in some areas to ensure that they took their share. West Country boys were put out from the age of nine, whereas in Devon they were apprenticed from eight years old. In Southampton it was twelve for boys and ten for girls. The compulsory binding of pauper children to farming until the age of 21 was frowned on by a governor of a House of Industry in Norfolk who commented that, with free labour (apart from bed, food and clothing) held over so many years, the master was less likely to use his apprentice well: 'surely to bind a young lad ... to twenty-one, to husbandry ... merely because he is out of work at the time is a harsh and violent measure.'[3] Many young children living at home first undertook part-time or casual work on farms – smaller farmers being unwilling to support a young child for a year when the need for their labour was seasonal. Only when they were older could they expect to be hired as living-in servants. The custom of hiring yearly living-in servants had more or less ended by the 1830s, farm servants and labourers being less welcome in the farmer's household – an indication, perhaps, of perceived class differences between farmer and labourer, besides the seasonality of the work.

In the late 1830s William Howitt described the work of young farm boys whose first job was often minding a field gate:

> to stop cattle from straying ... They are sent to scare birds from corn just sown or just ripening ... they help to glean, to gather potatoes, to pop beans into holes in dibbing time, to pick hops, to gather up apples for the cider-mill, to gather mushrooms and blackberries for market, to herd flocks of geese or young turkeys, or lambs at weaning time.[4]

Boy bird scarer: children as young as four scared birds with a rattle for over 12 hours. It was very lonely. (Mary Evans Picture Library)

They might help to drive sheep to market or to the sheep-wash at shearing time and they were useful in the farmyard too, shredding turnips and beetroot, carrying wood for the fire, 'They are mighty useful animals in their day and generation'. In mid-century a young boy of five or six might be employed as a bird-scarer, a long and lonely job sitting in a field with a rattle or gong. Some boys preferred shouting to swinging a rattle or banging a gong – at least it was a human voice even if it was his own: 'This method had another convenience, you couldn't cry while you shouted.'[5] He would be there from dawn until dusk, and there were no Sundays off. A Hertfordshire boy began to work as a bird scarer in the 1830s, aged seven. For part of the year he worked seven days a week from 4 a.m. to 8 p.m. for 7.5p 'plenty of work for little money and not much food'[6] was how he described it. A Lincolnshire boy, interviewed in 1866, worked from 6 a.m. until 6 p.m. bird scaring, and longer hours from 5 a.m. till 8 p.m. when the barley was sprouting and the hours of daylight longer, for 1.5p a day. Work varied with the seasons and this placed a strain on family budgets. Weeding, stone picking and setting potatoes were done in the spring, as was minding sheep and pigs in fields or by the roadside. One Warwickshire boy, in the 1870s, recalled how dreary the work was, particularly when the weather was cold. He said that he liked the pigs best and used to give them names. Weeding often involved children crawling between crops on their hands and knees to pull out long-rooted weeds, such as twitch grass, by hand. Stone pickers were paid by the load, eighty two-gallon pails comprising a load in Hertfordshire. A full bucket was heavy to lift and the children had to work long hours to earn a pittance.

Haymaking began in June and, where the grass was scythed by hand, two children walked behind each man, picking up the grass and sprinkling it around to dry. If cutting machinery was used children might be employed to lead the horses, rake up the hay and fetch ale from the farm. Girls were often employed in the fields at harvest time or were kept off school to mind younger siblings, whilst the mothers helped with the harvest. The prospects were grim and unremitting for any young person who could recognise alternatives: 'A black depression spread over me. This is what its going to be from now on, I thought ... Lifting, hauling, shoving, trudging about ... and no hope of getting out of it'.[7]

Ploughboys began their working days earlier than many other child farm workers. At 4 a.m. or 5 a.m. the horses had to be fed and made ready to begin work at around 7 a.m. A ploughboy could regularly walk ten miles a day 'driving the plough in wet, dirty, land'. One fourteen-year-old Gloucestershire ploughboy who had begun full-time farm work aged eleven, ploughed about ¾ acre a day. He would eat his dinner on returning to the stable in the late afternoon and would then help to look after the horses. He generally finished work at 7 p.m. and was home half an hour later. He was fortunate in not being required to 'supper-up' the horses for the night which would have taken him well into the evening.

Physical abuse and cruel treatment of bird scarers and ploughboys seems to have been fairly common practice. Sometimes a boy could identify the reason, while believing the violence to have been unmerited; at other times it seems that the adult, be it parent, immediate boss such as a ploughman, or farmer, randomly meted out violence, some seeming to take a delight in finding the most painful implement with which to flog. An orphan, having had a tolerable upbringing in a workhouse, was subjected to the most brutal treatment at the hands of his master when apprenticed by the Overseers to a farmer. He was pushed to the ground, his thigh broken and, when he crawled into bed, his master threatened to 'knock out his brains' if he did not get up to work. Eventually, severely disabled and bent double, he was returned to the workhouse.[8] Joseph Arch wrote: 'They used their tongues and their whips and their boots ... it is no exaggeration to say that ... life ... was not a whit better than that of a plantation [slave] boy.'[9]

On stock-raising farms the work involved carrying heavy loads of meal and turnips – one young Yorkshire worker recalled: 'I was too small to keep out of the muck, and waded through slop and cow-muck until I became absolutely lost. My breeches became so caked in pig-swill, calf-porridge and meal I believe they could have stood upright without me inside them.'[10] He later moved to a farm that concentrated on sheep and barley where 200–300 sheep were being fattened on turnips: 'we have no picture of the shepherd in the muddy turnip field ... sliding about in the muddy sheep-pen with skeps of sliced turnips.'[11]

In 1851, 5463 boys aged between five and nine and 73,054 aged between ten and fourteen worked as agricultural labourers in England and Wales; 53 aged between five and nine and 1020 between ten and fourteen worked as shepherds, while 451 from five to nine years and 25,667 aged from ten to fourteen worked as farm servants. Far fewer girls worked on farms – 193 aged between five and nine and 10,085 between ten and fourteen. But these were the full-timers and many more worked part-time, not being counted in the census. Younger girls were rarely employed in agriculture, one reason being that their long skirts regularly got soaked, resulting in rheumatics and other problems. This led to absenteeism and farmers did not think very young female workers were worth the trouble.

Farm labourers' daughters 'help their mothers ... in their cottages, as soon almost as they can waddle about. They are scarcely more than infants themselves when they are set to take care of other infants. The little creatures go lugging about great fat babies that really seem as heavy as themselves.' They could be seen congregating with others on green patches in the lanes, 'two or three juvenile nurses, with their charges, carrying them along, or letting them roll on the sward, while they try to catch a few minutes of play with one another' so wrote William Howitt.[12] As they grew older these girls would clean the house, feed the pig, run errands and, when they reached the age of ten or twelve, they became nursemaids at the farm-houses or, a little older still, would go into service, aspiring to be dairymaids or housemaids so they 'go on scrubbing and scouring and lending a hand in the harvest field till they are married.'

In many parts of the country grain harvest was the most important event of the farming year. It began in late August in a good year but later if the summer had been wet and cold. Grain had to be cut and dried, sometimes in adverse weather conditions, and both full-time and temporary labour was required, often working late into the evenings. Some children led the horses, others took refreshments to the men and the majority made bands of straw with which to tie up the sheaves of corn. Where reaping machines were used men, women and children were usually allocated to a specific machine. It was not unusual for a young boy to be hired by a small farmer to make bands for corn sheaves, then to lead carts for carrying the harvest, starting work at 4 a.m. and arriving home exhausted at around 9 p.m. There were other benefits to the family from work at harvest time, besides the children's meagre wages. Older boys could stand with the men as the corn was cut, waiting to knock down and kill rabbits that had become marooned in the ever diminishing standing corn. Rabbit stew or pie was a very welcome addition to the family diet. In the days before modern harvesting machinery, some corn was left in the fields for women and children to glean, gathering up the grain that was left behind – an activity that goes back to Biblical times.

Children gleaning after harvest to collect grain remaining in the field.

The father would then thresh the gleaned grain with a flail before it was ground into flour.

Children living at home and working on the land gave their wages to their mothers – it was 'an unwritten law'.[13] Rates of pay in agriculture varied by task and to some extent by age. James Hawker, aged eight, earned 5p for a seven-day week in 1844 : 'This sum Brought my Mother a four Pound Loaf.'[14] A boy bird-scarer typically earned 1.67p a day between the 1790s and 1850s, a ploughboy might earn 15p a week between the 1790s and 1820s but rates fell in the mid- to late-nineteenth century. A general labourer could earn between 30p and 45p a week in the mid-nineteenth century. And a teenage boy could earn as much as his father, becoming a second breadwinner, certainly earning more than his mother. A married women's daily pay in the seventeenth and eighteenth centuries was around 2.5p, and, in the nineteenth century from under 3p to 4.2p a day. Even if she worked five or six days a week she did not earn as much as a ploughboy or a teenage herdsman. Boys came to be regarded as a family's main secondary earners, girls earning significantly less than boys in all occupations in the nineteenth and for much of the twentieth centuries. Children who began as casual labourers in agriculture did, sometimes, become skilled farm workers. Joseph Arch began twelve hour shifts as a crow-scarer at the age of seven or eight, in the 1830s, earning roughly 2p per day. After two or three years he became a ploughboy earning 2.5p per day and, aged fourteen, a stable boy on 40p a week, earning as much as his father.

In the first half of the nineteenth century a great deal of waste land was brought under cultivation. During the French wars between 1805 and 1815 grain prices were high and the Lincolnshire Wolds were cleared of gorse, thistles and grass and put down to wheat and barley. Later in the century additional fen lands, such as Deeping Fen, north of Peterborough, were drained and cultivated. In the parts of England characterised by large farms and more dispersed villages, notably East Anglia, south Lincolnshire and Nottinghamshire and, to a lesser extent, Northamptonshire, Rutland and Bedfordshire, there was a large demand for labour at specific points in the farming year, depending on the crops grown. It would have been uneconomic for the farmer to employ large numbers all the year round, or to go in search of temporary labour.

Children in an agricultural gang. On large farms in the east of England, work was often undertaken by gangs. Many children had to walk some miles to a farm and became exhausted. (Mary Evans Picture Library)

Instead, he either organised his own private gang from women and children in the nearest village who would come at busy times in the farming year, or he would sub-contract particular work, such as potato picking or hoeing, to a gang-master who undertook to manage the task for an agreed fee. The gang-master, often an out-of-work farm labourer, employed between ten and forty young children, together with a few adults, to do the work. The gang system was well established by the 1840s, reaching its height in the '50s. By the 1860s the system was subject to intense criticism and was investigated by the Children's Employment Commission in 1866, it being believed that there was 'nothing more shocking ... than the sufferings incidental to the employment of young children in certain kinds of agricultural labour'.[15]

It was clearly in the gang-master's interests to have the work completed as quickly as possible, so as to be able to move on to work at another farm. In one Huntingdon parish, out of a gang of 40, 22 were aged between seven and thirteen years and five were under seven years old. The distances walked by the children each day could be as much as seven miles each way which added considerably to the length of the working day, besides the level of exhaustion. One observer noted in 1867 'You see the big ones dragging the little ones home, and sometimes taking them on their backs when they are overtired.' One girl said, 'I have walked home without my shoes, because we thought it tired us less.' Some gangmasters were cruel, resorting to whipping, beating with implements, kicking, knocking down or pushing a child into cold water.[16]

Gang work varied according to the season. In winter, when the demand for their labour was less, they worked at clearing stones or sorting potatoes. There was greater variety in spring; some cleared the long-rooted couch grass, painstakingly pulling out each root by hand; others planted potatoes, hoed fields or spread muck. The period of peak demand was summer when fallow fields were cleared of couch grass; fields of growing grain and root crops were hand-weeded, and hay had to be harvested. Children re-joined family members during the season of grain harvest in August and September, entire families going out into the fields together. And gangs re-formed in October for the potato harvest. In 1866, in the East Midlands and East Anglia, 6,399 people were said to have worked in gangs at some point in the year.

The Kentish hop harvest was undertaken by gangs of men, women and children recruited from the East End of London, supplemented by local children. The school year in Kent was subservient to the agricultural year with three weeks off in July for fruit picking, then a month back at school before another month off for hop picking, for which the payment was usually 5p for eight bushels. After each day's work the hops were weighed and the workers were paid at the end of the week. One girl recalled 'with the money we had earned, mother fitted us out with new clothes for the winter'. In Yorkshire a gang of women and girls 'in white smocks and rustic bonnets and kerchiefs' were seen potato picking in 1863. In some areas there was a sufficient variety of crops grown to keep children working on the land from spring through to the end of autumn: osier-peeling in May, pea picking in June, then hay and harvest, and finally potato gathering in October, followed by turnip pulling. Pulling turnips was described as 'perhaps the most pernicious employment to which a child can be set; it strains the spine, and often lays the foundation for chronic disease.'[17]

Agricultural gangs were disliked by many of those who worked in them, besides some of the more sensitive mid-Victorian observers who were shocked by the foul language used by adults and children alike and by the lack of segregation of the sexes. The rate of illegitimacy amongst gang females was said to be double that of Britain as a whole. Gang work interfered with school attendance and gang masters were not liked; a gang master was looked down on 'almost worse ... than a policeman.' For the gang master, there was no incentive to care about the children in his employ. It was in his interests to work them as hard as he possibly could and then to move on to the next farm.

An elderly woman reminisced about her East Anglian childhood in the 1860s. She left school at the age of eight to begin working in the fields with 40–50 other children – she being the eldest. They worked for fourteen hours a day, followed all day long by an old man carrying a long whip in his hand which he used frequently. They had a walk of two or more miles to the fields morning and evening and, in all the four years she worked in the fields, she never worked under cover. On one memorable day she and her workmates were invited into a small cottage during a sleet and snow storm. When it was dinner time the children were preparing to sit down under a hedge to eat their cold food when the shepherd's wife came towards them and invited them to her two-roomed cottage. There was only just room to stand but the shepherd's wife had such compassion for the freezing cold youngsters that she put the furniture out into the garden and the children sat in a ring on the floor. She then placed a very large saucepan of hot boiled potatoes in the middle and invited the children to help themselves. Not one meal eaten since then had ever seemed half as good as that meal.

In 1865 Lord Shaftesbury, amongst other politicians, persuaded the Government to require the Children's Employment Commission to investigate agricultural gangs. Some 500 witnesses gave evidence and the report on gangs was presented two years later in 1867. Gangs and gangmasters were heavily criticised, most of the latter being 'men of violent and drinking habits', older gang members being 'coarse and irregular' and the young people 'hardened by early association with vice.' In particular the Commissioners considered much gang work to be unsuitable for women and girls. Weeding a soaking wet field in a skirt was likened to wet spinning and Commissioners believed that it should be stopped. Moreover 'Field work renders them unfit for (domestic) service'. They were said to develop 'a love for unhealthy liberty ... they turn aside from service in farm or other houses, know little or nothing of sewing, washing, making or mending.' However one labourer's wife, in giving evidence to the Commission, said that her two daughters had both been in gangs before entering domestic service. Asserting that gang work both damaged the physical health and moral well-being of children and young people, the Commissioners' recommendations were framed as a Parliamentary Bill. Some evidence from older children was not negative, a ten-year-old boy acknowledging that he would not mind going again. Perhaps it was viewed as some relief from school – the Commissioners proposed a system of part-timing at school for children in gangs but Parliament did not accept this recommendation and the Agricultural Gangs Act was passed in 1867. A licensing system for gang masters was to be established; no child under eight years of age was to work in a gang, and men and women were prohibited from working in the same gang.

By the 1890s, competition from cheap imported grain and dairy products, besides refrigerated meat, reduced the demand for labour on farms, farmers putting their own children to work before and after school and changing from arable to pastoral farming, with machinery substituting, in part, for labour at harvest time. But, where there were labour-intensive jobs, farmers recruited their own private gangs of women and children (which were not subject to the Agricultural Gangs Act), children joining these from the ages of seven or eight. Jobs varied with the seasons: picking stones and sorting potatoes in January, spreading dung, singling (thinning out) turnips and setting potatoes in March, weeding in April, May and June, gathering hay in July, harvesting or pulling flax in August and September, gathering wood and gleaning, spreading dung, potato picking, and gathering turnips, carrots and mangolds until the frosts came. Farm hands were expected to supply additional labour from their families when needed and in the 1890s Dorset farmers advertised for labourers 'with a working family'.

In farming areas nearer to larger towns, market gardening was carried out, child labour being important for fruit picking, pea pulling, and potato gathering. In the mid-nineteenth century Kent children were paid 1.5p per day for picking gooseberries and currants and, later, plums, cherries, and hazelnuts. They were also hired for hop picking. Market gardening was particularly intense in the area between Dartford and London. In the Vale of Evesham, especially around Pershore, fruit picking, hop gathering and, from the mid-nineteenth century, the intensive cultivation of cabbage, rhubarb and strawberries, required child labour. One producer, alone, employed 200–300 women and children on 140 acres of gooseberries, currants and plums, paying the mothers for the quantity of fruit picked.

Despite the passing of the Agricultural Gangs Act in 1867 and subsequent Education Acts, the demand for child workers in agriculture continued, frequently at the cost of schooling. All schools in rural areas had to contend with high absenteeism during harvest and other demanding seasons in the farming year such as beating for shooting parties, pea and currant picking, hay and corn harvesting, school logbooks recording the frustration of head teachers. Head teachers seemed powerless to persuade parents to prioritise their children's education, log books recording high rates of absenteeism at different points in the farming year and particularly at harvest. In some instances the head teacher would close the school in desperation. Children of smallholders were the poorest school attenders of all, evidence that parents could require more labour from their own children than wage-paying farmers, paralleling the situation in many out-work industries. Education suffered, many teachers complaining that children forgot much of what they had learned in their absences from school. A concerned Buckinghamshire teacher recorded in November 1877 that two boys had returned to school after nearly three months' absence 'gone back terribly in their reading and writing.' A school master in Childrey, Berkshire, wrote on 1 October 1888 'Late harvest ... I opened school, only nine scholars came, the other schools closed for another week, so we closed for the week.'[18] A pattern of fitting agricultural and farm-house work around the school day and at weekends emerged, a pattern replicated in other areas of children's work too. One lad recalled milking five cows on the family farm before breakfast, delivering milk to several leaders in the community, cleaning his shoes 'because they were wet and the only pair I had' and then going to school. After school he got the cows in from the meadow, milked the same five, separated the cream and delivered the milk on his way home, arriving home at about 6 p.m. He worked from 6 a.m. to 6 p.m. on Saturdays.

The Agricultural Children's Act of 1873, implemented in 1875, prohibited children of under eight years of age being employed in agriculture; from the ages of eight to ten they were required to undertake a minimum of 250 school attendances and if certified as having reached this, they could undertake work part time. The Act was, however, poorly drafted and (mirroring the early Factory Acts) no agency was specified to ensure that its provisions were carried out. The 1870 Education Act required that adequate elementary education should be provided in all parts of the country. The 1876 Education Act required school attendance committees to be set up where there were no school boards (predominantly in areas serviced by church schools) but it was the 1880 Education Act, making education compulsory for five- to fourteen-year-olds, which was specifically concrete in its requirements to enable HMIs to inspect and report on non-attendance. This Act did not require full-time education beyond the age of ten, however (the age of eleven in 1893), children of ten to twelve being required to make 250 attendances a year and, from the age of twelve, to attend on 150 occasions.

Half timing was widely practised in the early twentieth century and, when the 1914–18 war broke out, farmers were quick to recruit child labour. It has been suggested that farmers did not like the idea that their labourers' children would receive a better school education as this would make them unwilling to work on farms for low wages. Under pressure from farmers, local education authorities allowed boys as young as ten and eleven to leave school to work on farms and, during the War, several hundred thousand elementary school children may have left school for farm work. Within a month of the outbreak of the Second World War some British rural education authorities decided to permit children to be withdrawn from school, and magistrates in some areas ignored the illegal employment of school age children. In April 1942 children aged twelve and upwards were allowed to miss up to twenty days of school (and more if necessary) to work on the land. Farmers saw this as a precedent and began to act as if they could 'get child labour for the asking'. Children were the cheapest form of labour available and could be hired and turned-off with ease. It took until the end of the Second World War for child labour in agriculture to cease to be regarded as a disposable commodity.

TWO

Climbing boys

CHIMNEYS ON HOUSES were introduced in around the thirteenth century and, being wide, they were relatively easy to sweep with brooms. This was a task for servants in larger houses and was most probably done by women of the household in smaller houses. But, from the mid-seventeenth century, narrower chimneys became fashionable and, by the early eighteenth century, master sweeps touted for the work, the task of sweeping being undertaken by children, almost always boys, from the age of five upwards. While, in comparison with other forms of childhood employment, the total number of child chimney sweeps was relatively small, the plight of climbing boys through accidents, disease and the cruelty of their masters made them the first child workers to be the focus of public campaigns. And it is from the various campaigners for the abolition of the employment of child sweeps that most of the evidence comes.

Young boys from large, poor, families were apprenticed – or rather sold – by their parents to sweeps; in addition, workhouse orphans were regularly apprenticed. One father told Henry Mayhew in the mid-nineteenth century that his son began climbing chimneys at the age of four years and eight months, while the youngest sweep on record was probably a three and a half year-old from Suffolk, identified in 1795. 'The best age for teaching boys is about six,' a master-sweep told the Children's Employment Commission of 1863. He continued:

> That is thought a nice trainable age. But I have known two at least of my neighbours' children begin at the age of five. I once saw a child only 4½

A boy sold by his mother; this occurred in cases of dire poverty.

years in the market-place in his sooty clothes and with his scraper in his hand … he began when he was four.[1]

In 1848 a boy was stolen in Nottingham and sold to a chimney sweeper at Hull. Another boy aged ten years was sold, successively, to five different sweeps and, when he was eventually brought before the magistrates, he couldn't walk. He was examined by a surgeon in court who removed his bandages, shocking the magistrates who learned that the boy had been carried from place to place and made to climb twelve chimneys on the previous Saturday. The mayor said 'Talk about slavery: there is no slavery in the world like that.'[2] A master sweep in the Staffordshire Potteries used to buy children from their parents, telling the Children's Employment Commission in 1862 'In Liverpool, where there are lots of bad women, you can get any quantity you want.'[3] Boys were frequently kidnapped in rural areas and children from more well-to-do families were warned by their parents not to wander with the threat: 'the sweeps will get you'.[4] A poem written in 1806 captures the scene:

> 'Sweep! Sweep! Sweep! Sweep!' cries little Jack
> With brush and bag upon his back,
> And black from head to toe ...
> But then he was not always black ...
> But, silly child! He ran to play
> Too far from home, a long, long, way ...
> So he was lost and now must creep
> Up chimneys crying sweep! sweep! sweep!'[5]

While most child sweeps were boys there were also some chimney girls. Two girls, working for their father, a master-sweep, swept the chimneys of Windsor Castle, while girl apprentices were noted by the 1819 Children's Employment Commission at Uxbridge, Brighton, Witham (Essex) and Headley (Herefordshire).

Chimneys could be as narrow as 23 cm (9 ins) in diameter and many had perilous bends in them. A good master would train a boy by sending him up with a more experienced sweep behind to keep him from falling, but many masters would make the boys strip and go up naked and alone. Since climbing a narrow and dangerous chimney was so frightening, the boy was often forced to climb by being beaten; pins were stuck into his feet by the person below, possibly a more experienced boy, and sometimes lighted straw was used to force the frightened child up the chimney. A boy sweep told Mayhew in the 1860s:

'In wide flues you climb it with your elbows and your legs spread out, your feet pressing against the side of the flue; but in narrow flues, such as nine-inch ones, you must slant it; you must have your side in the angles, it's wider there, and go up just that way ... you see how small you can make yourself. I niver got stuck myself, but a many of them did; yes and were taken out dead. They were smothered for want of air, and the fright and a stayin' so long in the flue.'[6]

A report on London sweeps in 1801 estimated that, of approximately 200 master sweeps, there were 'not above twenty who can make a decent livelihood by it.' In most cases the master sweep was a lodger with one room for himself, his wife and children and an adjoining cellar in which the apprentices lived with no bed but the bags of soot.

When a boy first began to learn the business of chimney sweeping his elbows and knees became very sore and, when the sores festered and broke, he couldn't climb chimneys without a great deal of pain. A considerate master would put pads over the sores but, more generally, sores were treated by rubbing in salt to harden the skin. A master sweep of Nottingham gave a statement to the 1863 Children's Employment Commission:

> No one knows the cruelty which a boy has to undergo in learning. The flesh must be hardened. This is done by rubbing it, chiefly on the elbows and knees with the strongest brine, as that got from a pork-shop, close by a hot fire. You must stand over them with a cane, or coax them by the promise of a halfpenny, etc., if they will stand a few more rubs.
>
> At first they will come back from their work with their arms and knees streaming with blood, and the knees looking as if the caps had been pulled off. Then they must be rubbed with brine again, and perhaps go off at once to another chimney.[7]

One witness, having acknowledged that he had kept a child up a chimney for four hours 'when he was so sore he could hardly move', wouldn't allow him down until the task was completed, added 'it has often made my heart wail. In learning a child you can't be soft with him – you must use violence.'

Most climbing boys went to bed unwashed, their eyes sore from rubbing them with sooty hands. They might have three to six baths a year. By the mid-nineteenth century, a weekly wash had become more common. In the worst living conditions, soot was ever-present, and sweeps were particularly prone to cancer of the scrotum – it was often called the chimney sweeper's cancer. A master sweep from Nottingham said that he had known eight or nine child sweeps lose their lives by the sooty cancer caused by sleeping black (unwashed) and breathing in the soot all night.

A sweep's home; many sweeps lived in poverty; they washed infrequently and soot was everywhere.

A surgeon, giving evidence before a Parliamentary Committee in 1817, spoke of the deformity of child sweeps' spines, legs and arms as a result of climbing chimneys when their bones were soft, besides being required to carry heavy bags of soot. Mayhew reported that the little chimney sweepers appeared to be 'pitiable in the extreme'. The boy sweeper trotted listlessly behind his master with a sack to contain the soot thrown over his shoulder or draped round his neck like a cape. The poorer masters clothed 'the urchins in any old rags which their wives could piece together or in any low-priced garment found in the streets'. Shoes and stockings were not included and were bought second-hand, if at all.

Some master sweeps looked after their apprentices well for the times. One of them was David Porter, of London, who campaigned for better conditions for child sweeps. He had once been a chimney sweeper's boy; his boys were 'kindly treated and well kept'; they were always 'cleaned and made neat' on Saturday evenings or early on Sundays, regularly attended church on Sundays and were never sent out on that day.[8] But there were publicised cases of extreme cruelty, in some cases the master sweep being taken to court. In 1801 two people walking along a south London street heard a cry and, on entering a house, found a boy hanging by one wrist from a beam, the other wrist tied to one of his feet. He had been flogged. He was rescued and taken to the local workhouse, the master sweep receiving a prison term of six months. In Yorkshire a boy was bought from a tinker by a sweep and his wife, who had both treated him cruelly, including hanging him from his wrists in a stable and tying one leg to a horse's leg. The sweep was charged with cruelty and sent to prison with hard labour. A Manchester sweep stated that he had been a climbing boy from the age of five and had been so cruelly treated that he ran away, but his master tracked him down 'and then he nearly killed me.'[9] He said that five to six boys slept in a kind of cellar with soot bags over them sticking to the wounds and all their bedding was straw.

Chimney sweeping was fraught with danger. In addition to the perils of inhaled soot and the possibility of cancer, child sweeps were accident-prone; not due to carelessness on their part, but largely to the design of chimneys, besides the cruelty of some masters. In 1794, a climbing boy suffocated in Suffolk; in 1808 a boy died of exposure on a freezing-cold day in February, having started work at 3 a.m.; in 1811, a boy in Wakefield fell down a flue onto a fire 'his flesh being completely burnt from his toes to his chin'; in the same year, another boy got stuck fast and was suffocated. A lame six-year-old London boy was so cruelly treated that he died and, at his inquest reported on in 1816, the sweep and his wife claimed that as the boy was their apprentice, they had a right to do what they liked with him. A Nottingham master sweep stated that apprenticeship, 'is as bad as the Negro slavery, only it is not so known.' He added that he had known boys as young as five and a half but was afraid they might die. 'They go off (die) just as quietly as you might fall asleep in the chair, by the fire there.' Climbing boys continued to be killed at, or as a consequence of, their occupation until the late nineteenth century although, from mid-century, in fewer numbers when the use of machines became more prevalent. George Brewster, an eleven-year-old Cambridge boy, became the last climbing boy to die as a consequence of his work – in 1875. His master was tried at the Assizes and sentenced to six months' hard labour.

The plight of climbing boys was first made public in 1783 when Jonas Hanway published *The State of Chimney Sweepers* and began to campaign for their better protection. But few master sweeps were sympathetic;

Jonas Hanway (1742–1786) was the first children's champion, publicising the dangers of chimney sweeping and campaigning for better conditions.

they had too much self-interest in continuing to use child sweeps. Hanway wrote letters describing the neglect of boys, publishing a book, *Sentimental History of Chimney Sweeps in London and Westminster* (1785). His letters impressed some humane magistrates – he published measurements of chimneys and made practical suggestions, advising that boys should not be forced up chimneys where a fire was alight, and that they should be properly cared for, fed and washed. A Commission of Enquiry was set up in 1788, after Hanway's death, to investigate sweeps. A Bill was introduced to Parliament but the House of Lords rejected it, a watered-down version being passed in preference. While the 1788 Act prohibited the employment of apprentices below the age of eight, and parental consent to their apprenticeship was required, the Act ruling that a child should be adequately clothed and housed, there was no provision for checking on whether, or how well, the law was kept; and it was widely violated. It was to be another 87 years before the nation prohibited the employment of child sweeps.

In 1788, David Porter, a master sweep and friend of Hanway petitioned Parliament on the conditions of climbing boys and, in 1792, published *Considerations of the Present State of Chimney Sweepers with Some Observations on the Act of Parliament Intended for their Regulation and Relief.* Porter claimed that the number of boys apprenticed to master sweeps in London had risen to 500, arguing that climbing boys should have a change of clothing, facilities for washing, a good dinner a week, be protected from catching cancer, and be taught to read and write. On no account should a boy ever be allowed to cry the streets of London. William Blake's poem 'The Chimney Sweep' captured the mood of those who sought to bring about change:

A little black thing among the snow,
Crying 'weep! weep!' In notes of woe![10]

Porter's writing informed the founding of the Society for Bettering the Condition and Increasing the Comforts of the Poor in 1796 and members tried to rouse opinion on the treatment of climbing boys. In 1803, William Tooke founded the London Society for Superseding the Necessity for Employing Climbing Boys, one of the vice-presidents of which was William Wilberforce, whose opposition to the slave trade was well known. A similar society was founded in Sheffield in 1807. Already the idea was emerging that the British were more kindly towards animals than children. In 1816 the Society for Superseding the Employment of Climbing Boys recommended to Parliament that a new Bill be passed, prohibiting the use of climbing boys altogether. But there was opposition from master sweeps who were afraid of losing apprentices and the Bill failed. The Sheffield Society for Superseding the Employment of Climbing Boys presented a petition to Parliament and, within a few days, the London branch sent a similar petition, the outcome being an 1817 House of Commons Committee to enquire into the working of the 1788 Act. Some master sweeps testified to the effectiveness of a sweeping machine and, in less than a month, an amendment to the 1788 Act was proposed but, on a technicality, was not passed. The Society for Superseding the Employment of Climbing Boys acted in 1818 to promote a new Bill to regulate the trade. This received support in many public meetings but, again, there was opposition from some chimney sweeps. Evidence in favour of legislation was given by a number of witnesses, including surgeons and architects; Dr Lushington spoke of the violent methods used to force children up chimneys, he described the sores on their knees and elbows rubbed with brine, he talked about accidents, the misshapen limbs, cancer of the scrotum and the boys' fear of suffocation. It was asserted that the few chimneys which

William Wilberforce (1759–1833), a campaigner against the African slave trade, also campaigned against the exploitation of child chimney sweep slaves.

could not be cleaned by machine could have soot doors inserted instead. But the House of Lords thought harm would be caused to the community if machines alone were used and they postponed the Bill. A year later the House of Commons was petitioned for permission to introduce a Bill for regulating the chimney sweeping trade. A newly elected MP was persuaded by master sweeps to oppose it, adding that many of the boys were 'cheerful and contented.' But it was passed in the Commons. When the Bill went to the House of Lords, Lord Lauderdale ridiculed the entire subject, telling a now famous anecdote of the practice in some parts of Ireland where a rope was tied around the neck of a goose and the bird dragged up the chimney which was swept by its fluttering wings. A wild goose story that was followed by hilarious uproar and the Lords voted against the Bill. Government had failed, once again, to protect working children.

Another supporter of the campaign to regulate chimney sweeping was a Sheffield man, James Montgomery who, in 1824, published *The Chimney Sweeper's Friend and Climbing Boys Album,* illustrated by Robert Cruickshank (brother of the more well-known cartoonist George). By the time Montgomery's book was published, a number of regional societies had been established specifically to champion the cause of child sweeps, sometimes encouraged by other bodies such as The Society of Friends (Quakers) in York, and the Cutlers' Company in Sheffield. The London Society continued campaigning, promoting the use of machinery for sweeping. Ten years were to pass before Parliament once more showed interest in child sweeps. William Tooke, of the London Society for Superseding the Employment of Climbing Boys, recommended that the 1788 Act be repealed, and that no child under the age of fourteen should be apprenticed to a sweep, or allowed to climb flues to sweep them. MPs were, as before, sympathetic to the cause, adding extra recommendations, the great change this time being the increased groundswell of public opinion. The Select Committee received petitions from all over the country. But the House of Lords still had to be persuaded; some members showing little concern for the boys' sufferings, while builders still erected chimneys that were virtually impossible to clean; a medical witness reporting to the Lords that he must have seen 100 cases of chimney sweep's cancer. The bill became law in 1834. The regulations appeared to be good; no boys under the age of fourteen were to be employed as apprentices and no master could have more than six apprentices at any one time. Moreover boys had to be willing to be apprenticed and appear before a Justice of the Peace for approval. There were loopholes, however and The Society of Master Sweeps took advantage of these; the practice of employing climbing boys continued.

In 1840, another Bill was presented to Parliament, putting forward more or less the same arguments. The subject was referred, as before, to Committee and the Chimney Sweepers and Chimneys Regulation Act was passed, the regulations becoming operative in 1842. One clause was that householders should see that all flues could be cleaned by machine. This Act would have been good, if powers for enforcement had existed. Lord Shaftesbury drew attention to the Act's weakness by reporting on a ten-year-old suffocated in Leeds, the master having escaped conviction because he was not present when the boy was climbing.

The case for effective regulation became more persuasive, not only because the cause of climbing boys had received so much publicity, but also because there had been developments on the technology front. The first effective chimney sweeping machine had been introduced in 1803, being invented by a carpenter named Smart. The machine was said to work in 99 cases out of 100, except where there were sharp angles in the flue. The adoption of these machines was promoted by the London Society for Superseding the Employment of Climbing Boys – the machine being donated by the Society to some master sweeps too poor to buy one. But, despite publicised experiments being conducted in several well-known buildings, little change took place. Philanthropists continued to promote the machine but the public at large showed little interest and, in 1817, the inventor estimated that there were no more than 50 or 60 machines in London. Henry Mayhew suggested that the greatest barrier to wider adoption of the machine was the opposition of servants who received 'back-handers' from master sweeps if the use of climbing boys was requested.[11] In 1828 Joseph Glass marketed an improvement to the Smart machine which was recommended by fire insurance companies. In his evidence to the 1834 Parliamentary Committee, Glass stated that he had managed to sweep all the chimneys in the House of Lords and most of those in Buckingham Palace with his machine. And it is this machine which, improved down the years, continues in use.

The campaign to ban the use of child chimney sweeps continued, finding an indefatigable supporter in Lord Shaftesbury. Appointed Parliamentary Adviser on child welfare in 1832 at the age of 31, he devoted the rest of

Lord Shaftesbury (1801–1855) was a campaigner against child slavery in a number of industries, including chimney sweeping.

his life to good causes, amongst which was the protection of working children, including climbing boys. He was in favour of the 1840 Chimney Sweepers Act, until he became aware of its weaknesses and tried unsuccessfully in 1851 and in 1852 to bring in bills to remedy the shortfalls. Lord Shaftesbury poured out his feelings of frustration in his diaries; in 1840 he wrote:[12]

> Anxious, very anxious about my sweeps ... should these poor children be despised by the lords, and tossed to the mercy of their savage purchasers.

Twelve years later, in 1854, he expressed,

> Great anxiety about Bill for relief of Chimney Sweepers. Have suffered actual tortures through solicitude for prevention of these horrid cruelties...

and, eighteen days later:

> Very sad and low about the loss of the Sweeps' Bill – the prolonged sufferings, the terrible degradation, the licensed tyranny, the helpless subjection, the enormous mass of cruelty and crime on the part of parents and employers, are overwhelming.

The publication, in 1863, of Charles Kingsley's widely read *The Water Babies* raised public awareness of the plight of child sweeps further. The story tells of Tom, a young child sweep, who runs away from his unkind master, Mr Grimes. He falls into a river and becomes a water-baby. After many adventures Tom meets up with his former master, now imprisoned and weeping in a chimney-top. Tom cries too, and the good fairy forgives and releases Grimes. In 1864 Shaftesbury proposed a Bill 'to amend and extend the Act for the Regulation of Chimney Sweepers' and this was rapidly passed. Police were given powers to arrest sweeps thought to be breaking the law, while severe fines or imprisonment were proposed for those convicted of breaking the law. But the Act did not totally ban human sweeps. Even in 1874 there were reports of magistrates, lords, squires and mayors allowing their chimneys to be swept by boys. In February 1875, twelve-year-old George Brewster climbed a chimney at Fulbourn Hospital and became stuck. He suffocated and an entire wall had to be pulled down to extricate him. He died a short while afterwards and his master, William Wyer, was found guilty of manslaughter and sent to prison for six months with hard labour. Lord Shaftesbury seized the moment and wrote a series of letters to *The Times*. In September 1875 Shaftesbury's final bill was presented to Parliament: 'at last they listened and so far as their undemonstrative natures would allow, applauded me ... The Times, may the paper be blessed, has assisted me gloriously.'[13] The Act was quickly passed, ensuring that chimney sweeps would be registered and their work subject to supervision. As Shaftesbury wrote: 'One hundred and two years have elapsed since the good Jonas Hanway brought the brutal iniquity before the public'; the use of child chimney sweeps finally ceased. After Lord Shaftesbury's death a picture was published showing ragged, barefoot children laying a wreath at his memorial.

Happy Families: that a version of this children's card game, published *c.* 1905, should contain the realistically depicted Soot Family, is a reminder that child sweeps had only finally been prohibited by Parliament 30 years previously.

THREE

Cotton

UNTIL THE LATE EIGHTEENTH CENTURY cotton was carded, spun and woven in the cottages of rural Lancashire, Cheshire, Derbyshire, Yorkshire and lowland Scotland. The eight-spindle spinning jenny, invented by Richard Hargreaves in 1764 and the sixteen-spindle version patented by him in 1770, increased cottage productivity and created the demand for more carded wool roved into slivers for spinning. The jenny was invented as a domestic machine, although power-driven jennies were available by the 1790s. By this time, however, Richard Arkwright had already succeeded in spinning cotton thread by power (his water frame being patented in 1769) and cotton spinning had become a factory-based industry. (Worsted thread could be spun by Arkwright's water frame and worsted spinning mills were built in Yorkshire and the Midlands, but the water frame could not spin shorter staple wool and so spinning for the woollen industry largely remained a cottage industry until the advent of the mule in the nineteenth century.) Arkwright's first cotton mill was in Nottingham, powered by a nine-horse wheel. This provided adequate power for an experimental factory, allowing him to observe how many machines could be driven by different numbers of horses – observable 'horse power'. And the preparatory process of mechanised carding was integrated into the factory system by Arkwright, probably adapting earlier attempts by others. Since steam power capable of generating effective rotative motion was not then a reality, Arkwright sought a good water power site and, in 1771, he built a water-powered mill at Cromford in Derbyshire, in partnership with a local hosier, Jedediah Strutt. He built other mills in the vicinity and sold licences for his patented spinning machine to cotton manufacturers who built water-powered mills on his principle in the valleys which bisected the Pennines, as well as in Scotland. Twenty years later, by the 1790s, the rotative steam engine had been developed and spinning mills were built in the rapidly growing Lancashire towns.

Carding and spinning machines could be tended by children under supervision, the cheapest form of labour. And, to recoup some of their initial capital outlay, many mill owners worked their factories night and day. But water-powered mills were often located some distance from towns and villages which could supply sufficient cheap child labour. Families could be attracted if housing was made available and Arkwright built rows of industrial housing in his factory village at Cromford but, for families to be attracted, this necessitated work being available for adult men and women. Other water frame spinners built factory villages, for example at Belper in Derbyshire, Styal in Cheshire, New Lanark in Scotland, and elsewhere. But there were not necessarily enough local jobs for adults, and children from local villages sent to the mills by their parents had to be paid a wage, however small.

There was, however, another source of child labour, pauper apprentices from urban workhouses, particularly London, and these did not have to be paid. Poor Law Guardians, anxious to keep poor rates low in rapidly growing towns, cooperated in apprenticing children, sometimes from as young as five, but more often from ten years of age. While some workhouse children were apprenticed to local town trades, many boys were sent to coal mines and girls to cotton spinning factories, sometimes well over a hundred miles away. These children were apprentices in name only. While children from relatively better-off families served meaningful apprenticeships, learning a trade for a term of seven years, pauper apprentices were often bound until they reached the age of 21, learning no 'trade' besides the operation of a specific piece of power-driven machinery. They received little or no payment but their clothing and keep, such as it was. The cotton industry provided a useful outlet for parish officials with many pauper children on their hands and large numbers of children were sent to midland and northern cotton mills from large London workhouses and the Foundling Hospital. Although the parish from which apprentices came had to pay an apprenticeship premium per child, it was far cheaper for them to do this than to support them in the workhouse. And, if the child was bound apprentice in another parish, it was that parish which became responsible for any future poor relief, so there was a great incentive to do this. In the 1770s and 1780s some overseers actually advertised in manufacturing areas that they had pauper children available. The usual premium paid by a cotton mill owner was between two and four guineas per child, the overseers providing a new outfit of clothes for each one. Some mill owners engaged the services of a medical officer, whose main task was to check that all pauper children bound apprentice were deemed capable of working long hours in a hot and dusty cotton mill. Any child found, within the first six weeks, not to be sufficiently fit was returned to their parish. Thereafter, all apprenticed children were the responsibility of the cotton mill owner who undertook to provide food, drink, clothing, washing and lodging in an apprentice house managed by a superintendent. The financial benefit to the parishes which sent apprentices out was clear – the child was off their books. Although wages paid to apprentices from workhouses were non-existent or low, there were certainly costs involved, however well or poorly the apprentice was treated, but had pauper apprentices not been available, labour for the mills would certainly have been more costly.

At Greg's Mill in Styal, Cheshire, the weekly cost per head of keeping an apprentice was 17.5p in 1790 and between 20p and 25p in 1822–40. While the cost of maintaining a child in a factory did not change greatly as he/she got older, the value of their labour increased. The minimal value of apprentices in their early years was attested by some manufacturers but, since many factory apprenticeships could be for twelve years or more, during which time the employer benefitted from non-waged labour, the benefits of the system to the early industrial revolution mill owner would seem to be evident. It has been estimated that, by the age of eight to ten, children could offset the cost of their upkeep and, thereafter, the factory owner benefitted considerably. The comparative 'wage' differential between parish apprentices and free labour became progressively starker as the apprentices grew older.

Many Birmingham paupers were sent to mills in Lancashire and Cheshire, besides the East Midlands; two Nottinghamshire mills having nearly 600 each in around 1800. Other mills had between 40 and 50. It was usual for children to be sent from parishes in batches, larger numbers of children being dispatched from London workhouses by waggon. Smaller mills, on the other hand, could be supplied locally with labour from nearby towns. Apprentice houses had separate boys' and girls' dormitories and the bedding usually consisted of chaff beds on flat boards, the chaff being changed twice a year. At better-run apprentice houses, there were sheets which were changed monthly. But there were anything from two to four children to a bed, two at the head and two at the foot and, where night work was done, the beds were constantly occupied by one shift or another. In these conditions fever was often rampant; bed bugs and head lice almost universal. Sometimes an epidemic of fever would break out amongst the mill children – probably due to unsatisfactory living accommodation and inadequate feeding. Arkwright's mill at Cromford, being the first successful water-powered spinning factory, was on the itinerary of numerous tourists, one of whom noted in 1776 that the mill hands worked on day and night shifts, spinning being done at night and preparatory processes during the day. But night work ended there in 1792. At the Peels' Radcliffe mills, near Manchester, the children on night shift worked for eleven hours and when, during an outbreak of putrid fever, Peel was asked to stop night work he considered it 'unprecedented a Requisition ... No man in his senses would have complied with it.'[1] However, within a few years he had changed his views and was instrumental in seeing the first Factory Act through Parliament in 1802.

Most children were given porridge made with water for breakfast, potatoes and sometimes meat for dinner and porridge for supper. Some masters provided bread and cheese as well. Water was the usual drink. Nantwich Mill appears to have been run by one of the more enlightened employers of pauper apprentices: 'Rise at 6 o'clock, wash and go to work – breakfast at the mill, dine in the house – one hour allowed for recreation. Leave work between 7 and 8 o'clock – sup – at liberty till 9 then return and go to bed.'[2]

In 1828 five weekly instalments comprising what became known as *The Memoir of Robert Blincoe* were published in a radical paper by a Bolton journalist, subsequently being published together in 1832. It is difficult to gauge how accurate Blincoe's account of the cruelty he sustained is, in the absence of direct corroborating evidence. He was born in about 1792 and, at the age of about seven, was dispatched, along with many other children, from St Pancras Workhouse to a mill near Nottingham. The horrors of his treatment – unremitting labour to meet production targets, combined with sadistic treatment by overlookers almost defy description; children

Death of an apprentice: an illustration from the novel by Frances Trollope, published in 1840, based on the story of Robert Blincoe.

were given tasks that they were too young or small to perform and then punished for failing to accomplish them. Blincoe alleged that he received regular beatings; he was kicked so violently 'it commonly lifted him off the floor'; heavy weights were hung on his body for the entertainment of supervisors; the children were almost always hungry; there were appalling accidents with machinery – a young girl whose apron was caught in a machine was whirled around until she was senseless and with many bones broken.

What is known is that both death and disappearance diminished the apprentice labour force at a number of mills. Apprentices absconded from some mills due, in large measure to exploitation, cruelty and under-nourishment, in addition to which females were liable to be subjected to sexual exploitation by masters, their sons or mill supervisors. Robert

Blincoe absconded twice, each time being caught and severely punished. Even at Styal, Cheshire, a mill with a good reputation, truancy was sometimes treated firmly, even severely. In 1836 Robert Hyde Greg ruled that any apprentice who ran away should have her hair cut off. Intervention by his sister, when two runaways were apprehended, prevented this from happening but one girl was locked in a room in the apprentice house, the windows being boarded up to prevent escape or communication with the outside world. When apprentices absconded, sometimes singly, sometimes in groups of three to five, employers went to considerable lengths to retrieve them. Each missing apprentice represented a cost to the employer,

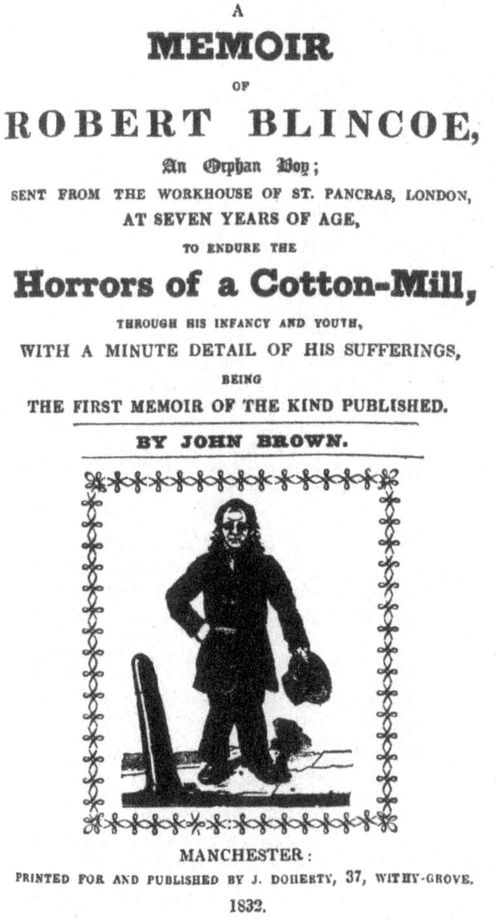
A
MEMOIR
OF
ROBERT BLINCOE,
An Orphan Boy;
SENT FROM THE WORKHOUSE OF ST. PANCRAS, LONDON,
AT SEVEN YEARS OF AGE,
TO ENDURE THE
Horrors of a Cotton-Mill,
THROUGH HIS INFANCY AND YOUTH,
WITH A MINUTE DETAIL OF HIS SUFFERINGS,
BEING
THE FIRST MEMOIR OF THE KIND PUBLISHED.
BY JOHN BROWN.
MANCHESTER:
PRINTED FOR AND PUBLISHED BY J. DOHERTY, 37, WITHY-GROVE.
1832.

Book cover of *A Memoir of Robert Blincoe,* originally published in book form, from five instalments, in 1830; the story of a pauper apprentice.

not only in terms of indenture fee to the parish, transport to the mill, housing, feeding and clothing, but also in lost productivity. It was not just a case of owners' and superintendents' anger at being disobeyed, apprentice children evidently had a value and were less expendable than might be assumed by the way that some were treated.

Early on in their apprenticeships, parish children in water spinning became responsible for machines in the main production processes; they were not just helpers. One factory master from Mansfield, Nottinghamshire, said 'We cannot work without the children ... children can do the work better than grown persons.' Unlike apprenticeships in later mule spinning

Scavenging apprentices, depicted in Frances Trollope's 1840 novel. Many apprentices were inadequately fed.

where a child might, for some years be a helper, in water frame spinning they soon became independent machine minders, under the supervision of overlookers.

Samuel Greg built his spinning mill in a remote area of Cheshire at Styal. He appeared to be in no hurry to build a community around his mill, instead, importing children from parish workhouses. The first parish apprentices to go to Styal arrived in the 1780s from a local poorhouse and, by 1790, the number had increased as Greg recruited children from further afield, requiring the building of an apprentice house. He reckoned that it was cheaper to build an apprentice house for 90 children at £300 and to support them, than to build housing for families at a cost of £50–£100 per house. And he may have been encouraged by the apparent availability of pauper children. By 1800 there were approximately 60 girls and 30 boys, comprising about half the total labour force. The proportion had dropped to 36 per cent by 1816. Some other cotton spinners relied even more on parish apprentices, including David Dale at New Lanark who had 500 in the late eighteenth century 'generally from the age of five and six, to seven and eight,' as did William Douglas at Holywell, Flintshire; the Peels at Bury had 1000. During the eighteenth century it was easy to recruit new parish apprentices and many cotton masters, even the more considerate ones such as Samuel Greg, turned children away at the end of their term and recruited a new consignment, although a few were retained, becoming valued long-term employees.

The new apprentices at Styal were given menial tasks at first such as sweeping floors, doffing (replacing bobbins) and piecing (repairing broken threads). Later, some became carders and spinners, while some boys became mechanics. Samuel Greg was a humanitarian employer (as was his son, Robert Hyde Greg), treating apprentices well for the times. His intention was to create a stable industrial community in which unrest and labour turnover were low. The apprentice house was clean, the floors regularly washed, rooms aired daily and the walls whitewashed every year. Two children slept in a bed and they had clean sheets once a month. Apprentices were provided with new clothes for Sundays every other year and new working jackets when they were worn out. Female apprentices at Nantwich Cotton mill were also relatively well cared for, having 'two petticoats, a shift, an upper garment called a brat, somewhat like a short bed gown, round in front and close; open behind with buttons at top, shoes and stockings, clean linen once a week – some of the girls had a kerchief round their neck.'[3] These children had extra clothes for Sundays.

Styal apprentices were provided with food made from locally produced vegetables, with meat and cheese from the Gregs' farm. If an apprentice fell ill he/she was visited by the village medical officer. They received a broad education for the time, being taught the three Rs; they received religious instruction and were taught music; girls also being taught to sew. To what extent any apprentice welcomed education after working for twelve hours is debateable, but what was provided was certainly enlightened for the time, due most probably to Mrs Hannah Greg, raised as a Unitarian and believing in educational entitlement for all. At Cromford, girls and boys alternated between church and school on Sundays, while at Belper and Milford, Lancastrian schools had been established by around 1807, but it was noted that girls were less frequent attenders than boys, often being required for domestic tasks. The Evans of Darley Abbey, Derbyshire, were reputed to be good employers, a number of the children living with their parents in the newly erected factory village. From about 1806 Cromford stopped taking children under ten years of age, the principal reason being that they should have learned to read before being employed. But, it was claimed, parents exerted pressure on the Arkwrights to take on their children, even if they were able to read only a few small words.

A report on New Lanark cotton spinning mills was published by the Society for Bettering the Conditions and Increasing the Comforts of the Poor in 1800. There were four mills, two of which contained 12,000 spindles for water twist on Arkwright's principles, the other two containing jennies. Five hundred children were fed, clothed and educated by the owner David Dale. The healthy appearance of the children attracted positive comments from visitors. Out of almost 3000 children employed at New Lanark between 1785 and 1797, only fourteen had died and none had been 'the object of judicial punishment'. The children – boys and girls were kept 'distinctly apart not only at times of rest and refreshment but also during the hours of work'.[4] They slept on cast iron bedsteads, the bed-tick being filled with straw that was changed monthly. After 7 o'clock supper the children attended school for two hours. The children wore cotton shifts – boys wore woollen clothes in winter and they all wore suits on Sundays. There was little variety in the diet, but food was plentiful: porridge for breakfast and supper with, in winter, a sauce made of molasses

New Lanark cotton mills, established by David Dale and taken over by Robert Owen, who created a model factory community.

and beer. For midday dinner they each had 7 oz of beef with barley broth or 5 oz of cheese and potatoes or barley bread. In Robert Owen's time at New Lanark, schools were provided for children until they were deemed old enough to work in the mills. And, to enable women workers to return to work, he built an Institution for Children, with an emphasis on physical movement through dancing and marching; natural history was taught using the local environment, rather than books. Rothsay cotton mills on the Isle of Bute were also managed with regard to the health – and morals – of the children. Carding machines were enclosed to prevent, in part, the carding dust being inhaled. As the workpeople lived nearby they went home for breakfast and for dinner. An innovative method of teaching was introduced whereby, rather than requiring the children to attend school after work, one or two were withdrawn at a time during the day and taught for ten minutes in an adjoining room.

Robert Owen of New Lanark

New Lanark school; young children of mill employees were taught in a very enlightened way for the times.

A few parishes began to question binding children as apprentices to cotton mills, Manchester being one of the first. In 1784 the parochial authorities prohibited the apprenticeship of poor children in cotton mills working at night. By the 1790s, greater public concern was being voiced for pauper apprentices sent from workhouses to the cotton mills of Lancashire, Yorkshire, and Derbyshire; their hours of work, living conditions and the discipline to which they were subjected. The Society for Bettering the Conditions and Increasing the Comforts of the Poor was founded in 1796 by a group of philanthropic evangelical Christians, including Sir Thomas Bernard (treasurer of the Foundling Hospital between 1795 and 1806), William Wilberforce, the Bishop of Durham, Frances Elizabeth King and others, some of whom were members of what became known as The Clapham Sect. The Society set out to develop a science from the study of all that concerned the poor, in order that principles could be derived, leading to the dissemination of good practices. Amongst the Society's original aims was the resolution that 'poor children, consigned in lots as apprentices to manufactories, and there left unprotected and forgotten, be placed under a system of inspection.' In 1796 the newly formed Manchester Board of

Health published a report on factory labour and Robert Peel 'struck with the uniform appearance of bad health and, in many cases, stunted growth of the children in his own mills, initiated a bill in Parliament which was passed as the Health and Morals of Apprentices Act of 1802 to regulate cotton or woollen mills where three or more apprentices or twenty other persons were employed. There were fourteen clauses, the key requirements being that each mill/factory be registered annually with the Clerk to the Quarter Sessions; all factories were to be washed with a solution of quicklime twice a year; apprentices were to be supplied with good clothing; no apprentice was to work more than twelve hours a day (excluding meal times) and no apprentices were to work between the hours of 9 p.m. and 6 a.m. All apprentices were to receive some education each day; they were to receive an hour's religious instruction on Sundays and to attend church once a month or, if the mill was too remote from a church or chapel, a service was to be held near the mill. The extent to which the law was obeyed was, however, very much up to the integrity of individual manufacturers, for the legislation did not provide for a factory inspectorate. Justices of the Peace were to appoint two visitors a year, one of whom was to be a J.P., the other a clergyman and, where there were more than six mills, the area was to be divided into districts, each with its two visitors. Fines were laid down for contravention of the Act. But no ruling was made as to checking on whether visits had been made, or on action that needed to be taken.

Two Manchester mill visitors, appointed by the Justices, 'inspected' eleven factories in a single day. In one weaving factory they found rooms crowded with too many looms. In one of the boy's dormitories there were seventeen beds, in another eighteen, while there were 42 in the girls' room; the food was basic, unwashed potatoes being boiled for dinner with their skins on, and eight cow heads being boiled in a separate pot. The privies were so noxious that the visitors declined to investigate further. In another smaller Manchester mill, however, the 36 apprentices appeared to be well fed and clothed and 'in the most comfortable Situation.' This was far from the case at a mill near Bury. The children received no education, whereas they used to go to a Sunday school, their clothes were so tattered that they could not go; they never went to church or any other place of worship. If a mill owner was warned of an impending visit, and this seems to have been the case sometimes, machinery was slowed down and, in a factory where the children were required to eat their dinner in the mill, part of the hour's 'break' being to be devoted to cleaning the machinery, the children were sent to an adjoining field to eat when an inspection was imminent. A Scottish mill owner expected the apprentices to attend church twice on Sunday, an enlightened observer commenting that they were hardly likely to be inspired by two hours of Scottish sermons each week.

While, in principle from 1802, pauper apprentices were under some protection, in practice things were very different. First, those who framed the Act seemed to have had no idea as to the scale of the factory system in the cotton and worsted industries for there were hundreds of mills in Lancashire and Yorkshire and many in Derbyshire. Second, there was not a sufficient number of J.P.s or their delegates to conduct inspections; third, there were plentiful opportunities for collusion between inspectors and mill owners who tended to mix in the same social circles, as a report of a Select Committee of the Society for Bettering the Conditions of the Poor made clear. While no grievance had been 'alleged' to exist regarding 'interference' with the legislation, the Committee claimed that there was no doubt that allegations had been made regarding grievances in many cotton mills. And, with respect to the 'health, and morals, the present and future hopes of thousands of children (were) being annually sacrificed in them.' Allegations had been made by visitors, families living nearby, 'and they have been frequently noticed by the magistrates.' There followed the detailed case of a cotton mill at Burley. The manufacturer set out his case, alleging that many of the apprentices in cotton mills 'are composed of the children of beggars, chimney sweepers and others, accustomed to live in total ignorance and idleness, and not infrequently addicted to stealing, swearing and other vices'.[5] In order that they could be effective mill children, he claimed, they needed to be 'reformed' and 'very strict discipline must be kept up' to ensure good order. It was alleged that about one sixth of cotton mill apprentices were required to work at night for 'free labourers cannot be obtained to perform the night-work, but upon very disadvantageous terms to the manufacturers'.[6] The Committee commented that it was cruel and unjust that the poor orphan or the deserted child should be compelled to undertake night-work which the free labourer could not be induced to do. The Committee disputed the claimed potential loss by the manufacturer. The manufacturer objected 'in very strong terms' to the power given by the 1802 Act to Visitors 'let the visitors conduct themselves with what discretion they may, the mills and factories will become a scene either of idleness and disorder, or of open rebellion',[7] the reason being that 'a considerable degree of authority must be exerted.' While Committee members wished that cotton mills could become 'a desirable seminary for children', they observed that this could never be the case while children were sent from London workhouses to remote places 'secluded from the eye of the magistrate'.

Night apprentices at Burley Mill worked from 7 p.m. to 6 a.m.; their dinner being brought at midnight. But the machinery was not stopped so the children had to take their food when they could. On ceasing work they had 'supper' and then, until 10 a.m. either schooling or exercise. Then they went to bed, rising at about 6 p.m. for 'breakfast'. The visitor's account concluded 'the night-workers are not changed, but do this work for four or five years successively.' The visit to Burley Mill was made less in the capacity of Visitor and more as a friend of the manufacturer; the mill and the children were prepared for his arrival. The Committee pondered whether, if the apprentices had been subject to abuse, what inducement would there have been for them to make this known? Rather, there would have been fear of retribution. Moreover this visit was carried out after the magistrates of both Lancashire and the West Riding of Yorkshire had passed resolutions, in 1784 and 1800 respectively, refusing to allow parish apprentices to be indentured in cotton mills and other works where they were obliged to work at night. This led the Committee to ponder whether, if this had been an historical account of a part of Asia or Africa 'should we not shudder at the perusal?' The Committee asserted, but provided no evidence, that the continued practice of night work by the same children for years did not occur in many cotton mills, and concluded by recommending that cotton and woollen mills be placed more immediately under the inspection and control of magistrates so that apprentices be prevented from working at night, besides ensuring that the other requirements of the Act were met.

The Visitor to a mill in Bury, an eminent surgeon from Leeds, obtained evidence from the apprentices. The night workers were all boys, five out of six of them saying that they would prefer to work during the day. The reasons given included not being able to sleep so well during the day, not being able to work so easily by candlelight, or being woken to begin work at just after midnight on Sunday nights. He reported that the girls seemed healthy and happy. Finally, the Visitor commended the religious and moral education of the children, which he believed did the mill owners credit.

The 1802 Act appeared to do little, save to publicise the issue. Until a Factory Inspectorate was created – and this would be a further 30 years away – the management of pauper apprentices would be more effectively regulated by the attitude of individual manufacturers, technology and the state of the trade.

There were also independent initiatives to investigate the conditions of pauper apprentices. The Foundling Hospital, and Overseers of the Poor in towns from which workhouse pauper children had been apprenticed to mills, began to send Visitors to report on the state of apprentices' well-being. Some visits began in the 1790s and there were more from the early nineteenth century. The workhouse at St James, Piccadilly, was prepared to fetch children back if reports were bad. Several overseers from St James visited Strutt's cotton mill and found that some children had been severely punished for trifling offences, besides which they were all inadequately fed and worked for excessively long hours. St James' children at two Cheshire mills were visited every few months in the early nineteenth century. Whilst, in the late 1780s it was said to be the duty of magistrates, rather than Overseers, to investigate the condition of apprenticed pauper children, the concern being that Overseers might not be as attentive as a parent, in practice it was more usually the Overseers or their delegates who visited. Birmingham Overseers began to send Visitors out to inspect the condition of their parish apprentices in mills in the 1790s, as did many other town Overseers, as the extent of the problems faced by some children began to be recognised. Inevitably, some parishes were more dedicated to enquiries and seeking solutions than others. At a mill in Bury the Birmingham Visitors found that the children's clothes were 'very bad, only one ragged suit each, their feet extremely dirty – no shoes or stockings – some have wooden clogs ... On enquiring the reason why they had not shoes we were told "if we gave them shoes they would run away."[8] Officers of a parish in Middlesex ruled that parental permission was to be obtained before children were sent to work in distant mills and this was generally declined. Visitors from the London parish of St Clement Danes, on inspecting Holywell cotton mill, in 1792, found that apprentices worked all night and required the children to be returned. Other parishes were, seemingly, less concerned; Doncaster, despite objections from family members and the apparently high death rate of apprentices at Arnold Mill, Nottingham (27 children died there in 1801), nevertheless continued to send children there.

65 children died at Cuckney Mill, Notts, between 1786 and 1805. A Visitor to Blantyre cotton mill on the Clyde described his concern for the children who worked a fourteen hour day:

> I need not commemorate their, in general, forlorn and squalid looks; they are, God knows, painfully enough impressed on my mind. What a beginning, gracious heaven! For the dawn of human animal life and human intellect ... God help them poor souls. Never to be blessed with the fond endearment of any creature caring for anything but their mere existence and their labour, and condemned to pass the playful years of childhood in a wearisome sameness of employment to which childhood is so particularly averse.[9]

With the adoption of the rotative steam engine from the 1790s, cotton and worsted spinners were freed from dependence on water power in the more remote Pennine valleys, and the associated need for pauper apprentice labour in areas with a low population. Mills to contain the newly invented spinning mule, began to be built in large numbers in Lancashire and Yorkshire and, while mill owners still depended on cheap labour, the children generally did not come from workhouses living, instead, with their families. Many of the child workers in Manchester cotton mills and Yorkshire worsted mills lived in great poverty in slum dwellings. And, in a paper published in the late 1790s, Dr Ferriar, a Manchester physician, set out his advice to poor families. He advised families to avoid cellar dwellings but, if there was no alternative, to make sure that the windows were in good repair. He emphasised the importance of keeping houses clean and of airing bed clothes weekly. With respect to working children:

> Always wash your children from head to foot with cold water, before you send them to work in the morning. Take care to keep them dry in their feet, and never allow them to go to work without giving them their breakfast, tho' you should have nothing for them but a crust of bread, and a little water. Children who get wet feet, when they go out early fasting, seldom escape fevers or severe colds.[10]

He chided parents who neglected to get their children vaccinated against smallpox at the infirmary. Then he added 'there is scarcely any thing [*sic*] more injurious to the health of children than allowing them to work at night in the cotton mills.' He did not, however, see that there was any danger in their working during the day in 'clean, well-managed cotton-mills.' Some forty years later spinners and weavers in the vicinity of Blackburn were still said to be living in abject poverty and filth.

In Manchester, with its large urban population and a ready labour force, a sub-contracting system was in operation. In many mills, only the spinners were employed by master manufacturers, the spinners themselves employing the piecers and scavengers, preferring younger children to do the task for 5p rather than older ones for 15–30p a week. By 1803 one writer estimated that only one in ten children employed in Manchester cotton mills was an apprentice; it not being uncommon for four or five to be hired from one family. When Robert Southey visited Manchester in 1802 he was told that children were employed from the ages of seven or eight, a typical working day beginning with the arrival of the first shift at 5 a.m. They were given breakfast in the mill, had an hour off for dinner, leaving work at 6 p.m., to be relieved by the night shift.

Employers and some doctors were keen to emphasise how easy and untiring the work was: 'I know of no employment whatever less laborious than that in the cotton factories.' A number of employers claimed that the children had both the time and energy to play after their shift. Others were less sure. By 1819 a greater body of evidence was forthcoming on the length of time at work and the damage done to children's health. Children's bodies suffered damage due to the long hours spent looking after machines, often standing in awkward positions. At a period of major physical growth, this could lead to permanent 'deformity'; many had crooked legs and were stunted in growth. If the apprentices were subjected to cruelty, they were additionally physically and psychologically damaged. Mill fires were also a hazard.

Child labour declined in cotton spinning in the early 1820s, but this trend was reversed with the introduction of larger self-acting spinning mules which required child piecers to mend the yarn breakages. The carriage containing a row of spindles moved on a 'rail', coming to its maximum extent for the twisting part of the process, then moving back to join the main body of the machine, a process that could not be stopped mid-journey. Piecing was a high risk task as the child dodged in at the side of the machine to pick up both ends of a broken thread, twisting them together, and getting out before the spindle carriage moved back. By the 1830s mechanisation of the cotton industry, together with the adoption of steam power, had reached almost every stage by which raw cotton was made into cloth. This required operatives to be machine minders, but not particularly skilled, save for a specific operation, so that there was, apparently, little transfer between departments. On the other hand, with the advance of mechanisation, there were far fewer heavy jobs to do in textile manufacture, so that tasks previously performed by men could, in principle, now be done by women and children. The exception seems

"Love conquered Fear."

Mule spinning; this machine had a frame on a 'rail' which moved away from the body of the machine to enable cotton thread to be drawn out and twisted. The threads sometimes broke and it was a small child's role to dodge in at the side, gather up the two ends of the thread, twist them together to join them, running out before the frame returned to the fixed base. The machine could not be stopped if a child was not sufficiently quick and major accidents could occur.

to have been mule spinning which became the preserve of men (with younger children as 'little piecers'), while the preparatory processes of carding, drawing, slubbing and roving became firmly the tasks of women and teenage girls. The largest mules in Manchester mills needed between three and five piecers each and gradually, younger children were replaced by adolescents. In 1833 most of the boys in mule spinning were employed by the machine operative.

The employment of parish apprentices in the cotton industry declined from the early nineteenth century and by 1833 few mills employed them, the Gregs at Styal being amongst the last. In 1835, a Manchester cotton spinner bought a factory in Derbyshire, complete with apprentices and decided to keep them on, imagining there to be a benefit on account of their low wages. However the costs of housing, feeding and clothing, and their low standard of work, added to which the apprentices complained that they were working for nothing, led him to re-think, believing them to be 'troublesome, inconvenient ... objectionable in almost every point of view.'

There are several reasons for the decline in numbers of pauper apprentices in cotton spinning. First, there was increasing public disquiet on the number of children apprenticed and the great distances they were sent, besides the abuses to which some children were subjected: exploitation, excessive hours, maltreatment, insufficient food and poor lodging. Second, changes in legislation made their employment less attractive – night work for children in cotton and woollen mills had been prohibited by the 1802 Health and Morals of Apprentices Act and, by the early nineteenth century fewer parishes were prepared to make pauper apprentices available. Finally, with the development of steam power, mill owners were no longer tied to remote locations by fast-flowing rivers and steam mills could be built in urban areas where the labour of families was more readily available. In 1816, London parishes were forbidden to apprentice children any further than 40 miles away. But other children, those not recruited as parish apprentices, could continue to be exploited – and they were.

Cotton weaving remained largely a cottage industry until the widespread adoption of the power loom in the 1820s. While town weavers had a greater potential choice of employer and employment, the country weavers often had no alternative so that they were imprisoned in their trade and obliged to survive on the pitiful wage rates paid in the second quarter of the nineteenth century. Most plain cotton weaving was relatively simple to learn and did not require great strength, so could be undertaken by children, besides adult men and women. Most rural children probably learned the trade by watching father and/or mother and gradually acquiring the necessary skills. And many of these weavers may have been part-time, with other demands such as domestic duties demanding their attention.

The pressure on the Government in the 1830s to take action to regulate child labour resulted in the 1833 Factory Act, prohibiting the employment of any children under the age of nine and also limiting the employment of children under thirteen to nine hours a day, besides requiring attendance at school for two hours a day. The extent to which the Act was observed depended on the degree to which parental pressure was exerted on young children to contribute to family earnings, the extent to which the requirement for parents and children to provide documentary proof of age and school attendance was observed, and the levels of enforcement possible with an under-staffed factory inspectorate and many mills to inspect. The 1844 Factory Act instituted what was known as the half-time system. In addition to lowering the age at which a child could begin work to eight, and limiting the hours of work for a child aged between eight and thirteen to six and a half hours a day, it required three hours' school attendance each weekday but, since schooling was not free, this clause was largely ignored except by more philanthropic employers. The proportion of the cotton industry workforce that was under the age of thirteen fluctuated; from the mid-1830s to 1850 the proportion fell to 4.6 per cent but by 1874 it had risen to 14 per cent and, thereafter, dropped steadily. In 1874, the age at which half-timers could begin work was raised to ten (becoming effective in 1876), eleven in 1893 and twelve in 1899. While workers and unions opposed all attempts to raise the age at which part-timers could begin work, the cause was won by reformers, including educationalists, in the twentieth century and the Education Act of 1918 abolished 'half-timing'. Child labour in the cotton industry had finally been eliminated.

FOUR

Bleaching and printing

Bleaching

BEFORE THE DISCOVERY of chlorine bleaching in the late eighteenth century and its wider adoption early in the nineteenth century, woven cotton goods were bleached in a lengthy out-door process, being spread out in fields to lighten, with the aid of buttermilk and sunshine. It 'took from six to thirteen weeks to bleach what would now be done in two or three days.'[1] Chemical bleachworks, were established in the West of Scotland, Lancashire and near Dublin in Ireland, particularly from the early 1800s, often still being referred to as 'bleachfields' despite the change from an out-of-doors to an indoor process. The throughput of work in bleaching was dependent on the calico printers – a distinct and separate business; the bleacher did not keep stock but worked on commission, the goods belonging to others: 'he is their servant, and only works to their order.'[2] Because of this, he was frequently subject to greater pressure than other employers in the textile industries. If he declined a job, due to pressure of work, he was likely to lose that customer for good. Some 63 girls and 27 boys under the age of thirteen were employed in nineteen bleachworks in the West of Scotland in 1842, together with 248 girls and 89 boys aged between thirteen and eighteen. Most of the women and girls had come from the Highlands of Scotland, many speaking only Gaelic, 'English being to them a foreign language.'[3] A local surgeon reported that few girls remained at a bleachworks for more than a few years 'their great object being to amass some clothing and articles for a house.'[4]

Children worked particularly in starching, clearing and drying muslins which had been chemically bleached and washed by the men in the bleaching house. Cotton or muslin cloth for printing was singed, by drawing the cloth (even the finest muslin) over a red-hot iron cylinder, to remove the loose filaments which would impair the smooth application of designs and colours. Then it was bleached. The goods to be bleached arrived by cart from Glasgow or Paisley, were dumped on the floor and tied up in bundles by young girls. This was one of the few cool operations involving girls. It was then soaked and boiled in chemicals by men and afterwards washed. Girls worked in pairs taking opposite ends of the pieces, twisting them to dry in a heated room. Then starch and blue was put on the cloth and the fabric was dried in heated rooms called stoves or stenters. Some of the youngest boys were employed to swing fans in the roofs of the stenters with handles to aid the drying process. The work was generally light, none of the tasks requiring great physical exertion; nor was the air laden with dust as in textile spinning. But the long hours and high stenter temperatures, in contrast to the outside air temperatures, took their toll. On the other hand, in the absence of machinery there were very few, if any accidents. Nor were there reports of physical punishment being inflicted.

The hours of work were longer than those of any other industry in Scotland, regularly being from eleven to thirteen hours a day, excluding meal times. Unlike some other occupations, there were no opportunities for

Dash wheels in which cloth, after having been singed, was washed in drums which were rotated (an early form of washing machine).

Bucking kiers; once chemical bleaching was established at the end of the eighteenth century, the time take to bleach fabric became much shorter. Assisting with the processes involving chemicals was a job in which only boys were employed. The cloth, after having been washed, was boiled with lime (*c.* 450g of lime being used for every *c.* 13,000–18,000g cloth).

sitting down and children worked in temperatures of from 90 to 120°F. Girls were liable to suffer from 'inflammatory attacks' which could prove fatal. These were caused by the sudden changes in temperature either by a girl going out of an excessively heated stove building or by drinking cold water when perspiring from the heat. Because the work required the girls to stand all day, the feet and ankles would swell and ulcers could result. Girls slept in 'women rooms' – a kind of dormitory – with two or three to a bed, some thirty to forty beds in the room. Two or three blankets were provided – not a lot for a cold Scottish winter – and the mattresses were of straw.

Considerate employers hired a woman to cook the frugal food – potatoes, porridge and rarely, if ever, meat. Others expected the girls to buy food from a local truck shop (employer-owned) where the provisions were more costly than in other shops and sometimes of questionable quality.

When the Scottish cotton spinning industry declined in the latter half of the nineteenth century, printing and bleaching, with the exception of a few major firms, migrated to Lancashire.

Calico Printing

Children usually began work in the print-works of the West of Scotland between the ages of eight and nine but the Assistant Commissioner had heard of instances of them beginning work aged between six and seven and of one beginning at five and a half years. In Scotland the children were employed by the adult printer, in Lancashire being, typically, hired for a year, the term being extended further if required. Some of the latter, particularly those who had little schooling, were said to cause problems and were thought to be untrustworthy, besides being rude.

By 1842, calico printing was undertaken in four different ways: by the age-old method of hand printing with wooden blocks, by flat plates, by power-operated engraved cylinders, or by the discharge process (in which the part of the material not to be printed or coloured was covered with a substance which would not admit the dye and, when the fabric was washed after dyeing, the pattern was revealed). After the cloth was printed it was subjected to a variety of processes, depending on the colours employed and whether it was to be subsequently dyed.

The regular hours of work for both block and machine printing in Scotland were 6 a.m. to 6 p.m. But 'overhours' were frequently required, depending on particular orders and the patterns required, for which some tables were working 24 hours, whilst others were standing idle. These changes seemed to be caused both by the seasons of the year and by changes in fashion. During rush periods in the trade the system of

Children helping at different printing machines; no parts of the machine were guarded.

'twelving' operated, namely two end-on shifts of twelve hours each, the printer keeping the same helper for the whole time, meals being taken in the workshop. Twelving usually took place in winter when much of the work was done under artificial light, which provided added strain. But it had already become clear that, under this kind of pressure, much of the work was faulty and night work came to be regarded as a false economy. The techniques of calico printing were probably introduced to England from France towards the end of the seventeenth century, some of the words applied to tasks and the people who undertook them, being derived from the French. The child who spread the colour onto a sieve for the printer, was called a 'tierer' or 'teerer' from the French word tireur. The youngest children in the major Scottish print works, Lancashire, and Ireland began as tierers, about 5000 being employed in the whole of Scotland. The child stood on a stool behind the printer, the job being to apply colour with a brush to a piece of flannel laid on a sieve, onto which the blocker dipped his block. After each application of the block to the cloth being printed, the blocker turned to get more colour from the sieve. The tierer had to wash the printer's block, often during mealtimes, and at the end of the working day. And on Saturdays the tierer washed all the printer's tools. Since each adult blocker needed one tierer, the children had to do the same hours as the adult blockers. If shawls were being printed, the child tierers were required to go round the printing table to assist the printer to turn the shawl and this was more tiring. If the tierer was careless in stirring the colour or bespattering the patterns, he would be beaten with a rod and sometimes knocked down. A printer could sack a tierer 'any day or hour he chuse'.[5]

One Dublin factory employed 78 children under the age of thirteen. The children were reported as generally looking well, healthy, and happy. Girls earned from 5p to 10p per week; boys rather more. A twelve-year-old girl described her day: she arrived at work at 7.30 a.m., and worked till 8 p.m. in winter, and in summer she worked from 6 a.m. to 6 p.m. with 1.5 hours allowed for mealtimes. A 40-year-old man who had been working at a print works for 32 years had eight children alive, six of whom were employed in the factory where he worked: 'I cannot afford to have myself or give my children more than two meals a day; we generally have potatoes and milk; I cannot afford meat.'[6] He believed that 'employment in factories tends to stint the growth of children and young persons'. Very few of the

Child tierer at a printing press; the girl is distributing dye across the container so that the printer takes up an even quantity when he needs to re-charge the dye.

children received any education, the parents seeking to get them employed as soon as possible. Few accidents were said to occur – although one fifteen-year-old boy overbalanced and fell into some boiling water and died and another inadvertently put his finger on a printing cylinder – the finger was drawn in and had to be amputated: 'this was the boy's fault entirely, as he had no business near this machinery; there is no machinery where the children are employed'. A twelve-year-old Scottish girl tierer said that she sometimes had a headache from the smell of the colour and the heat of the room, whereas she had always had good health before she began work at the calico printing works. No punishment was permitted in Duffy's large Dublin print works, although it was admitted that, 'they are sometimes slapped by the blockers for inattention, but even this is interdicted, and any persons discovered ill-treating the children are liable to be fined.'[7] A thirteen-year-old boy who, having said that he was never beaten by his blocker, acknowledged that if anything was done wrong, the blockers turned them away and refused to employ them, with the likelihood of more severe punishment when the child went home.

A print works was a complex organisation. An order for a particular pattern, then in fashion, might arrive from London, or a large order might be required for dispatch by a particular ship, or there might be a limited number of blocks with the requisite pattern on them, or only a few printers might have the particular skills required to undertake a certain job. In these cases only a small proportion of the hands could undertake the work. Children's hours could, on occasion, be from 107 and 116 a week. Manufacturers agreed that the hours were excessive and that children deserved an education, but the competition between businesses meant that none would reduce hours unless it was a legal requirement. A print works owner explained the dilemma: 'If ... it is enacted that children shall not be employed between certain hours, say 9 pm and six am in summer and 7 am in winter, it will be the source of almost insurmountable difficulty in many departments of a print-work, and very much interfere with the operation of that trade.'[8]

Excessive hours were recognised as contributing to poorer quality work – cylinder-printing workshops might employ children for between 94 and 114 hours per week. Some girls worked in the stenter-stoves or dry sheds, hanging the printed goods to dry over brick flues, the temperature ranging from 85 to 100°F. Other girls were employed in cloth drying by a different method in which the fabric was passed over and under steam-heated cylinders called steam-cans. This task, being one of the final operations to be performed, was often undertaken into the evening. Instances were recorded of girls working at the steam cans for 38 hours continuously. In Turkey-red works the stove-girls' task was to hang goods across the barred floors in the two or three-storey stoves and there the temperature was 110°F, the steam rising from the wet goods being more suffocating and oppressive than dry heat. These girls worked bare-footed and wore hardly any clothing, carrying the goods on their backs. Stove girls generally had to be at work by 5 a.m. and often as early as 2 or 3 a.m. Children who worked in the heated atmosphere of print shops, turkey-red stoves and stenter stoves were usually pale, and rather delicate; most of them, on first entering the works, suffering from sickness and loss of appetite. The Assistant Commissioner noted that children generally went shoe-less out of choice, rather than from poverty.

Neither bleach nor print works were covered by the first factory acts and the introduction of regulations in spinning and weaving tended to make conditions worse in printing since there was a larger supply of young children needing work. A pamphlet written by one of the Factory Inspectors in 1840 cited thirteen-year-old children who were required to have a certificate in order to work full-time, being rejected, even when they had previously worked for seven years in a print shop. The long-term effect of the fatigue of standing for many hours as a tierer in a warm and humid

Mechanised cotton printing – note the small child standing behind the man on the left.

atmosphere had taken its toll. Three years later it was reported that 5642 children under thirteen years of age worked in print works in Lancashire, Cheshire and Derbyshire.

Lord Shaftesbury brought a bill to Parliament in 1845 to cover bleaching, dyeing and printing and it was bitterly contested. To seek to ensure that it passed, he compromised and the Act of 1845 applied only to print works, prohibiting the employment of children under eight years of age; no child under thirteen was to be employed between 10 p.m. and 6 a.m.; and 30 days' school attendance a year was required. Lord Shaftesbury sought further action but the opposition grew in strength, as much or even more, being from his Parliamentary colleagues rather than from the industry. In 1852, he introduced a bill to the House of Lords for the regulation of bleach works but it was withdrawn in the Commons after a Commissioner was appointed to review the trade. Several further bills were introduced and in 1857 a Select Committee was appointed but out of this arose two reports, one in favour of legislation and the other against. The issue was again raised in 1860 and this time an Act was passed, placing dyeing and bleach works (except open-air bleaching) under the Factory Acts. But when, in 1867,the Factory Extension Bill was being considered, it was said that insufficient information was available as to the operation of print works, bleach works and dyeworks and yet another Commission was set up which recommended the levelling-up of the regulations. This was achieved in 1870. As in other industries, piecemeal factory legislation was only one of the means by which child employment was controlled, education acts being, in the longer term, more effective.

FIVE

Silk

THE ENGLISH SILK INDUSTRY received a great boost in the late seventeenth century with the immigration of French Huguenots who had suffered religious persecution, some 13,000 settling in London, many in Spitalfields. A Spitalfields weaver generally had two looms and children were set to work from the ages of six or seven to wind silk onto quills for the weaver. When they were nine or ten they picked the silk to remove dirt and knots and, by the age of twelve, they were put to the loom and could soon learn to weave plain silk fabrics. By the mid- to late-seventeenth century there was an established silk button trade in Macclesfield, a cottage industry employing women and children. In 1698 the corporation decreed that poor children (or other poor) should receive instruction in button making and could then be outworkers for Macclesfield merchants who supplied the raw materials and sold the finished product. A child of six was said to be able to support by helping in the preparatory processes. It became the chief industry of Macclesfield until silk buttons were superseded by horn buttons but the workpeople, skilled in silk preparation, were able to transfer to the emergent silk throwing industry of the town, children on a three-year contract earning 2.5p a week in their first year, 3.75p in their second and 5p in the third year.

Silk, having already been 'spun' by the silkworm, required cleaning, 'throwing' and 'doubling'. In the throwing process the thread was given a full twist and, in doubling, the thread of three or more bobbins was wound together. Until the early eighteenth century thrown silk was imported from Italy but, in about 1720, Thomas Lombe succeeded in throwing silk in a water-powered factory in Derby and the town became a centre for silk weaving. By the mid-eighteenth century, when Lombe's patent had expired, silk throwing mills began to be erected in a number of areas. As with early cotton mills, factory owners depended in part on pauper apprentice labour. Parish children were sent from St Martin in the Fields to a silk mill at Watford, complaints of ill-treatment being received in 1796, that were not upheld. Officials reported that 'it appeared to them that the children were all perfectly satisfied, very well treated and comfortably accommodated ... the complaints (being) malicious and unfounded.'[1] Islington parish had made a decision not to apprentice its children to factories, only agreeing in 1814 to bind children to Courtauld's silk mill in Braintree.

By the nineteenth century the number of silk throwing mills in Britain had grown considerably, some locations having previously been centres of woollen cloth manufacture, such as around Bocking in Essex and in Somerset. By 1838 there were 263 silk mills in Britain, the largest number (92) being in Cheshire, seven counties having more than ten mills. Silk mills were one of the main sources of work in Watford in the early nineteenth century and by the 1830s there were four mills in the town. Children as young as five and many more from the age of six began work in the mills, beginning at 6 a.m. and working until 7 p.m. with less than an hour and a half for meal breaks. In one mill 'if the children are not tall enough, stools are got for the infants'; the children were 'regularly urged to do their work by beating; they use canes in that mill to beat the children.'[2] Silk throwing mills had one of the highest ratios of child to adult workers and, when the minimum age for children to begin working in textile mills was specified, in the 1833 Factory Act, an exemption was made in the case of silk mills, as the silk throwing industry was 'dependent almost exclusively on child labour.'[3] Because silk mills could take children from a younger age than cotton factories, and the children could be made to work longer hours, the possibility of accidents was greater – small children's clothes being caught up in machinery which could result in death.

Silk throwing was undertaken by the child standing the whole day and legs and back ached as a consequence. It was acknowledged that punishment was often necessary, a Hertfordshire mill supervisor giving evidence to a Parliamentary Select Committee in 1832 acknowledging that 'I was obliged to make them strain every nerve to do the work and I can say I have been disgusted with myself and with my situation. I felt myself degraded, and reduced to the level of a slave-driver in such cases.'[4] Another respondent said: 'they are regularly urged to do their work by beating; they use canes ... to beat the children.'[5]

But throwing also continued as a hand process involving an adult turning a wheel (the gate) which twisted four threads, while a child ran and hooked the threads on stationary pins some 30 to 35 yards away. The process was described in detail in the 1841 Children's Employment Commission:

> For twisting it is necessary to have ... shades which are buildings of at least 30 or 35 yards in length, of two or more rooms, rented separately by one, two or four men having one gate and a boy called a helper ... the upper storey is generally occupied by children, young persons or grown women as 'piecers', 'winders' and 'doublers' attending to their reels and bobbins driven by the exertions of one man ... he (the boy) takes a first rod containing four bobbins of silk from the twister who stands at his gate or wheel, and having fastened the ends, runs to the 'cross' at the extreme end of the room round which he passes the threads of each bobbin and returns to the 'gate'. He is dispatched on a second expedition of the same kind, and returns as before, he then runs up to the cross and detaches the threads and comes to the roller. Supposing the master to make twelve rolls a day, the boy necessarily runs fourteen miles a day, and this is barefooted.[6]

Silk weaving was, initially, widespread in the eighteenth century, some areas producing all-silk fabrics, others using silk with cotton or worsted as in Norfolk and the West Riding. Silk weaving only began in Macclesfield

Child running to wind thrown silk.

in about 1790 but by 1817 there were twelve manufacturers of woven silk and 26 silk throwing mills in the town. Silk ribbon weaving grew fast in Coventry, Derby, Leek and Congleton and, in the first two decades of the nineteenth century the development in East Anglia was remarkable. The 'Spitalfields Acts' of 1773, 1792 and 1811 were intended to protect wages of silk weavers but they brought about, instead, a paralysis of the silk trade in Spitalfields and, had the Act not been repealed in 1824, the trade would have been utterly ruined. As it was, by 1816, some two thirds of weavers were without any means of support and had deserted their houses in despair, unable to bear the sight of their starving families. London manufacturers, anxious to avoid the restrictions and high labour costs imposed by the Spitalfields Acts not only established throwing mills but also put out weaving to towns and villages on the Essex/Sussex borders, attracted by the availability of women and children, besides which there were unemployed woollen and worsted weavers from a long tradition of textile manufacture in the region.

Before 1820 the British silk industry had been protected by a high tariff imposed on imported silks from France, and the easing of this caused much anxiety amongst silk producers. A House of Commons Committee on the Silk Trade in 1831–2 estimated that approximately 50,000 people, with between 14,000 and 17,000 looms (4–5000 of which were unemployed due to trade depression) were dependent on the silk industry in Spitalfields alone. Silk manufacture elsewhere, however, expanded not least due to the application of steam power to throwing. The weaving industry became largely located in Cheshire, Derbyshire, Kent, Hampshire and Gloucestershire and in this industry more girls than boys were employed: 950 girls and 672 boys in Cheshire and 295 girls and 72 boys in Derbyshire, in 1837, for example. The Cobden Treaty of 1860, however, more or less killed off the British silk throwing and weaving industry by abolishing the import duty on French manufactured goods. Fine quality French woven silks, were preferred in the market.

Although silk weaving continued for some years, there were only 548 silk weavers left in London by 1901. And by then child labour in the industry was a thing of the past.

SIX

Wool and worsted

At the end of the seventeenth century, the mayor and the vicar of Leeds decided to use a legacy, bequeathed to the town for the benefit of the poor, to buy wool and tools for making woollen cloth, and poor children were 'taught to mix woolls and perform other parts of that manufactyre'. By the 1760s, 'many poor girls and boys (were) taught to scribble, a new invention, whereby different colours in the dyed wool are delicately mixed.'

In his southern Tour Arthur Young passed through Sudbury, Suffolk, 'an exceeding dirty but a great manufacturing town' noted for its woollen textiles, particularly a cloth known as 'say' and also 'burying-crape'. Young described spinning as 'poor business', meaning not well paid, 'a stout girl of 15 or 16 not being able to earn above *6d.* (2.5p) a day.'[1] Besides this there was employment in weaving ships' flags in which women and girls earned between 12.5p and 15p a week. Says were also made at Bocking and Braintree and here 'stout girls' aged sixteen or seventeen years could earn up to 2p a day spinning. Girls of seven or eight earned 5p a week rolling weavers' quills and, in the summer, supplemented their earnings by hoeing turnips and wheat, making hay and helping with the harvest. When he arrived in Oxfordshire, Young remarked how few women and children were employed in manufacture, although 'some few spin'. But at Witney, he noted its blankets which were exported to Spain and Portugal, while kerseys and coarse bearskins were exported to Canada. Boys could earn as much as journeymen – 50p–60p a week, working from 4 a.m. to 8 p.m., much of the time in winter by candlelight. A child of seven or eight could earn between 7.5p and 8p a day spinning. In Romsey a variety of lighter cloth called ratinett was made. Here, a sixteen-year-old girl could earn 5p a day weaving 'but in the neighbouring villages, by spinning, not above half as much … the children are employed at quilling (winding spun wool ready for the weaver's shuttle) very young.'[2]

The Yorkshire woollen industry in the eighteenth century was largely in the hands of small independent farmer-clothiers, many of whom combined cloth production with small scale subsistence farming. The father would purchase wool in a local market and it would be carded and spun by his wife and children. 'Scarcely anything above four years old, but its hands were sufficient for its own support,'[3] as Daniel Defoe noted. Yorkshiremen 'either from thoughtlessness or necessity, have seldom spared their children, and one cannot doubt that many young workers were kept at tasks beyond their strength for long hours daily.' The wool was dyed with the help of a son or apprentice and then woven. Two pieces of cloth were produced per week by some clothiers but many managed only one. The woven cloth was taken to a local fulling mill to be felted and then, after being dried and in its rough and unfinished state, was sold in the cloth hall. The clothier might take on an apprentice to assist in the family business; this might be an unofficial apprenticeship for his son who would be taught all the clothier knew about cloth making or it might be the son of a neighbour or friend in which case a formal apprenticeship indenture would be drawn up, a premium sometimes paid, the apprentice serving for a term of thirteen years. A third form of apprenticeship was when the overseers of the poor needed to find a place for a poor child and on some occasions the overseers almost compelled a person to take on an apprentice. Clothiers had been known to refuse, preferring to pay a fine rather than agree. The apprentice became a member of the master's family, an unpaid servant and it was fairly common for them to abscond when they reached an age at which they could become journeymen. Newspapers regularly carried advertisements describing a runaway apprentice (promising kind treatment if they returned.)

Towards the end of the eighteenth century, spinning schools were established in several parts of Britain, particularly in rural locations where there were no other local manufacturing employment opportunities. One was established at Oakham in Rutland (now part of Leicestershire) in 1787. There, the young worked from 8 a.m. to 1 p.m. and from 2 p.m. to 7 p.m., with a half day on Saturday. They learned to spin jersey and linen as well as to knit. Dinner was provided at midday for which parents were charged 2.5p a week and 'the children do more work in the week by these means and get a much better dinner than they could at home.'[4] A new poor house at Boldre, Hampshire, was equipped with machinery for spinning and weaving and, at Bamburgh Castle, Northumberland, 60 poor girls were taught to spin jersey, and flax as well as to sew, although 'twelve of the youngest are only taught reading and knitting.'[5] In the Lewisham School of Industry children were employed in spinning, wool winding and knitting, one boy aged nine, being engaged in weaving. A School of Industry was opened in Kendal in 1799 with two mistresses for knitting and spinning, together with a master shoe-maker. A schoolmaster and a fourteen-year-old usher, with the help of the older and more intelligent boys, provided instruction for 112 children.

In the then, uncontrolled, context of domestic textile work, children often began to assist parents at a very young age, beginning by winding bobbins and assisting with carding, 'graduating' to handloom weaving as soon as their legs were long enough to reach the loom treadles. An old Yorkshire woman described how, in the mid-nineteenth century women and children from the Dales would still go out on sunny days to some favoured spot with their spinning wheels to work.

Hargreaves' spinning jenny originally had eight spindles and was devised as a hand-operated machine which would fit into larger cottages, the number of spindles increasing to sixteen in the 1770s. Some clothiers who owned mills, particularly those in the West Country, began to install larger jennies in workshops at the mill and, from the 1790s there was a powered version, although it does not seem to have been very widely adopted. Carding and slubbing (preparation of the wool, into slivers for spinning) had been mechanised before the end of the eighteenth century and this process was increasingly undertaken in mills in the West of England. Slubbers could earn about twice as much as handloom weavers in the mid-nineteenth century but the young boys and girls who were piecers (rubbing the carded ends together) earned a pittance – 15p–17.5p for standing all day for a working week of some 90 hours.

The condition of some of these children in early to mid-nineteenth-century Yorkshire mills was pitiful. Some of the slubbers beat them cruelly and in winter time fathers might be seen carrying their children on their backs at five o'clock in the morning through deep snow to their work at the mills. Many had crooked legs as a result of standing fifteen, sometimes sixteen, hours a day piecing.

Mechanisation of the woollen industry took place in a piecemeal fashion. Wool preparation was largely being done on scribbling and carding machines by the end of the eighteenth century, a Wiltshire clothier complaining in 1806 that these had taken away much children's employment, although there were more jobs for women (probably in jenny spinning). Spinning continuing to be done on the jenny until the mule was adapted from cotton to woollen spinning around 1820. Some aged weavers considered that children's work conditions under the domestic system, before the introduction of spinning and weaving factories, was worse than under the factory system, parents being the hardest task masters.

The organisation of the woollen industries in Yorkshire and the West of England differed; in Yorkshire the family was the unit of production, whereas in the West Country fulling mills were largely owned or occupied by clothiers with a larger capital, who owned the cloth at all stages of its production, including spinning and weaving in the cottages. Gradually, integrated factories evolved as mill owners brought spinning and weaving on site (the preliminary carding process having already been mechanised). This led to great distress amongst women and children in the former spinning villages up to twenty miles distant from the mills. That the mechanisation of spinning had taken its toll in rural areas is evidenced by the 1824 House of Lords Select Committee on the Poor Rate. Overseers of the Poor in Acton, Suffolk complained that absence of employment was one great cause of the (poor) rates being so enormously high. A similar complaint was heard in Framlingham, Suffolk, where it was said that the women and children had little or nothing to do since hand spinning, which used to employ so many, had been superceded by machine spinning in Yorkshire. William Cobbet reported that the mechanisation of wool spinning for the Witney blanket industry had destroyed domestic spinning in many Cotswold villages causing 'decay and misery'.

Weaving continued to be undertaken in cottages on the hillsides and moorlands in Yorkshire and the West of England well into the nineteenth century. In the 1820s in the villages near Leeds, weft yarn, being softer as it was less tightly spun, was wound onto bobbins on a one-spindled wheel, ready for the weaver. Wool winders, mostly women, boys and girls, used to have 'blood dripping off their fingers caused by the friction of the yarn in winding these bobbins.' Handloom weavers worked into the evening by candle or oil lamp light and it was common to see a boy or girl standing on one side of the loom watching to see if a thread broke (the weaver watching on the opposite side) because, if a broken thread was undetected in the dim light, several more might break as a consequence. But, as hand looms and later, power looms, were installed in mills, the cottage handloom weaver fell on very hard times such that, in 1837 a Parliamentary Commission was set up to investigate, reporting in 1840/41. The overwhelming evidence of poverty was shocking, affecting the entire family, for children had continued to work in the home alongside parents. While, in the earlier 1830s, there had been an estimated 400,000 handloom weavers in Britain, by the time the Commission reported, the number had fallen to 100,000. The Assistant Commissioner for Gloucestershire spelled out the plight starkly in terms of family income. Whereas a factory weaver might earn 65p a week, his wife at weaving or burling 35p and a child carding 12.5p, the entire family income of cottage-based handloom weaver, including the labour of wife and children, was 50p. 'The outdoor weavers are undoubtedly in deep and severe distress.'[6]

'Many weavers have declared that they consider the condition of a prisoner to be superior to their own, inasmuch as he is supplied with food and clothing, and they can scarcely obtain the one or the other.' The governor of one prison confirmed this, saying that 'they leave prison with regret, not knowing where to obtain the next meal.'[7] A petty constable described a weaver's wife who 'had a child at the breast, and declared she had had no food for the whole day (it was 5 p.m.) and that she had three children; there was not a table or piece of furniture in the room; everything was sold.'[8] The truck system of payment (in tokens redeemable at a designated shop) predominated in some clothing villages, with the consequence that many weavers paid their cottage rents in goods too. While an advantage of the system was that a large part of the wage could not be consumed in drink, the disadvantage was that many truck masters valued their goods at higher prices than were paid in local shops and markets and the quality was often poorer.

One of the final operations in the production of a piece of woollen cloth was burling, being the inspection and, where necessary, mending of a piece. This was a task undertaken by women and younger girls who might be seen going to and fro fetching cloth on their shoulders to burl, and

Hungry children, better dressed than some.

taking them back when done. It was one of the non-mechanised processes which was brought into the mills as they were enlarged or entirely rebuilt to accommodate the increased number of machines. In the West of England burling shops were usually located on the top floor of a mill, lit by long rows of windows. In Yorkshire much of the burling continued to be done in cottages until the mid-nineteenth century. Burling workshops were great sources of gossip of what people were doing and saying; people's circumstances. A writer in the 1880s reflected that if the burlers had had a chance of a decent education, and had chosen to follow it up, the burling shed might have become a kind of college.

The 1802 legislation limiting the number of daytime hours which could be worked by a child in cotton and woollen factories did not entirely apply to water-powered factories, a number of which still existed in the 1830s in the West Country and in more rural districts of Yorkshire. Water-powered mills suffered from two causes of water shortage: dry summers and, for those located lower down valleys, the fact that the mills upstream held-back the water first, with the result that it did not reach downstream until midday or even later. These factories were permitted to make up for lost time by working late and, sometimes all night. By 1830, when mill night working for children was less common, Richard Oastler took up the cause of the length of a child mill worker's working day, writing a series of letters to a Yorkshire newspaper entitled Slavery in Yorkshire, pointing out that the 1819 and 1825 Factory Acts did not cover woollen mills and that children were working for fourteen and fifteen hours a day and without proper breaks for meals. The owners of water-powered mills opposed any regulation on the grounds that night work or extended hours, when water power was inadequate in the day, was the only means by which orders could be met. For water-powered factories situated in the lower reaches of valleys, late evening and night work was said to be essential.

Mill children; a somewhat romanticised image of two reasonably well-dressed children walking to work at the large mill in Yorkshire.

Richard Oastler (1789–1861), a Yorkshire children's champion who campaigned for the ten-hour day.

By 1850 the number of children under thirteen years of age employed in the woollen industry was low: 645 boys and 422 girls in Yorkshire; twenty boys and fifteen girls in Gloucestershire. As the woollen industry became more factory based – by this date only a few handloom weavers were continuing to eke out a miserable livelihood in cottages – factory children were largely employed as piecers for mule spinning.

In 1862, Henry Mayhew, author of *London Labour and the London Poor,* published a detailed account of a three-day visit to one of the remaining woollen factories in Gloucestershire in *The Shops and Companies of London and the Trades and Manufactories of Great Britain.* The factory, consisting of two mills under single ownership, was located near Stroud, producing high quality superfine cloth. Superfine broadcloth took five months to produce and was said to be 'as soft and homogenous in their texture as a baby's skin'. Young people were employed in some of the processes: a 'small boy in a very short coarse white smock' beat a bundle of fleeces on the floor with a wooden implement, making the wool more easily handled by the adult wool sorter. Some of the wool was dyed (other cloths being dyed after weaving) and then boys in sack-cloth jackets 'all be-smudged with indigo' and with fingers and faces 'the colour of blue mould' worked at the blowing machines and the twilley – which separated the wool fibres in preparation for spinning. The entire workshop was 'hazy ... with clouds of blue dust for ever flying about the place.' No comment was made concerning the inevitable threat of lung disease. The spinning mules 'like enormous harpsichords fitted with some hundreds of the finest strings' were operated by men, assisted by girls whose hair was encased in nets to prevent it becoming caught in the machines, wearing spotted bib-and-tucker aprons. The girls walked to and fro carrying bobbins from the slubbing machines (which imparted a loose twist to the wool) to the mules, two girls working at each mule. They would have walked a number of miles each day.

Arkwright's water frame, invented for cotton spinning, was adapted to spinning longer, combed, worsted thread in the 1770s, but it could not be used for spinning the shorter-stapled wool used in making woollen fabrics. For this reason the organisation of the worsted industry more closely paralleled that of the cotton industry, in that water-powered mills were built (mainly) in Yorkshire and Derbyshire for carding and spinning from the 1770s onwards, whereas powered spinning in woollen manufacture largely took place from the 1820s when the self-acting mule was adapted to shorter staple wool. More women and children were employed in worsted weaving than in wool (although not so many as in cotton). And, as in the Lancashire cotton industry, they were more numerous in the country districts where there was little alternative employment.

There were larger numbers of children under thirteen working in worsted mills for, in this industry in the late eighteenth and earlier part of the nineteenth centuries, spinning and weaving were conducted as distinct enterprises, as they were in the cotton industry. Integrated mills, incorporating all the main manufacturing processes, became a more usual feature in both the worsted and cotton industries in the second half of the nineteenth century. Children were required to clean machinery while it was in motion, this being a frequent cause of accidents; girls, in particular, being vulnerable with their skirts and long hair which could be caught up in machinery. Limbs were frequently broken and deaths occurred. When, in 1842, Lord Ashley was seeking evidence of child exploitation in different manufacturing industries, he sought the assistance of William Dodd, a former worsted piecer, who had been crippled by his work as a child. Dodd travelled around Britain collecting evidence which he sent to Lord Shaftesbury and, in Bradford, interviewed Benjamin Gomersal who had begun work as a piecer at the age of nine, working from 6 a.m. to 7 or 8 p.m. with only a half hour lunch break: 'We had no time for breakfast or drinking. The children conceive it to be a very great mischief to be kept so long in labour; and I believe their parents would be very glad if it was not so.' He described the effect on his body of the long hours at work:

> We had to stoop, to bend our bodies and legs. I was a healthy and strong boy, when I first went to the mill. When I was about eight years old, I could walk from Leeds to Bradford (ten miles) without any pain or difficulty, and with a little fatigue; now I cannot stand without crutches! I cannot walk at

> all! I found my limbs began to fail after I had been working about a year. It came on with great pain in my legs and knees. I am very much fatigued towards the end of the day. I had to attend the mill after my limbs began to fail. I could not then do as well as I could before. I had one shilling a week taken off my wages. I had lost several inches in height. I frequently had to stand thirteen and fourteen hours a day, and to be continually engaged. I was perfectly straight before I entered on this labour. Other boys were deformed in the same way. I am sure this pain, and grievous deformity, came from my long hours of labour.[9]

Gomersal was beaten by the overlooker in the mill:

> I have been beaten till I was black and blue and I have had my ears torn! Once I was very ill with it. He beat me then, because I mixed a few empty bobbins, not having any place to put them in separate. We were beaten most at the latter end of the day, when we grew tired and fatigued.[10]

A thirty-four-year-old man, crippled since the age of seventeen and eking out a living by woolcombing which he could only do for an hour at a time, told Dodd that he had often wished he had been born a horse, a cow, or a dog – anything but what he was, a human being. In 1850, 2222 boys and 2556 girls under thirteen worked in Yorkshire worsted mills and in the combined spinning and weaving mills there were 1779 boys and 2932 girls. Numbers declined sharply thereafter. Factory legislation and the later nineteenth-century Education Acts prohibiting factory work for young people under thirteen, unless they had a certificate of educational attainment, together with a larger factory inspectorate, effectively put an end to the employment of young children in woollen and worsted factories.

SEVEN

Coal mines

COAL DEPOSITS ARE WIDESPREAD in Britain and the Romans located and exploited the main deposits in the Scottish Lowlands, Northumberland and Durham, North and South Wales, Cumbria, Yorkshire, Lancashire, and the Forest of Dean. In the Middle Ages 'sea cole' was collected on the shores of North East England and drift mines and bell pits were cut where the coal outcropped. Early shafts were lined with timber and, by the mid-eighteenth century, brick-lined shafts were common. By this time the North and South Staffordshire coalfields were also being extensively exploited. By the late eighteenth century deep shaft mining was extensive and the industry rapidly expanded during the nineteenth century, peaking in the early twentieth century.

Children had probably been employed in coal mining for some hundreds of years before the Industrial Revolution but pre-eighteenth century mines were neither so large nor so deep as they had become by the 1760s. A treatise on mining in the North East of England, published in 1708, mentions adult male miners and describes the issue of ventilation and the causes of mine explosions but does not mention children. This does not, of course, mean that there was none in the mines at that time. But by the later eighteenth century both boys and girls worked underground, some from the age of five. The proportion of the mining labour force made up of children varied according to the depth of the coal seams and the techniques employed, the largest number of children being employed in areas with narrow seams and the most primitive technologies, locations where adults could only enter with difficulty.

Child trapper, one of the most crucial jobs, and perhaps, the loneliest in a coal mine, waiting for the sound of a waggon in order to open the door to let it through and to close the door afterwards, to prevent a rush of gas which could cause an explosion.

A 1798 report on the mining poor of Tyneside suggested that coal mining was an industry in which the youngest children worked. Some coal mines were located in inhospitable or remote places where there were few alternatives to pit work for children or adults. A traveller writing of a visit to the mines at Whitehaven (Cumbria) in 1813 wrote of a horse pulling a line of baskets 'driven by a young girl covered with filth, debased and profligate, and uttering some low obscenity as she passed by'.[1] It was not until the 1835 Select Committee on Accidents in Mines and the 1842 Report of the Children's Employment Commission that widespread evidence of the extent and state of child employment underground became widely known. The 1842 Report revealed in horrifying detail the conditions under which some children worked, the impact being all the greater as it was the first Parliamentary report to be illustrated. In the early to mid-nineteenth century boys and girls entered underground workings at the age of six or seven, working as 'trappers' from twelve to eighteen hours a day, a job which varied little from one coalfield to another. It was tedious and lonely, involving sitting for hours on end by a closed door, listening for the sound of a waggon, opening the door to let it through and closing the door after it had passed. Despite their young age, the trapper had a crucial role in the maintenance of pit safety for, if the door was left open, gases could travel along the tunnels and cause explosions. And doors were left open when the child fell asleep. These small children acknowledged that they saw no daylight on weekdays, only on Sundays. Many found the job not only lonely but frightening. They were not provided with candles, so sat in the dark for twelve or more hours a day. One young girl admitted that she liked to sing but was too frightened to do so in the dark. This was a life passed in solitude, damp and darkness. On one occasion, in 1841, as a Mines Commissioner was passing, a young boy trapper begged for some grease from the Commissioner's candle. The child had scooped out a hole in a great stone and, having obtained a wick, had made a crude sort of lamp which he kept going as well as he could by begging contributions of melted tallow from the candles of any kindly passers-by. At the age of ten or twelve the boys became 'lads' or 'foals', taking coals on a tram, from where the miners had hewn it, to the shaft. They were often subjected to abusive language and blows, being required to perform more than they were physically able.

Colliery owners rarely, if ever, went into the mines. Mine agents/stewards were more knowledgeable but were, on occasion, reluctant to disclose the ages of the younger children. Evidence from the 1842 Mines Report shows that the ages at which children were employed above and below ground varied from one part of the country to another. A Sheffield pit boy reported that he first went into the pit aged five, as a trapper, then hooked coal baskets onto the gin and then, aged thirteen, helped to fill the baskets or waggons before pushing them. He acknowledged that, sometimes, the work was too hard. An orphan girl, who didn't know her age, but was probably around twelve or thirteen years old, worked on a pit bank at Wednesbury. Her father was dead and her mother had run away, leaving her when she was very little. She had strayed around searching for her mother and had walked away from Coventry on her own, asking for the road to Lancashire. She arrived at a pit bank to warm herself near a fire and then said that she was lost. She was told to wait until a man came up out of the pit and, when he came up, he took her home to his wife and they looked after her.

One Black Country surgeon reported that children who began work in collieries as early as seven or eight, often met with accidents before they were eight. In Shropshire a child of four regularly accompanied his father down the pit, as did a three-year-old in Yorkshire. It was said to be common practice for children to begin work in the mines at between the ages of five and six in Durham and the West Riding. A six-year-old Durham boy got up at 3 a.m. and was at the pit for 4 a.m. He returned home at 4.30 p.m., was given dinner, washed and went to bed. He had almost no time in the week for eating, let alone playing. In Eastern Scotland children began pit work between the ages of five and six and employers seemed to be, on the whole, unconcerned. In South Wales and Monmouthshire children were quite commonly taken down the pits at the age of four, many young boys being taken into the mines as soon as they could stand, sometimes when they could merely crawl. But in North Wales they did not generally work underground before they were seven years old. A boy who had begun work in the pits aged four said that he could hardly keep his eyes open but found that smoking a pipe helped. For these children childhood hardly existed. In the mines of Southern Ireland, on the other hand, the work which was done by very young children in England, was undertaken by children in their teens aged between thirteen and eighteen.

In the South Durham coalfield children were said not to be taken to work in the pits before the age of nine, but the Commissioner found 'overwhelming evidence' to the contrary, children being taken down as young as five or six. And it was often the parents who sought to get their children into mine employment under the age of nine. In times of brisk trade fathers would threaten to leave, if the colliery refused to comply. Returns made by fourteen South Durham collieries for the 1842 Report showed that, out of 235 trappers, 135 were under the age of ten. Overall the Commissioner estimated that between 12,000 and 15,000 people were employed at collieries between the rivers Tyne and Wear, of which some 1040 were under thirteen years of age and 1356 aged between thirteen and eighteen. Underground workers at one pit described how they came up at the end of their day's work in a tub, men and boys together, laughing all the way. But conditions were not so good at other pits. A seventeen-year-old from Jarrow described how he began to drive a horse at the age of eight but was badly used by the waggon-way men who repaired the waggon road and he was afraid to complain in case he was whipped again. The tubs at this colliery were heavy, weighing 9 cwt and workers were not allowed time to sit down and eat between 5 a.m. and 5 p.m.

In the majority of coalfields, children were taken into the pits by their parents. Where a child was one of a large family he/she might be taken as soon as they could understand instructions. If several siblings were already earning, the younger child might be fortunate enough to be kept out of the mines until the age of nine. Most of the children in West Yorkshire coal mines were employed by the colliers. This led to an abuse not seen by the colliery owners, namely that of children being left in the pit after the colliers had left. This was reported in the northern part of the West Riding coalfield, the collier sometimes even leaving the child to finish his stint, besides having to fill and transport two or three baskets after the collier had left.

Some children were apprenticed to coal mines by a local workhouse, in a similar fashion to the system of apprenticing paupers to cotton, worsted or silk mills. This system was prevalent in the Black Country but also in Yorkshire, Lancashire and the West of Scotland. In Thornhill, West Yorkshire, a case was reported of a workhouse child under five years old being sent to a pit. Birmingham Workhouse apprenticed boys to the South Staffordshire mines, for example. The South Staffordshire coalfield was characterised by a system of subcontracting in which the colliery owner paid a subcontractor or 'butty', the butty in turn hiring and paying the labourers. Pauper apprentices were entirely in the power of the butties and they were greatly in demand, being sent on trial between the ages of eight and nine. At nine years of age they were apprenticed for twelve years, without pay. It was said that there were hardly any boys in the workhouses at Walsall, Wolverhampton, Dudley and Stourbridge.

The butty system was pernicious, the men being prepared to send a boy where they would not go themselves, resulting in more than occasional broken limbs and lost lives. Some parishes would not let the butties have their pauper apprentices. There were no apprentices in the South Durham coalfield, but children were at the beck and call of the men. A fifteen-year-old boy described how, having been a trapper for two to three years, he was employed to clean the track way and sweep the rail with a brush. The men used to beat him, one man telling him to clean one place and, while he was doing it, another man would tell him to clean another place. He could not do both at once and one of them would hit him.

Apart from trapping the most usual task for children in the mines was pushing, pulling or carrying corves (a kind of basket sometimes with wheels attached) along 'roads' (passages) from the coal face to the main shafts. In many coal workings the seams were too narrow to accommodate pit ponies, some being no more than 50–60 cm high. Baskets of coal were often pulled (or sometimes pushed) along by boys or girls. The child would have a girdle put around his or her naked waist from which a chain

Hurrier in a Halifax mine, hauling a waggon.

attached to the corve was hooked, passing between the legs. The boys or girls then crawled on hands and knees, drawing the corve behind them. This was extremely painful, as the girdle and chain caused blisters and knees became very sore. The work was less hard in mines where rails had been laid but where there were none the work was a hundred times more slavish. One old miner, when asked for his views replied 'Sir, I can only say of it what the mothers say, it is barbarity, barbarity.'[2] Some children were required to load the waggons, having to lift weights of up to 40 kilos. One of the men gathering evidence for the Royal Commission wrote 'I have no hesitation in adding that were they galley slaves their work could not be more oppressive.'[3]

Hurriers in a Lancashire mine, pulling and pushing on an incline.

Wages of children aged from seven to about fifteen years were paid to the parent(s), some children being unaware of what they earned. The Parkend Coal Co., in the Forest of Dean, paid 20p per week for the labour of young boys, although boys in Yorkshire more often earned only 2.5p per week, which was increased to 15p between the ages of nine and eleven, and 42.5p between the ages of ten and fourteen. By the time the young person had reached the age of fifteen they sought to be independent of their parents, either leaving home or continuing in the parental home for an agreed rent. A fifteen-year-old Forest of Dean lad, who lived with his widowed mother, earned 70p a week, all of which he gave to his mother and she sometimes gave him a little of it to spend.

There were variations in practices from one region to another, partly due to geology, whether there were any alternatives to pit work and partly to local custom. One of the Yorkshire pits visited by a Commissioner was worked both day and night. The day shift arrived between 6 a.m. and 7 a.m., leaving work at 5 p.m. The night shift worked from 7 p.m. to 5 a.m. The Commissioner was told that the men took who they liked to work in the pit with them, the steward never asking their age, although children under the age of nine could not work at night as they got too tired. At the time of the enquiry there were seven boys on day shift and seven on the night shift. In the Stainborough area lads went into the pit at 2 and 3 a.m., only having twenty minutes for dinner. In the Birstall district of West Yorkshire the average distance the children had to drag corves was 150 yards each way and they were worked so hard that if there was the least pause, they immediately dropped down asleep. A Forest of Dean mine manager who had begun work in a Nottinghamshire mine, driving a horse working a winding gin, had worked from 6 a.m. until after 8 p.m. and, by comparison, considered the eight-hour day of boys and men in the colliery he managed to be a great improvement on his own earlier experience.

While some children ate bread and butter, sometimes dry bread or bread and cheese and, on occasion, red herrings and potato, others were less fortunate being given just bread and a bit of fat for dinner. For water the children drank the water that ran through the pits. The sons of widows were singled out as being less likely to eat their fill. The parish priest of Attercliffe, Yorkshire, said that he had seen many boys bring nothing to eat for days on end, only getting what they managed to beg from others. A fatherless lad was, on the whole, looked after by his work mates who were called on to share. Other children were reported as being, on the whole well-fed, having milk porridge and bread for breakfast, Yorkshire pudding with a bit of meat or bacon and bread or potatoes, some beer and cheese on coming out of the pit or, if dinner was cold, they might have meat and potatoes and milk porridge for supper before going to bed.

Yorkshire pit children received little day-school education and few of those interviewed by the Assistant Commissioners could read or write. The Yorkshire Commissioner was scathing about the county school instruction, suggesting that education in the proper sense of the word scarcely existed amongst collier children. Many children went to Sunday School but they appeared to learn little and the teacher was referred to as 'only a lad.' A twelve-year-old boy said that he would prefer to go to school but was forced to go into the pit; he could not go to evening school because it was too far to travel. A fourteen-year-old girl who could read but not write said that she read and taught herself when she returned home in the evening but an eleven-year-old girl said that she could not read and had never been to school as she had no shoes to go in. Girls were sometimes prevented from attending Sunday school, being required to do domestic work in the home, in addition to their work at the pit.

A Yorkshire colliery agent considered that the children's education was lamentably bad, and that the adults set no example, since only three out of 50 men were able to sign their own names. There was a single reported exception to this dismal tale where, at Flockton, Yorkshire, a school was erected by the colliery owner and his wife who provided a Christian education on Sundays and, with a monitorial system, ensured the children could read and spell. On Monday afternoons the school re-opened and children were taught the three Rs, besides geography, drawing and, for the girls, sewing. Working long hours for six days a week left only Sunday as 'free time' and, in Yorkshire, Sunday play was frowned upon. John, from a Sheffield pit, said that he didn't play and only ambled around. Another child said that he had never been to (day) school but went to Sunday School where he was taught writing, adding that he went to chapel every Sunday. James, aged thirteen began work in the pit aged seven, and said that he never played at all. But opportunities for play were found at some of the pits. The Vicar of Attercliffe described how boys could be seen playing together at quoits with horse shoes, to pass the time. Sometimes they made cages for mice to take them home for the cats. Whenever the engine stopped, the boys played. But this was at pits where the coal seams were wider and machinery was more widespread. The Forest of Dean Commissioner, commenting on the dullness of being a trapper (called door-boy in the Forest), observed them enjoying rides on the coal waggons as far as the trap door nearest their own, being ready to ride back with the returning train, and perform their task as soon as required.

Pit clothing was sparse. At one Barnsley pit the Commissioner found a group of men, boys and girls, all naked to the waist, the girls' hair bound in a tight cap. At two other pits, while the girls were dressed, the majority of men with whom they worked were stark naked except, perhaps, for a waistcoat. A seventeen-year-old girl who worked in a pit at Barnsley as a hurrier, reported that she generally worked naked to the waist and regarded the work as very hard. Her back and ankle had been strained. One father commented that he preferred his daughters to work at the pit than to be in domestic service, believing there to be less immorality in the pits, saying that if a man were to offer any insult to a girl in a pit she would raise her fist and give him a blow in the face. However, a sixteen-year-old girl who wore a petticoat, shift and stays said that the man she worked for was stark naked and she did not like that.

Corporal punishment certainly took place. If a trapper fell asleep he or she was beaten; if a child swore or misbehaved they were flogged, for the mine owners were said to be angry if stewards were not severe. One boy reported that he was not ill-used unless he missed marking the corve and then they would beat him with a pick handle. William, aged ten, from Tinsley, Yorkshire, said the boys were given conflicting orders and then one party or other would 'thump' them. Other punishments included putting candles in their mouths or making the boys drink oil. Older children learned to mimic adult behaviour and would beat the younger ones for the slightest misdemeanour.

The risk of serious accidents was high where very young children worked as trappers, yet this was universal practice. Doors were shut to control draughts and the passage of gases, either of which could cause a serious explosion and fire. The employment of the youngest children as trappers put them in a position of huge responsibility of which they were, probably, only dimly aware; and some fell asleep from exhaustion or boredom or both; they were sometimes the cause of terrific destruction to others. Children sometimes propped doors open or left them ajar; they frequently fell asleep in the warm atmosphere and, because of this, regular patrols of ventilation doors were instituted in North Eastern collieries during the 1830s and early 1840s. Corporal punishment was the likely outcome, the children being continually liable to the checks and reproof of those in authority. Failure to understand the gravity of shutting an open door and thereby diverting the air current, bringing up gases from the coal face to where children sat with naked candles, could lead to an immediate explosion. The 1842 Commissioners' Report concluded that a frequent cause of fatal accidents in coal mines was the almost universal practice of entrusting the closing of the air-doors to very young children. And there were other dangers for young trappers who could be injured by the wheels of trucks and trolleys, as well as from the horses.

Larger mines were at a greater risk of accidents from methane gas (fire damp) than smaller ones. This could cause explosions; an additional hazard being a mixture of carbon dioxide and nitrogen, known as choke damp. The role of the trapper was crucial since the ventilation door in their charge maintained the direction of underground air currents. A number of mine explosions were caused by the child trappers' inattention and this led to calls for them to be excluded from pits. If the accident was small-scale, mine stewards would often seek to keep the incident from the colliery owner. There was nothing more dangerous than the sudden shutting of a trap door which had been left open, for that could drive a body of gas to where children or colliers had candles and cause an explosion. It was hard to devise any other really safe system than that of having a much older, better paid, and responsible person to perform so vital a task. Colliers, finding that the Davy lamp provided inadequate light would often unscrew the lamps or take naked candles into the mines. A Sheffield mine steward reported that none of the men would work with Davy lamps if they could help it, candles giving far better light, besides being handy for sticking in holes and places where they were needed. In some mines in the north of England, lamps were padlocked but the men managed to poke holes in them. Effective ventilation was the best accident prevention, in addition to which an inspection was recommended before work began each day.

In some Scottish mines girls carried the coal in baskets strapped to their backs, ascending to different levels by ladders. They frequently did this in twos, the risk to the lower girl being hit by falling coal being very great. In shafts of from 40 to 95 fathoms in depth, a breaking rope was almost always fatal. The Forest of Dean Commissioner reported that frequent accidents occurred in the smaller pits where ropes continued in use after they had become too rotten to sustain heavy weights. One boy was killed by working under a partially worked coal vein, after enquiring whether there was any danger and having been assured there was none. A crack suddenly opened and the coal fell on him and buried him.

Occasionally pits were flooded, the cause generally being excessively bad weather, as at Silkstone in 1838. It had been raining hard during a thunder storm to such an extent that the water came into the sough of the engine house. The engineer gave the alarm to the banksman who shouted to put the light out and come out of the pit. The children and people were frightened, not knowing what was the matter. A number of children ran from the shaft towards the pit-rail and were met by water escaping from old workings. Having passed a trapdoor, the children were driven against it by the water and, being unable to open it, eleven girls and fifteen boys were drowned.

Notwithstanding the long hours, the dark and damp, some alleged that Yorkshire colliery children were more robust and healthy in their

Girls carrying coal in baskets up a ladder from the mine, with many possibilities of serious accidents.

appearance than manufacturing children, except where the work was badly ventilated; or the children worked with the belt and chain, crawling on all fours in thin pits. However a local surgeon disagreed, stating that they were prone to asthma and other chest ailments caused by the damp working conditions, besides the coal dust. One collier believed that girls' health was badly affected by the heavy weights they had to lift; they acquired a stoop and had internal complaints. One girl, a hurrier, described how she sometimes had to push the corve with her head and it made her head, which was soft, sore.

Most of the significant improvements in mining technology were made in ventilation and underground haulage; both occupations in which the majority of workers were children and young people. By 1842 wheeled cabs were beginning to replace the baskets and wooden sledges which had been laboriously hauled and pushed, while iron rails were replacing wooden planks and cast iron tram plates. In North Eastern collieries, where height permitted, there was an increase in the use of pit ponies, with the added advantage that they could haul heavier loads. The introduction of hauling machinery was governed by the height and slope of coal seams. In West Yorkshire, parts of Lancashire, Shropshire and south Staffordshire, where the coal seams were thin and the passages narrow, the use of children as bearers or 'hurriers' continued.

Geology and, linked with this, the mining methods that were feasible, were determining factors as to whether young children were recruited in large numbers. There was great variation even within a single coalfield, depending on the height of the coal seams. In those parts of the West Yorkshire coalfield where the seams were wider children aged under thirteen comprised 16 per cent of the recorded labour force in the 1840s, whereas in the small pits with narrow seams they comprised 24.7 per cent of the labour force.

By the 1840s putting young children in charge of mine ventilation was increasingly regarded as unsafe practice. The Vicar of Attercliffe, Yorkshire, devised two ways of opening trap doors either of which would succeed, although he had little expectation of their being adopted. Agents for some of the larger mines thought that legislation prohibiting the employment of young children in coal mines would come as a relief to the coal owners, but would affect the interests of the workmen who would think this to be against their interests. Opposition to the proposed restriction on children's

Lord Shaftesbury investigating child labour in a coal mine, a task that few Mines Inspectors were prepared to undertake. (Mary Evans Picture Library)

employment underground came from areas where the coal seams were thin and it was more difficult to introduce improved technologies for carrying coal from the face to the surface.

The Mines Act, prohibiting the employment underground of all females, and boys below the age of ten, was passed in 1842. Historians do not all agree as to the reasons for the legislation or its timing; some have argued that the level of public outrage forced the government into action; others have suggested that mining legislation was part of the general social progress of the time. What has become clear is that the Mines Act reflected developments which had already caused a reduction in child employment underground, namely economic and technical changes which made child employment underground less necessary or economically viable.

Initially after the passing of the Mines Act, only one inspector was appointed to cover all the mining districts of Britain, and any intending inspector often had to disguise himself as a collier in order to avoid being attacked. Seven years after the passing of the Act, the Inspector, on being examined by a House of Lords Committee admitted that he had never actually been in a mine. As late as 1866 the Mines Inspector for Lancashire reported that he would only enforce the Mines Act when mine owners knowingly employed under-age children or if an underage child had been killed underground. Since most children were employed by members of their own family, the penalty would fall on the parent or guardian of the boy rather than the mine owner. The Mines Act was easiest to enforce in the North East where, uniquely among British coalfields, the majority of children were directly employed by the coal owners. Meanwhile in marginal coal districts, where working conditions continued to be harsh, some of the conditions which Children's Employment Commissioners had complained about in the mid-nineteenth century, lingered on into the early twentieth century, the leather harness for dragging wooden sledges in thin seams persisting in use in the Forest of Dean and some Somerset mines as late as 1908.

EIGHT

Tin, copper, lead

WHEREAS COAL WAS HEWN fairly readily from rock and, after being sorted for quality and size, was sold and used in the state in which it was mined, metal ores were extracted from veins in hard rock and, once mined, had to be broken up, washed and then smelted. The use of gunpowder underground, from the late seventeenth century, restricted the tasks undertaken by children working underground, but they comprised a significant element of the labour force engaged in washing and dressing the mined ore on the surface. Various methods were used to dress the ore, depending both on what the ore was and the region in which it was mined. While lead was smelted near to the mines, copper smelting migrated from Cornwall, where there was no coal, to South Wales and the north Midlands where locally mined coal for the furnaces was cheaper.

Copper and tin

'The shafts of Cornwall', wrote A. K. Hamilton Jenkin, 'could they all be numbered, would prove as the sands of the sea, while the underground tunnels alone extend into thousands of miles.'[1] Tin was mined in Cornwall in Roman times and, by the early Middle Ages, profits from the trade were of great value to the Crown; King John granted a charter to the tin miners of Cornwall and Devon, confirming their 'just and ancient customs and liberties' and their independent Stanneries Court. Generations of men and boys worked in these mines from the early days when the miner's tools were a small iron pick and shovel, to the late 1670s when gunpowder was used to blast the rock and, from the late eighteenth century, when increasingly sophisticated means were used to pump water out from great depths.

Tin was the highly valued ore; copper was worked on only a small scale at the end of the sixteenth century and seems to have been regarded as being of little value in the following hundred years. Only in the last decade of the seventeenth century did copper begin to be regarded as, possibly, being of some value. By the mid-eighteenth century copper mining was of greater importance than tin and by 1787 around 7000 people were employed in Cornish copper mines, working at depths well below 100 metres. The Cornish copper industry suffered severe competition in the 1780s and '90s from the hugely productive Mona and Parys mines on Anglesey. This led to a degree of over-production and a considerable fall in the price paid for copper. The industry revived in Cornwall during the early to mid-nineteenth century. Thereafter the industry declined in importance.

Botallack Mine, Cornwall, now a Heritage Site. Tin, copper and arsenic were mined here.

By the end of the seventeenth century there were at least twenty tin mines around St Austell, employing more than 1000 men and boys on day and night shifts. Until around the end of the eighteenth century tin was obtained by two methods: streaming and mining. Streamers worked in the valley bottoms, sifting the clay, sometimes sinking a shaft from five to twelve metres deep through the clay bed which lay on top of tin bearing gravels. Men and boys were both employed. From the late seventeenth century onwards most of the ore dressing was undertaken by boys aged between seven and seventeen who, according to William Borlase, writing in 1758, were 'taken in so young, become healthy and hardy by using themselves to cold and to work with naked feet all day long, summer and winter alike, and learn early to contribute to their own maintenance.'[2] With the development of more intensive mining came developments in ore dressing. Tin ore was first broken with hammers and then taken to a stamping mill, after which it was ground between stones in a 'crazing' mill until it was as fine as sand. The resulting material was washed by being moved to and fro in dishes in order to float away the waste and retain the heavier ore, this often being done by boys who stirred up the material with their feet.

By the eighteenth century large copper mines dominated the lives of men, women and children in the mineral bearing areas of Cornwall. From around the age of eight both boys and girls were apprenticed, doing light work at the surface. By the age of twelve or fourteen boys became underground miners, going down with their fathers to learn the trade, while girls became 'bal maidens', doing the heavier work of breaking the copper ores with long-handled hammers.

The 1780s were lean years for both the tin and copper trades of Devon and Cornwall and families experienced great want, contemporary writers describing the wraith-like figures of some of the miners. But, in the early nineteenth century conditions had improved. In 1801 there were 75 working mines in Cornwall, around 16,000 people owing their livelihoods directly or indirectly to tin and copper. By 1818 mines in the area of Camborne and Chasewater, alone, employed 8000 people, while by 1838 more than 200 mines employed more than 30,000 men, women and children. Numbers increased in the 1840s and 1850s and, by 1862, 340 mines were recorded employing almost 50,000 people. Cornish miners were either 'tutworkers' or 'tributers', their status being determined by whether or not they held a share in the profits. Tutworkers were contracted workers, often being responsible for sinking shafts, whereas tributers were employed at the mineral-bearing lodes and worked not for piece rates but for a percentage of every pound's worth of ore sent to the surface. While the risks and hardships were similar for both, the tributer stood to earn more and held a slightly higher status. The more ambitious boys always wanted to become tributers.

Men and boys experienced considerable hardship working underground. Accidents were possible on the long ladders to the mine, some mines went out under the sea and the miners were continually drenched with salt water which seeped in, their clothes becoming stiff with salt. Other mines were hot and ill-ventilated. A miner might have to descend some 360 metres of ladders, do an eight-hour shift, climb back up to the surface and walk home. It could take three quarters of an hour to descend and an hour and a quarter to ascend the perpendicular ladders to and from the workface, sometimes carrying mining tools with them. To miners who had been doing this from boyhood, climbing ladders seems not to have presented particular difficulties and boys used to consider it a matter of honour not to pause or give way to another on the ascent.

The 1842 Children's Employment Commissioners found that the youngest child working underground was eight years of age, but children may have worked underground at younger ages in earlier times, one miner describing how, before he was eight and being unable to climb the ladders on his own, he was often taken down the mine on his father's back. By the early 1840s, the more usual age for beginning to work underground was between nine and twelve years. The main job for these children was working air machines or fans. When tributers found a good vein of ore, boys would work 'a double core or stem' (shift), sometimes to earn more for themselves, sometimes as a kindness for a friend. One witness in 1842 described how 'when about fifteen, I used to stay once or twice a month for three twelve-hour courses in succession, merely coming to surface for a short time between each stem of twelve hours to take some food ... I was so much fatigued at the end of the time that when I got home to bed I often found it impossible to get to sleep for hours.'[3] Another boy was said to have worked 'five double-stems out of six days' in a week, in all around 80 hours.

Some boys were employed in 'rolling' or wheeling stuff in barrows in mines, where underground tramroads had not been laid. One witness in

1864 said that he had wheeled 'many a time when my fingers have been ready to go right out, when I was not able to hold anything and the weight was supported by a sling round my neck.'[4] When a level was long, an empty barrow being brought from the shaft might have to be lifted over a full one going towards the shaft.

Conditions such as those known in coal mines where very young children sat in the dark minding a door, or 'hurried' the coal through passages little more than eighteen inches high, were unknown in the tin and copper mines of Devon and Cornwall. Boys were said to be ambitious to go underground, where the wages were higher and the hours shorter than for work at the surface. The 1842 Commissioners suggested that, on the whole, 'not only is there no tyranny exercised by the men over the boys but ... there is a very general consideration ... of the age and powers of their young fellow-labourers, and a disposition to relieve them of any excess of toil even at the expense of increased exertion of their own.'[5] The fact that many children worked with their fathers or near relatives contributed to the promotion of a generous community spirit. One miner described how he was working in a section of the mine when the news was brought that his twelve-year-old son had fallen off a ladder and was hurt. He rushed to the scene, imagining the worst and when he arrived at the scene, the boy was sitting on a man's knee, looking quite cheerful, only crying a little. The tributing system operated in a number of mines. Under this system boys were enabled 'at an early age to acquire that knowledge of their dangerous calling which afterwards made many of them miners of unrivalled skill and intelligence.'[6] It was claimed that corporal punishment was unheard of in Cornish mines, although there were instances of children picking on one of their number who was particularly poorly dressed or unable to defend himself.

Accidents were quite frequent. Some boys who experienced serious ones returned to work eventually as did a sixteen-year-old boy who fractured his skull by falling down a shaft in 1841. In 1860, ten-year-old William, following his father down ladders into a mine, fell and died instantly. Accidents apart, the dust, damp, changes in temperature and the long walks home contributed to lung and heart disease, besides digestive problems, 'those who labour in the mines have a very pale sallow appearance, and this they seem to acquire even after having worked underground only a few months.'[7]

Breaking and sorting ores.

As in other mining regions, specialised terms which seem to have been more or less unique to the region or to the mineral, were used by the Cornish miners and ore dressers for the different processes. Copper ore was brought to the surface in buckets known as kibbles and broken into smaller pieces by men, the kibbles being hauled up the shaft by a horse-whim, in which horses walked round and round a wheel on the surface, the horses sometimes being driven by boys.The separation of the ore from waste rock was known as spalling and this was done by women and boys. The spalled and riddled ore was then picked, a job for the younger children and then sieved, large lumps being sent back to the spallers for further breaking.

These processes were usually carried out on areas of cobbles near the top of the mine. Waste material was separated from the ore by washing and jigging (ore being heavier than the waste sank to the bottom of the jigging boxes), the purpose being to have a fine 'slime' of ore which could be graded.

Much of the work of dressing both tin and copper ores was contracted for by a tributer who agreed to provide ore fit for smelting in return for a percentage fee. The tributer, himself, employed the women and children required to do the work, children ranging in age from seven or eight to twelve or fourteen. Sometimes a parent, perhaps with a large family, would beg a tributer to take a younger child that they were finding it difficult to afford to feed. The tributer would sometimes agree, taking the child in for very light work. The younger children earned less than 1p a day to begin with but by the age of nine or ten they would make their own contracts with the tributer. The youngest girls were usually employed in picking pieces of copper ore and the youngest boys in washing it. Though the work was not very heavy, in most cases, the hours were long: ten in summer and nine in winter. Sometimes, if engaged in piecework, workers at the surface could get off at 2 or 3 o'clock once or twice a week. But at other times a boy or girl aged between nine and twelve was required to get up at about 4 a.m., have a quick breakfast and, after a walk of an hour or more, reach the mine at 6 a.m. and work without a stop until midday. Then, after half an hour's break for dinner they worked until 8 p.m., then had the same long walk as the morning (some three to six miles), ate supper and went to bed by 10 p.m. Some children worked in this way for around a third of each summer month. In some mines a system of overtime over-exerted the children even more, although it was not in operation for so long or affected so many. In these cases boys were engaged in ore preparation from 7 a.m. of one day until 2 p.m. on the following day, working all through the night. However it was not usual for children to be employed on the surface at Cornish mines during the night. On going home in the evening, the children rarely got out of their wet clothes, wearing them again the next day.

By the early nineteenth century much of the ore dressing was undertaken by women and older girls, the 'bal maidens' who undertook spalling, breaking up the larger rocks with long-handled hammers. Then the smaller pieces of copper ore were broken into yet smaller pieces by 'bucking' on an anvil. This was said to be harder work than spalling; the girls sat in cramped positions which allowed little movement and the sheds in which they worked were open to the elements, winter and summer. When working very hard a girl could earn 5p a day. But on average it was around 3 to 4p. Bal maidens generally ate their dinner together but sometimes 'some of the girls steal away ... to eat their meal behind a hedge, being ashamed of the meanness of their fare.'[8]

While the hamlets and villages in which mining children lived were often located several miles away from the mines, the cottages were cramped but many were clean and warmed by an open fire. The lodging shops of the Northumberland and Durham mining areas were unknown in Devon and Cornwall. Young people married early and, as a consequence, families were large. Infant mortality was high and surviving children had to be sent to work at an early age. The only education mining children received was acquired at a dame school or Sunday school but by the 1860s it was claimed that all children could read, although many could not write.

Around 6,795 young children and teenagers worked at the Cornish mines in the 1840s, almost all of them at ore dressing. An estimated 1600 boys under thirteen were working in mines in 1841; it was said that children were being employed at a younger age than before, due to the increasing poverty of their parents. Boys who worked underground, although of a similar age to surface workers, had a certain kudos and kept themselves apart from those who worked on the surface. Despite increased mechanisation during the mid- to late-nineteenth century, children were still employed at Cornish mines in the 1870s and, in 1872, the young people working on the surface at Cardon Hill, on the edge of Bodmin Moor, struck for more pay. Copper mining had been beset by problems from mid century – falling prices in the markets, proposals for Government inspections, and the notorious five-week month – a flat rate of pay per month, whether there were four or five weeks in it. This practice was only abolished in 1872 after the formation of the Miners' Protection Society. In May of that year 300 girls and boys in the Liskeard area struck and were awarded an additional penny per day, but in other places children struck for an additional 1p per day – without success – resulting in a disgruntled return to work.

It was not until 1872 that the employment of all girls and boys under the age of ten was prohibited in metalliferous mines and, six years later, in 1878, the Factories and Workshops Act gave protection to surface workers, stipulating that women and children were not to work more than a twelve hour day – the Act also prohibited night working on ore dressing, a process that was more efficient and cost effective with continuous working. Even after the passing of the 1880 Elementary Education Act requiring school attendance for children aged between five and ten years, it was known that some children of school age were employed illegally in the mines. But copper mining in Cornwall and Angelsey had been eclipsed by other countries, leaving landscapes permanently changed by past industrial activities.

From the 1850s and '60s and still more in the 1870s and '80s, a stream of young Cornish men went to the mines of North America, Australia and South Africa, taking their knowledge and skills with them. Some emigrated permanently, others returned to tell tales of the Californian gold rush and of pioneer mining in distant lands.

Lead

Lead mining was largely undertaken in Derbyshire, Durham, Northumberland and Cumberland. The Derbyshire lead industry peaked in the eighteenth century and, by 1830, most of the mines had closed. The 1842 Commissioner in the Northern region noted 'Very few strangers come to settle in these vales ... the miners, therefore, are as much as possible an unmixed race and are likely so to continue.'[9] One illustration of this was that many of the words used in the 'lead country' were unlikely to be encountered in the south of England.

In the 1840s, the London Lead Company leased extensive mines in Teesdale, Co. Durham, employing 1200 adults, 240 teenagers between thirteen and eighteen and 40 boys under thirteen, plus twenty girls aged between eight and thirteen. Boys who worked for the Derwent Company were hired by the men, usually their fathers, as subcontracted labour. At the age of eleven or twelve they received around 3.5p per day, rising to between 4 and 5p until the age of eighteen. Most boys worked at loading separate vehicles with waste stone and ore. The miner drilled a hole in the rock and then inserted a cartridge of gunpowder. Drilling the hole was, however, often performed by boys and youths but they were seldom trusted to charge it with gunpowder. As the fuse was lit everyone would run from the site as the shot went off with a great deal of noise, smoke and dust. A few boys were employed either to drive a horse in the mine at a wage ranging from 35–40p a week, or to drive a horse working at a winding whim on the surface. Boys worked for five days a week, from 7 a.m. until 6 p.m. with an hour off for dinner. Some mines worked double-shifts and a few worked three, with more or less non-stop working.

The geography of a lead mine comprised different levels and air circulation could become a problem, not helped by the smoke and dust. Mine ventilation was said, in the early 1840s, to have been 'good and efficient', compared with earlier in the nineteenth century but, nevertheless, miners were breathing in air which contained minute particles of dust, smoke and other effluvia. As with coal mining, candle light was an indicator of the quality of the air and, when miners were far from a current of fresh air, foul air could enter, putting the candles out. Then it was time to leave. Miners found that they could continue for a while, if they held the candles at a slant but this was seldom done: 'We have the most foul air when the weather is dull and the clouds hang low.' In mines where there was bad air boys were not employed as 'they 'cannot stand it'.[10] In some mines machines, known as fanners, were operated by boys to carry air along pipes to places where it was slow to penetrate; forcing pumps were also used to force the air along.

Until the mid-eighteenth century boys were employed underground, as in coal mining, to drag ore from the seams to where it could be hauled to the surface. Horse drawn waggons on rails reduced the necessity for this and, by 1842, 'there was none of the wholesale exploitation of child labour found in coal mines. The reason, however, was economic, not humanitarian.'[11]

Boys were, however, employed in ore washing and this depended on a good supply of water and could be stopped by frost or drought. One of the consequences of this was that boys worked fewer hours or none at some points in the year and made this up with longer hours when water was available. In the eighteenth and early nineteenth centuries the operation of ore washing was very simple. The ore was put into a 'buddle', a shallow excavation in sloping ground, about the size of a door, so that water entering at the upper end flowed slowly through the buddle, carrying away loose dirt and clay. The solid pieces of ore remaining were broken by a 'bucker', a kind of mallet. At smaller enterprises in remoter valleys, this method of washing and ore breaking continued into the mid nineteenth century. Ore crushing mills were introduced in around 1800, with a considerable saving in lead wastage, although boys were still required to pick out the larger pieces of ore by hand:

The ore's awaiting in the tubs, the snow's upon the fell,
Canny folk are sleeping yet but lead is right to sell,
Come my little washer lad, come lets away,
We're bound down to slavery for four pence a day.'[12]

Few of the ore-washing places had any kind of shelter, men and boys often getting wet early in the day and continuing to work all day in wet clothes. Only their feet might remain dry as they wore thick clogs. For dinner, they sat where they could, very seldom having any additional covering over them. In the mines the men and boys had a 'hasty' meal when they could. The London Lead Company hired the boys for ore washing but in other mining concerns, boys were hired by a contractor who was paid by the weight of dressed ore. It was up to him whether he employed ten boys or forty. Joseph Fleming, aged fourteen, began working at Stanhope Burn Works washing ore when aged eleven. During the winter he worked underground in the mine but said that 'washing is easier.' He got up at 6 a.m., had some coffee and dry bread and was at work for 7 a.m. He had a little white cake and more coffee for dinner (called 'bait') and went home after his eight hours work to wash his face and neck; 'on Saturdays I wash down to my navel'. Supper consisted of potatoes with mutton or bacon, 'We have a rather better dinner on Sundays and have some meat to it.'[13]

After being washed and crushed, the ore was taken to a smelting mill. While few mining concerns admitted employing teenagers at a smelting mill, sometimes a man would take his own son, or perhaps another boy to help him, while a youth of sixteen might be employed in roasting the ore if he was strong enough.

In comparison with coal mining, accidents at lead mines and the associated processes were relatively rare. Occasionally death was caused by a roof fall in a mine and there was report, in the 1840s, of a ten-year-old boy killed in a stone-crushing machine; but these accidents were infrequent. A far more common cause of death was consumption and this was usually contracted in adulthood; the life expectancy of a lead miner being lower than the average.

Some of the larger mining companies built villages to house their employees – even so, many men and children had to walk three miles or more to work and back each day. Where mines were more remote, lodging houses were built by the companies. These seem to have been uniformly foul. Men and boys would stay there for four nights a week, two men to a bed, with a boy sometimes across the end. The Commissioner described the smell of one sleeping room as 'utterly intolerable' despite the fact that the beds had not been slept in for three days. They would bring provisions each Monday and these were locked, together with the miner's wallet, in an individual cupboard. The Commissioner's view of lodging houses was made clear: 'I should think it no hardship to have to remain 24 hours in a mine, but I should be terrified at being ordered to be shut up a quarter of an hour in the bed-room of a lodging-shop.' This evidence was corroborated by a miner who said 'Our lodging-rooms were ... not fit for a swine to live in.'[14]

The London Lead Company had a large school at Middleton, two teachers being paid by the company. All children over the age of six were expected to attend until they began work and, when ore-washing could not be undertaken in winter, children up to the age of fourteen were required to attend school. Most of the boys who were interviewed could read and write and had some general knowledge and would attend church sometimes; one, however, could neither read nor write, having played truant at school. Perhaps a measure of the working conditions in lead mining was reflected in the fifteen-year-old who had visited Newcastle and said that he would like to be a sailor.

By the 1860s Britain was importing lead and the northern industry had halved its output. Wages fell and, by the 1880s, were around half the level of the 1860s. Were it not for the smallholdings that many mining families had there would have been even greater destitution. Work for children at the lead mines had become, more or less, a thing of the past.

NINE

Pottery and bricks

Pottery

THE GREATEST CONCENTRATION OF POTTERY WORKS (or potbanks, as they were called) in the eighteenth and nineteenth centuries was in North Staffordshire, but pottery was also made in many other places including London, Worcester, Bristol, Swansea, Derby, Newcastle, Liverpool, Leeds and Glasgow. The industry used machinery, but most of it was hand-operated and many different craft skills were involved in producing earthenware or fine bone china. The only power-driven operations were the heavy tasks of clay mixing and flint grinding and, more occasionally, colour grinding for glazes.

In the sixteenth and seventeenth centuries, many farmers made simple pots at home, which they took to market with their agricultural produce. But, by the eighteenth and nineteenth centuries, pottery was increasingly being made in a series of workshops around a courtyard, with the 'bottle' oven(s) located on the perimeter or centrally. Potbanks were highly adaptable units which could be incrementally extended far more easily than, for example, a multi-storey mill.

Children were employed in large numbers in the North Staffordshire industry in the nineteenth century. The industry was investigated in both the 1843 and 1863 Children's Employment Commissions and the evidence provides detailed descriptions of working conditions. The 1843 North Staffordshire Potteries Assistant Commissioner visited 173 works, listing 127 pottery firms, some of which had more than one potbank and, after

Small craft pottery in the early eighteenth century.

initially considering writing itemised reports on each one, he divided them into three categories, in recognition of their similar characteristics. The first group, comprising 25 potbanks consisted of the most recently built works with 'large, well ventilated, light, airy, commodious rooms', including such firms as Wedgwood, Minton, Alcock, and Mason. The second group, 'by far the most numerous', comprised 63 works each employing anything from 50 to 800 people. Typically, these works had:

> been erected many years and, as the trade has increased, so the rooms appear to have increased ... some here and there, upon, around, and about the first premises, so there is neither order, regularity, nor proportion; the consequence of this is that men, women and children are to be seen passing in and out, to and fro, to their respective departments all hours of the day, no matter what the weather, warm, cold, wet, or

dry; the rooms with very few exceptions, are either low, damp, close, small, dark, hot, dirty, ill ventilated, or unwholesome, or have all these disadvantages.'[1]

One of the larger second category potbanks extended over fourteen acres with nineteen bottle ovens, 272 workrooms, nineteen slip kilns, 42 warehouses and 33 other offices, a steam engine for clay and flint grinding, which also drove some lathes and throwing wheels, and another engine for breaking down broken saggars (in which the wares were baked) as well as driving some machinery. There were, in all, 454 workpeople, of which 77 were children under the age of thirteen. An office worker stated 'I cannot tell how many rooms we have for working in, they are all so in and out.[2] The third group was 'even still worse'[3] but few children were employed in these potbanks and in many there were no children at all.

Child employment in the Staffordshire Potteries was of two kinds. First, there were apprentices aged between eight and seventeen years, boys seldom being taken before the age of fourteen. These were employed

Josiah Wedgwood's first pot bank, built around a square with bottle ovens in the centre.

Diagram of various processes in a mid-nineteenth-century pottery.

directly by the pottery master. Apprenticeships were for seven years. However the legal binding was nominal, since parents were often unable and always unwilling to pay the requisite £1 stamp duty, or even to ask the master to pay half. Occasionally, where a particularly competent and active youth was apprenticed, the employers would sometimes provide the stamp duty themselves. Since the majority of so-called apprentices were this in name only, many youths would move on after around three years, seeking higher wages in a new situation and leaving the parental home. The second form of child employment was the more numerous, the child being subcontracted to an individual pottery worker who might be his/her parent. It was customary for the men to stop work at midday on Saturday and not to return until Tuesday or even Wednesday the following week; then requiring their child assistants to work late on Wednesday, Thursday and Friday nights. Moreover when order books were full and trade brisk, the oven men, printers, plate-makers and others might require children to arrive as early as 4 a.m. and remain at work until 8 or 9 p.m.

The number of different processes involved in pottery manufacture meant that entire families might be employed – father, mother, and children. The men for whom the children worked were paid by the piece but the boys were paid by the day and were only very rarely given extra for working longer hours. Girls, too, were paid by the day, although at a lower rate. A fourteen-year-old male dipper earned 27.5p a week; a twelve-year-old jigger earned 10p a week; an eleven-year-old figure-maker earned 15p a week; a twelve-year-old press room boy earned 20p a week. Others earned less: an eight-year-old boy was paid 7.5p, the same as a ten-year-old girl. Payment was weekly; the employer would give the head of each department a list of men, women and children, with the sum due to each alongside, together with a 'wage bill'. This then had to be changed for cash, usually in one of the numerous local beer houses. The landlord brought in sufficient cash in advance but would expect either a percentage, or that a certain amount of beer be drunk. Heavy drinking was endemic and, in times of poor trade, parents were keen to get their children to work, however young.

Pottery throwing: a girl turning the wheel and a small boy standing on a block of wood to pass clay to the potter.

If all the family was employed, earnings could be £3 or £4 a week, sufficient for a more than adequate living. But the strong culture of drinking resulted in families having nothing to fall back on in times of ill-health, short-time working or in times of strikes.

The first Potters' Union was founded in 1824 and, in the following year, a number of workers struck for higher wages. The strike was ill-timed, since the pottery industry, along with much manufacturing industry in Britain, was suffering severe depression, and Potbank owners were only too glad to close their works. The strike and the union soon collapsed. Trade revived, but many manufacturers complained of reduced profits, and wages were kept low. A new union was established in 1833 and, in 1834, the men who were employed by those master potters who declined to negotiate, came out on strike. In the weeks that followed, the manufacturers who had acceded to some of the workers' demands were seen to be gaining business at the expense of those whose works were closed. Eventually the latter manufacturers gave in to the workers' demands and, nearly four months after the beginning of the strike, the potbanks were re-opened and an equable rate of wages agreed.

Potter turning a large vessel on a wheel operated by a boy.

But industrial peace was short-lived for, in 1836, the men set out to change the basic terms under which they were employed: annual hiring and being paid only for goods which came in perfect condition from biscuit-firing. By November nearly 20,000 workers were out on strike and 64 potbanks were closed, around half the total number, including those of some of the largest employers. While the union members were men, the potbank closures affected women and children equally and families experienced great poverty; union funds allowing only 5*s.*–6*s.* per head to men who had families – single men receiving 3*s.*–4*s.* Women and children had no share in the funds provided by the union. Distress rapidly spread throughout the entire region for, since there was little money to spend on food, drink or fuel, many others, besides pottery workers, suffered. The effect of the strike on families was pitiful. Mothers wrote in desperation asking for their child apprentice's pay, with little hope of receiving anything.

When the union's resources, including generous gifts and loans received from sympathetic workers in other regions, were exhausted, the men, facing starvation, gave in. 'Ruin descended on the homes of many a working potter. The savings of years were scattered in the space of twenty weeks ... (and) irreparably lost.'[4] Charles Shaw remembered how, on bitter winter days, he went to work without food and how 'Old Rupert' would give him some of his own; Shaw could remember 'many Saturday nights coming home when there was not a morsel of food in the house, and the next day Sunday and all the shops to be shut'.[5] One Saturday 'when the younger ones were crying for food and hardly any fire in the grate' a young potter knocked at the door, slipped his hand between his rolled up apron and waistcoat and handed over a gleaming coin 'and in a very few minutes I saw bread and butter on our table.'[6] On 20 January 1837, the men returned to work, but not before many, including Shaw, had had to go to the Workhouse.

At the time of the 1843 Commission, the pottery industry was suffering from a severe trade depression, on account of the trading situation with America, besides which many pottery workers were still suffering from the aftermath of the 1836–7 strike which 'contributed to reduce those who were in a previous state of prosperity ... to one of dependence, humiliation and poverty from which they have never recovered.'[7] The Assistant Commissioners found examples of children starting work as young as three and four years of age, 'not infrequently' at five and more generally between seven and eight. A large employer, John Ridgeway, believed that children should not be employed in manufactories under the age of ten.

In all cases where the very young were employed it was the parents who put the children to work at some process under their own direction. Young females, potentially, had an additional burden, that of child care. One nineteen-year-old, who scraped off the uneven dipping of wares when dry, looked after younger siblings after her day's work at the potbank, when her mother went to evening school.

Charles Shaw worked as a 'mould-runner' from the age of seven and, a year later was sent to another potbank to work as a handle-maker. The work was not so heavy but the hours were longer. He had to work six days a week but 'the place in which I worked bore a holiday atmosphere on Monday and Tuesday ... throwers would be away drinking ... Sometimes half the turners would be away drinking too.' And sometimes the men managed to bring drink into the works, evading the eyes of the overlooker. On Mondays and Tuesdays the unsupervised boys indulged in play and went home earlier. If a man came into work on Wednesday and found an insufficient number of handles ready, he would often brutally flog the young handlemaker; pots had to be made and:

> from Wednesday to Saturday they worked themselves, and worked others, boys and women, like galley slaves. From four and five in the morning until nine and ten at night this fierce race for wages was run ... Many a time after fourteen and fifteen hours' work, I had to walk a mile and a half home with another weary little wretch ... No wonder ghosts were seen in the dark, gasless 'Hollow' ... Oh yes, I have seen ghosts and heard their wailings on such nights, when my senses were dazed with weariness ... The children were weary for sleep, weak with hunger, and worn out with hard work.[8]

Hours of work varied, although most children arrived at or before 6 a.m. The more fortunate ones left at 6 p.m. and had half an hour for breakfast and an hour for dinner. One boy, who worked in the dipping house, brushing wares from the biscuit oven, had to be at work at 5 a.m. 'to get the fires in; and the place warm.'

The production of a piece of tableware or a decorative figure involved many different processes, children being employed in all but the most strenuous, largely in supporting roles. Some processes required only a few children, whereas others needed more. Very young children were to be found particularly in the throwing, plate, saucer and dish making, dipping, scouring and printing departments. Dish, saucer and plate makers required boy 'jiggers' and 'mould-runners' who worked from 5.30 a.m. until 6 p.m. and frequently as late as 8 or 10 p.m. Each man employed two boys. The boy 'jigger' turned a horizontal wheel all day for the journeyman potter who formed flat wares in a mould which was rotated by the 'jigger'. The 'mould runner' carried the pressed ware to the hot-house, bringing the mould back for more wares. The hot-house was an enclosed room within a room, without windows and with a central iron stove. The temperature could reach up to 130°F. In such temperatures the boys wore little clothing, even when it was freezing weather outside. They laboured 'like little slaves' and their work was acknowledged to be the hardest and most exhausting of all. Many children in these occupations died of asthma or consumption. The Assistant Children's Employment Commissioner estimated that, during a week, the mould runner would carry a total weight of 3840 lbs each day over a distance of seven miles 1120 yards, or over 45 miles per week. In addition, the adult required a boy to arrive more than half an hour before the potter to bring coal into the workshop, remove the ashes, then wedge clay in the yard, and collect half-dried pieces from the shelves, all this in addition to his other tasks. And he probably had a mile to walk to work in the morning and back home in the evening.

Very young children were engaged in making handles for cups (they were known as 'little handlers') using two plaster of Paris moulds which were brought together by pressure. The children threw themselves with all their strength against the mould then wriggled, horizontally on it, exerting great pressure on their chests. There was potential for lasting damage in children whose bones were still developing and relatively soft. A ten-year-old boy who looked 'very pale and phthiscal' [sic] worked as a handle presser and while 'I do not think the jumping on the moulds hurts me; feel no pain from it'[9] he had had a cough for three or four years.

Dipping and scouring were regarded by the 1843 Assistant Commissioner as 'the most pernicious and destructive in the whole process of potting'. It was in these processes that dangerous substances were used. The dipping liquid comprised borax, soda, potash with whiting, stone, and carbonate of lead, all finely ground and mixed with water. Coarse goods had a higher proportion of lead in the dip and, in some cases, arsenic (which had been in more widespread use earlier in the nineteenth century). In dipping, the boys' task was to bring the ware in its rough ('biscuit') state from the warehouse or painting room to a tub. With constantly handling rough pottery the hands became almost sandpapered and so delicate that they could bleed, enabling the body to absorb more chemicals. Dipping was performed by a man, while a boy would take the article to be shelved and dried. Both men and boys had their hands and clothes constantly saturated with the dipping mixture and 'reckless of the danger ... seldom or ever change, or use precautionary measures, frequently taking their meals in the same room, sufficiently satisfied to wipe their hands on their aprons.'[10] Boys and men who worked in the dipping area were susceptible to a range of potentially fatal diseases, largely due to the failure to wash properly or to change clothes, epilepsy being the disease to which children were most susceptible, besides persistent constipation. And, when fathers were asked by the Assistant Commissioner whether they would bring their own children into the dipping room the answer, invariably, was 'No'. One youth began work in the dipping house at Minton's earthenware factory but the lead quickly affected him and the foreman moved him to the warehouse. A 69-year-old working at Boyle's pottery in Stoke said 'Some of the occupations of the children are very pernicious; those, for example, in which lead is used; they are not so bad as formerly; there is not so much lead and arsenic used.'[11] He added that he had children of his own and 'I would not bring up either in the dipping or scouring-house.' A nineteen-year-old related how he fell ill in the dipping house:

> I was going to work one morning, as I thought pretty well, but was taken with giddiness in my head, and felt as though Is [sic] going to fall down; I found my way back home, and told mother to make haste down stairs as I was bad. She sent for the doctor, but before he came I had a bad fit, and was confined to my bed two months. The doctor tried to bleed me but did not succeed. I have had fits since; have fits now every day; have sometimes ten or twenty. My right side is useless to me. They tell me I shall never recover the use of my limbs.[12]

A smaller number of boys worked as stokers at the bottle ovens, carrying coal to the fires. Ridgways employed two boys each night at the ovens, together with two men; altogether there were 26 oven-men and sixteen boys who worked nightly in rotation.

Girls between the ages of eight and seventeen and boys from fourteen upwards served seven-year apprenticeships in painting and burnishing, working in separate rooms under the supervision of masters and mistresses. These were 'literally schools of art' in which the young people sat at clean tables in well-ventilated rooms, heated by a stove on which they could warm their dinners. A 40-year-old woman, who managed the children in the painting room at Minton's earthenware factory, said that the girls were all healthy but, over the years, many had died from illnesses caused by the vapour of turpentine and paint in an unventilated room. One girls' supervisor described how she tried to inculcate a spirit of good feeling and kindness between children and she knew of no cases of punishment, but rather of reward for good work. While, in the printing room, the work was not strenuous, the girls also had to carry water, make fires and clean, besides working for many hours. Some women used their child workers badly, young girls being made to carry water from the yard to the department on their heads.

Many children had too little to eat and were not always allowed the stated meal breaks when working as a direct employee of a pottery worker. More considerate employers allowed hearths on which children could cook or heat their dinners. Other children went home for dinner. Many children were poorly clothed and went without shoes. A seventeen-year-old apprentice, who had been a handler for eight years, had no father – his mother worked at the potbank – reported that he had had no dinner that day; he could neither read nor write and said that he didn't go to Sunday school because he had no clothes to go in. A few children at the potbanks were, however, reasonably well-dressed and had sufficient food. A twelve-year-old girl at Minton & Boyle's earthenware factory said that she had three frocks and good shoes and ate beef and potatoes every day. She was an exception, however.

The state of education, diet and clothing of potbank children was largely dependent on the home context. Working children generally handed their earnings to their mothers and, if there were many siblings, the mother was unlikely to work. Thus William, aged eleven, could neither read nor write, he did not go to Sunday school as he had no clothes to go in. His foreman explained that the child's want of clothes was due to the improvidence of the father and the mother being 'badly used by her husband'. An eight-year-old with a mother and stepfather did not go to school ''cause I've got no trousers'.

Because so few of the tasks in making pottery required moving machinery and, where machinery was used, it was largely hand operated, the 1843 Assistant Commissioners found little evidence of industrial accidents. But there was plentiful evidence of punishment. Girls were far less subject to corporal punishment than boys and some supervisors rewarded good behaviour by reducing the required output on occasion. In the printing department at Minton's earthenware factory, the children were said to be well behaved and seldom beaten by the printers since the master, if he heard of it, would be angry. One twelve-year-old boy at Adams Cliff Bank potbank was strapped twice by his contracting employer for turning the jigger too quickly for fun and throwing the clay off the wheel, but neither the master nor the overseer found out. He added that he would rather be at work than at home, for he would be strapped there. A ten-year-old mould-runner said that his master never hit him but another sometimes strikes his back with cutters (a wire with wooden handles at each end to cut the clay). A ten-year-old mould runner said that his father, for whom he worked, flogged him if he dropped a mould or broke a saucer. An eleven-year-old mould-runner was severely punched by his employer for taking time over his breakfast (although not the full allowance of half an hour). He added that his father, 'a totaler', was very good to him. A twelve-year-old mould runner said that his master never thrashed him and they did not throw cockspurs or hot coals on the floor for him to tread on, but he have seen that done many times to other children.

There were around fourteen potteries on Tyneside. Children generally worked twelve hour days, including meals, but one diminutive boy aged about ten worked several times a week from 6 a.m. to 8.30 p.m. and, on the day the Assistant Commissioner visited the works, he had been there since 4 a.m. As in the Staffordshire Potteries, male pieceworkers employed their own child assistants at whatever age they liked.

Where punishment was meted out it was at the hands of these journeymen rather than with the knowledge of the proprieter. An eleven-year-old boy said that the men and lads beat him with their hands many times, perhaps once or twice a week and made him cry. One twelve-year-old was beaten and had stones heaved at him by his half-brother on an almost daily basis, making large bruises. He was also frequently punched by another adult who accused him of not working sufficiently hard. One thirteen-year-old was regularly beaten by his master with a rope and then suffered regular pains in his side. An eleven-year-old girl who worked in the transfer department of a North Shields pottery was always paid 15p a week, whatever the number of hours worked. Her master used to beat her almost every day, making lumps on her head with his knuckles.

A great many of the North Staffordshire children were illiterate and even those who claimed to be able to read were, upon being questioned, found to have a poor grasp of reading. The Assistant Commissioner commented that, in the cases where children claimed they could read, they were not very proficient. A number of children also claimed to be able to write, but had no idea of how to hold a pen – and as evidence, the Assistant Commissioner published an indecipherable scrawl which a girl claimed was her name. It was not only the long hours and state of exhaustion of the children, but also their inadequate clothing, which were given as reasons for non-attendance at evening or Sunday school. Joseph Clementson, a pottery owner, commented on the parents' neglect of child education. The provision existed but, parents did not, he alleged, appreciate the value of education. One twelve-year-old, however, reported that he could read and write; he attended the Mechanics Institute every evening and, despite working from 7 a.m. to 6 p.m. for six days a week, claimed that he did not feel very tired after work and could study for two hours.

A number of the employers giving evidence in 1843 were adamant that very young children should not be employed at potbanks; that ten should be the minimum age at which a child could be hired and that all children should attend school. By the 1860s employment conditions had worsened in some places and, in the 1862 Report on Children's Employment in The Staffordshire Potteries, the Commissioner focused particularly on Longton, the town in which there was the largest number of workmen who had become small manufacturers in rented premises. The landlords, too, were poor and either unwilling or unable to improve the potbanks, which were of all sorts, shapes and sizes, crudely built and which from the inside, looked more like rabbit warrens. The surgeon and Mayor of Hanley said that employment in pottery was one of the most destructive of human life in the country. At the 1861 census there were 4,605 children under the age of ten working in the Staffordshire industry, 593 of whom were five years-

Child working in a pottery in the late nineteenth century. (Staffordshire Record Office)

old and more than half were girls. This was almost 14 per cent of the total Staffordshire Potteries' labour force.

The groundswell for change gathered pace, supported by the leading pottery manufacturers, 26 of whom petitioned Parliament for legislation to control the employment of young children in the industry. Among the signatories were Wedgwood, Minton, Ridgway and Adams, who argued that employment caused moral and physical evils in the young. There was opposition from those who argued that a half-time system for children would delay making up time in lost orders, one manufacturer arguing that he and his colleagues were perfectly competent to manage their own affairs. When a Commissioner looked at the thermometer on a stove at this man's factory it registered 120.5°F.

The pottery industry was included in the Factory Acts Extension Act of 1864. Maximum working hours were to be ten, no child under eight years was to work in potteries and those under thirteen were required to spend half a day in school for each half day worked in the factory. No child, young person, or woman was to eat in the dipping room, dippers' drying room or china-scouring room and potbanks were to be kept clean and well-ventilated. One of the factory inspectors, reporting in 1865, acknowledged that new buildings would be required in a majority of the potbanks so that employment in the industry could be free from danger. Two years later the inspector reported on improvements in the better factories. Steam power was rapidly being introduced and, by 1871, there were only 2971 children under thirteen working in the Staffordshire Potteries. But ten- to fourteen-year-olds continued to make necessary contributions to the family economy of the North Staffordshire Potteries into the twentieth century, Stoke on Trent being the second largest area of juvenile employment in Britain after Lancashire in 1907.

Brickmaking

In those parts of the country deficient in stone for building, bricks were used for most construction work. And, wherever a sufficient deposit of clay could be found, bricks were produced as near to a building site as possible, on account of their weight. Chimney pots and roof tiles were also made at brickfields. Brickmaking tended to be a seasonal occupation when the ground was neither frozen nor saturated with rain, although clay was dug by men during the winter and left on the surface so that it could be broken up by the frost. It was then further broken up – a process known as puddling – in a horse-powered pugmill. If there was no pugmill this task was performed by children stamping on the clay with their bare feet.

In the nineteenth century children of both sexes were employed from the ages of seven or eight – it was said that a moulder's child was born with a brick in his mouth. Children undertook extremely heavy work at brickfields, often working a sixteen-hour day from 5 a.m. to 8 or 9 p.m. in the summer, carrying the puddled clay on their heads from the pugmill to the brick moulders (often their parents), who worked at tables. They also took the moulded clay to the kilns and moved the baked bricks to be stacked. This was some of the most strenuous work undertaken by children in the nineteenth century and was not covered by factory legislation until late in the century. Contemporaries sometimes favourably compared this work, undertaken in the fresh air, with the conditions experienced by children in cotton factories, but many brickfield children had twisted limbs and spines, as a result of carrying heavy loads, before their bones and muscles were fully grown. An Inspector to the 1867 Agriculture Commission related that both the vicar and schoolmaster in an agricultural area suggested that regulation was needed in the brickfield, where children

SIFTING THE DUST

Girls sifting clay at a brickworks in the 1870s. (Mary Evans Picture Library)

of six and seven worked barefoot all day. A man who had worked as a child in brickfields in his youth described the 'monkey-like faces, the shrunken, shivering, cowering, scared looks of many of the children are things not to be imagined.'[13] Violence was one way of achieving the production totals required: 'I myself have seen, over and over again, the black eye, the unhealed sore, the swollen head, the bruised body, in little, very little children ... punishment within not an inch but a hair-breadth ... of life.'[14]

Factory inspectors and those giving evidence to various parliamentary committees of enquiry in the nineteenth century, commented critically on child labour in the brickfields but, as with child sweeps and children who worked in textile mills, it was a children's champion who campaigned relentlessly for change. George Smith of Coalville, Leicestershire, had worked in a brickfield during the 1840s, beginning work at the age of nine and being made to carry clay and bricks weighing around forty pounds for thirteen hours a day, walking up to fourteen miles a week in the work. In adulthood he determined to rescue children from this labour and began a campaign in 1869. Boys were employed from around the age of eight, girls from between nine and ten. Girls did not carry clay on their heads the entire day, being partly occupied in carrying bricks to the kiln. Many of the children worked almost in the nude. In his evidence, Smith calculated that an average brickmaker would produce 3,500 bricks a day and a child with the brick mould (which weighed 4½ lbs) and, containing bricks weighing 10½ lbs, would be required to walk to and fro twelve yards, making nearly 24 miles over a working day. Smith asserted that girls should not be employed in brickyards at all and boys should not be employed at such young ages or for so long each day for, at the end of a day's work, they were completely exhausted. At the Social Science Congress of 1870 Smith exhibited a lump of wet clay weighing 43 lbs which had been taken from the head of a nine-year-old child three days before. The child weighed 52½ lbs – he was carrying the equivalent of more than three quarters of his body weight. Smith wrote to the Home Office in early 1871 pointing out that employment in agricultural gangs, printing, pottery and brickyards

Child working at a brickworks in the late nineteenth century.

George Smith (1831–1895), the brick children's champion.

employing 50 or more workers, had had their hours restricted by legislation and that, if a Factory Act was good for regulating places employing 50 people, it must be good for those employing twenty or fewer. In a debate in the House of Commons, one speaker observed that 'ignorance, vice, and immorality prevail to a greater extent amongst the employees in brickyards than in any other trades.'[15] Smith kept the subject in the public eye, writing letters to newspapers, making speeches and seeking to keep the matter under the eye of Parliament. He was not averse to resorting to poetry to make his point:

I saw a little brick-yard boy
With body almost bare
What clothes he had were thin and torn,
And matted was his hair;
And such a little boy was he,
In years, no more than three times three.[16]

A series of illustrations of barefoot children working in brickyards was published in 1871. They were intended to shock and, as with the earlier nineteenth century depictions of children working in coal mines, they succeeded. The Factories and Workshops Amendment Act of 1871 banned the employment of boys under ten and girls under sixteen from working at brick and tile works. George Smith was in the Public Gallery of the House of Commons (at *c*.1.30 a.m.) to hear the Bill passed, admitting that, such was his tension, his blood seemed to be freezing in his veins. And, in January 1872, 10,000 brickyard children were taken from their slavery and sent to school. But, despite the provision of inspectors, Smith could write, seven years after the passage of the Act,that he knew of 'a number of large brick and tile works ... upon which an inspector has not set his

Children queuing up to be paid at a brickworks in the 1870s.

foot, nor is there a notice to be seen.'[17] While some inspectors fulfilled their obligations, others were more neglectful. Smith contested the notion that inspectors needed to be 'gentlemen', saying that such men would be better employed as police officers, parish officers or other be-suited occupations, rather than being required to 'make the most visits, carry out the Act thoroughly (and) with the least annoyance'[18] The Factory Act of 1878 further strengthened the protection of children and young people in brick and tile yards and, in 1879, the Earl of Shaftesbury, the great nineteenth century children's champion, presented a testimonial of appreciation to George Smith.

TEN

Black Country trades

THE BLACK COUNTRY, those towns to the north of Birmingham where coal seams come to the surface, including Walsall, Dudley, West Bromwich, Bilston, Tipton, Wednesbury and Cradley Heath (but to purists not Wolverhampton, Stourbridge and Smethwick), was described by Abraham Lincoln's Consul to Birmingham (apt. 1864) as 'black by day and red by night ... (it) cannot be matched for vast and varied production by any other space of equal radius on the surface of the globe.'[1] An 1851 travelogue said 'blackness everywhere prevails; the ground is black, the atmosphere is black, and the underground honeycombed by mining galleries stretching in utter blackness for many a league.' The buildings were also black; 'perpetual twilight reigns during the day, and during the night fires on all sides light up the dark landscape with a fiery glow.'[2] The people, too, appeared to be black, being unfairly described as: 'Savages, without the grace of savages, coarsely clad in filthy garments, with no change on weekends or Sundays.'[3] The region seems to have acquired this name in the 1840s, although it may have been so-called by locals earlier than this. Nowadays the term Black Country includes most of the Metropolitan Districts of Dudley, Sandwell, Walsall and Wolverhampton. The name Black Country described how the landscape appeared and its inhabitants appeared. But it could also be a metaphor for the conditions of child employment in the area for, when the Children's Employment Commissioners visited in 1841, their reports were amongst the most shocking of all the reports on British regions.

A multitude of trades involving metal working characterised the Black Country, different towns specialising, to some extent, in different trades.

Wolverhampton was noted for ironmongery 'in nearly all its branches', as well as japanning, tin plate and brass. Besides a large iron foundry and an edge-tool factory, the main industries in Wednesbury were gas-pipes, coach-springs and axles, gun-locks and screws. In Stourbridge there were 'great numbers of nailers and chain-makers', besides the largest iron-works in England, glass works and fire-brick and fire-clay manufacturers. Willenhall specialised in locks and keys; Wednesfield in keys; Darlasaton in coach-springs, files, hinges, gun-locks, bridle-bits and nails; Bilston had coal pits, besides japanning, and screw manufacture; Dudley had a brass foundry, glass works and coal mines; the principal trade in Sedgley was nailing, with some locksmiths and in Walsall there was a bridle-cutting factory, an iron foundry, plating, and buckle works. In terms of numbers working in the various small metals trades, nailers and chain makers were the most numerous.

The Assistant Commissioner for Wolverhampton began his report by writing that 'Great numbers of children and young persons' were employed

Black Country coal mine; one of the Earl of Dudley's thick coal pits – compare this with the images of children crawling in mines with narrow coal seams in Chapter 7.

in ironmongery, japanning and tin-plate. All working-class children were working by the age of eight 'with the exception of those few who remain at home to nurse infants.'[4] Many of these children worked for 'small masters', whose businesses were so small that in many cases they were only known to the men to whom the masters took their work for sale. Of upwards of 260 locksmiths, there were probably only six or so who had their workshops in the front of a street. The same was the case with the 60–70 small master key-makers, as well as the 20–30 small masters in each of the screw, latch, bolt, snuffer, tobacco-box, spectacle frame and case making trades. These were all hidden away in backyard workshops appropriately described as hovels. The courts and blind alleys contained from one to four houses, one or two of which were workshops or had a room in them used as a workshop. 'In one of the hovels ... it appeared that a man, his wife and child and a donkey all slept together. The hovel had but one room.'[5] Some single-storey hovels had had an upper floor added 'when they could bear it' but this often caused large cracks to appear in the masonry. Many of the yards had gutters with stagnant water in them and 'perhaps with a general dunghill not many feet from their windows.'[6]

The hours worked each day by children varied according to the different trades. Japanners, the relative aristocrats of the Black Country trades, worked from 7 a.m. to 7 p.m. in summer and from 8 a.m. to 8 p.m. in winter. Tin-plate workers, iron braziers and founders worked from 5, 6 or 7 a.m. to 7 p.m. Nail makers worked from 7 a.m. till 8 p.m., children working overtime – from one to three hours – as much as twice a week, usually because the adults declined to work on Mondays and sometimes Tuesdays, a habit often referred to as St Monday, which was spent in drinking. Some small masters, working at home, worked well into the night – sometimes due to pressure of trade but more often on account of St Monday. Children had no option but to work alongside their employers, whatever length the working day. The children employed in japanning and tin-plate working undertook painting, lacquering, varnishing, polishing and carrying light weights. Children employed in the range of small metals trades did not do heavy work, except the few who worked at the presses, although boys were hard worked in the heavy steel goods trades, lifting heavy weights and using heavy hammers. Children aged between nine and ten operated bellows, while boys of thirteen to fifteen operated a hammer as well. Boys who worked in casting shops often complained of sickness and headaches; while boys who worked at edge-tool grinding, although not appearing to be injured by the mixture of stone and steel inhaled in the process, were laying a foundation of harm, as men who worked at it rarely lived to be old. An even more harmful occupation for boys was working in the casting shop of brass and bell-foundries for they were often ill, frequently vomiting, and had a yellow tinge to their faces.

At one nail and boot-tip factory at least 60 children and young people were employed. With a great number of heavy machines on each floor 'the building was in so shattered a condition that every particle of it was in a constant state of creaking and groaning vibration.'[7] There were great gaps in the broken flooring so that it was possible to look to the floor below. The Assistant Commissioner mentioned this to the occupier and was greeted with a smile. A few days later part of the upper floor fell, killing a small boy instantly, another boy having both his thighs and an arm broken. Three others boys were injured. And, besides the unsafe structure, the rooms were 'all crowded with dangerous machinery, so close that you can scarcely pass'. None of the machinery was guarded; 'little boys and girls are here seen at work at the tip-punching machines (all acting by steam power) with their fingers in constant danger of being punched off once in every second, while at the same time they have their heads between two whirling wheels a few inches from each ear.'[8] But not all factories were like this. At another nail and boot-tip factory there were hardly ever any accidents and a guard was placed in front of the nail machine to prevent a child's fingers from being damaged.

Two forms of child apprenticeship were found in Wolverhampton. One was legal, the other not. The first involved indentures from magistrates or Boards of Guardians; the second involved taking a child to a lawyer to be bound apprentice without reference to the proper authorities. Many more apprentices were bound by this illegal means and in both cases a child was bound until the age of 21, even if the apprenticeship began at the age of seven. Apprentices were given no regular pocket money, but an indoor apprentice was lodged, fed and clothed by the master. Non-apprenticed children and young persons were hired by the adult whom they assisted and most were paid by the piece. Some were paid by the day or week – termed 'work-and-play' which led the Assistant Commissioner to remark ruefully that, of the latter, 'there is consequently but little among the children.'[9] Children received very little reward, a few receiving a small amount for working overtime. The one 'grand stimulus is that of necessity. The parents count the money; the employers estimate the work; the child must do it.'[10]

Punishment was meted out by the master to whom a child was apprenticed, or for whom he/she worked and consisted of beatings, going without a meal or being made to work over-hours. While it was likely that some children behaved badly on occasion, the small master locksmiths, key, bolt makers and screw makers made 'extortionate demands ... upon their labour.' Only the japanners treated their child workers differently 'Children and young persons are treated best by the japanners and worst by the small locksmiths.'[11]

The health of children and young people who worked in Wolverhampton was 'very poor indeed,' partly on account of the inadequate diet on which they had to subsist. Much of the meat available in local markets was notoriously bad; indeed some butchers dealt only in diseased meat, particularly veal. Children seldom washed more than once or twice a week and then only their hands and faces. They were very badly clothed, no difference being made between winter and summer wear. Many of the children were 'very delicate, some sickly, many ill-formed, meagre ... some badly deformed. Many of the girls had displaced shoulder-blade bones which jutted out giving them the appearance of the back of a grasshopper. Nearly all children examined were stunted and appeared younger than the ages they gave.'[12]

Many parents were improvident, regularly drunk, and in the numerous cases where both worked, childcare was left to older siblings from the age of seven upwards. Many infants died in accidents by being left by the fireside in winter, the mother or sibling having given the child Godfrey's Cordial (a mixture of opium and treacle) as a sedative. Few children attended school beyond the age of eight, at which point parents could find work for them, so that few could read and almost none could write. Only the better-off working class children remained at school until the ages of eleven or twelve. The Commissioner commented: 'The excessive labour of children at the tender age of seven, eight and nine, is positively injurious to them.'[13]

Payment was, as in the Staffordshire Potteries, either in cash via a local public house, where each adult was required to consume 1*s*. worth in drink and then received the cash (boys being required either to consume 6*d*.

worth or to give this to an adult), or in kind via a 'Tommy' or truck shop. While the price-equivalent given in food at the latter was high, it did mean that women and children received food through the week for otherwise, where all wages were paid via the public house, the likelihood was that they would be consumed in drink by the men, leaving families destitute and starving by the middle of the week.

During the visit of the Assistant Commissioner to Willenhall in 1841, he found record of:

268 locksmiths
76 keymakers
18 latchmakers
12 file, grid-iron and chafing dish makers (cooking utensils)
14 bolt makers
10 curry comb manufacturers (for grooming horses)

He acknowledged that there were probably more key-makers and locksmiths than recorded 'but so many of them live in holes and corners that they are scarcely discoverable.'[14] Keys were made at a forge and stamp, children commonly operating the forge bellows. No girls were employed in these trades. It was estimated that there were between 900 and 1000 boys at work in the town, including those working for their fathers. They began work from the ages of eight or nine, or even earlier if they could hold a file, sometimes working at a vice from the age of seven, standing on blocks so as to be able to reach it. Most children were apprenticed until the age of 21 and directly a boy's time was up he was turned out, the master getting another apprentice. Boys who were apprenticed from a workhouse often had the clothes given to them by the parish taken away and given to the master's son. 'Saint Monday', and often Tuesday as well, were days in which the adult males generally did not work. Instead they made up for it later in the week, for 'as long as they can possibly stand',[15] sometimes standing at the vice from 4 or 5 a.m. until 11 or 12 p.m. A thirteen-year-old boy said that his first master: 'used ... to beat him with a currant stick; when he wore out the stick he got another out of the garden ... He often had only one meal a day and this was potatoes, or gruel or dry bread and sometimes no bread at all. Had nothing some days.'[16] The boy ran away. His second master, although he didn't beat his apprentice, made him work from 6 a.m.

until 10 p.m. and did not always give him enough to eat, or clothe him well, or give him the 6*d* (2.5p) a week as promised.

Since adults were paid by the piece, it was of little consequence to the manufacturers when and how long they worked. The more responsible larger manufacturers sought to exert some control and opened their works from 5 or 6 a.m. in summer (or when light in winter) until 9 or 10 p.m. Whatever hours the men worked, boys were required to do the same. This was not only extremely bad for their health and development but accustomed them to the work regimes to which they would adhere when adult.

One respondent considered the condition of children in Willenhall to be 'very bad', the parish apprentices being the worst treated – after they were bound there was no guardianship over them and they were often bound to masters who could not afford to feed them; they often had no beds. Sometimes an apprentice would feel sufficiently bold to complain to the magistrates. One complainant said that his master regularly took his clothes to the pawn shop on Monday and was sometimes unable to redeem them on Saturday. Apprentices in Willenhall often worked from 6 a.m. to 11 and 12 p.m. An innkeeper spoke of how a thirteen-year-old boy went to him (when he was constable), crying and covered in blood. His master had been beating him because he would not let the mistress remove his shoes to pawn them. The boy's head was cut open. Another boy, one of two apprentices, described how his master beat the other in bed at 5 a.m. because he had not yet got up to work and 'set about him with his fist'. He, too, had been beaten with a whip handle and wished that he could be released from this master 'who's never easy but when he's a-beating me. Never has enough to eat at no time; ax him for more, he wont gie it me.'[17] A fourteen-year-old youth was beaten regularly with the hand, a hammer or anything the master could get hold of. He attended Sunday school, could write his name, and could read easy words. In response to the commissioner's questions he had heard of Adam and Jesus Christ who, he said, was an angel in heaven. One sixteen-year-old youth, described as having a look of indignation marked in his hard-worked face, was ill-treated and had insufficient to eat; he had to work from 6 a.m. until 10 or 11 p.m. and if he did not complete his work he was beaten and went without supper – his head has been cut open five times. Not all masters ill-treated their apprentices; one who made cabinet locks had six apprentices who were given plenty to eat and shared three feather beds between them, they were well clothed; although they were occasionally beaten with a strap. The respondent went to Sunday school, could read easy words but couldn't write. Sometimes it was not the master who ill-treated an apprentice, but the journeymen and when, the apprentice complained to the master, he did nothing about it. One child, despite being clean and well clothed, was described as looking ill-treated; his mind seemed stupifed by constant worry. Of those ill-treated children who were brave enough to seek a summons from the Wolverhampton magistrates, it appears that little happened, since the local constable declined to serve it.

Punishment was said to have been worse in about 1800 than it was by the early 1840s. One master had run his apprentice through the body with a red-hot iron bar (and was hanged for the crime). In the mid-1830s an apprentice had been required to wear an iron collar around his neck, while another walked around the town with a great wooden log attached to one leg to prevent him from straying. But, even by the 1840s, boys could be cruelly beaten with a horsewhip, a strap, or a stick. Some, at the Assistant Commissioner's request, stripped to the waist to show scars, bruises and sores. One boy said that his master beat him with a whip with four lashes to it, and tied in knots. It was not only the masters who could be cruel; some apprentices were 'shamefully' treated by the master's wife; and it was all the worse for them if they begged for mercy. A common method of punishment was what was known as 'clamming', making boys go without a meal or meals, when their diet was generally inadequate anyway. In summary, the Assistant Commissioner reported that the treatment of apprentices was atrocious, no care whatever being taken of them. Parish apprentices who worked in the collieries and stone pits around Willenhall were said to be much better treated than those bound to trades. They regularly worked twelve hours a day in the mines, whereas most of the boys working in the local industries worked from twelve to eighteen hours a day.

The Assistant Commissioner reported that, having entered the hovels of journeymen locksmiths and keymakers unannounced, he had seen 'the utmost destitution; no furniture in the room below but a broken board for a table, and a piece of plank laid across bricks for a seat; with the wife hungry, – almost crying with hunger – and in rags, yet the floor was perfectly clean.'[18] Upstairs, in a room 7 ft long 6 ft high at one side, slanting to nothing like a wedge, a husband, his wife and three children slept. There was no proper bedding but an old bag laid upon sacking. Yet everything was spotlessly clean.

A local surgeon, reporting on the health of the working population of Willenhall, suggested that up to one third of adult males suffered from hernia; truss makers in the area had made a fortune. There were also 'innumerable cases' of joints distorted from standing at a vice for long periods and from holding a file in a particular way. Shoulder blades were dislocated and the right knee bent from standing at the vice for long periods. One witness called this the 'hind leg' as it seemed to him so similar to that of a drudging animal.

The main outwork trade in Wednesfield was the manufacture of steel traps – mainly for rats, but also for foxes and badgers. By 1841, the trade was declining and all had to work for longer hours to make a bare livelihood. A local innkeeper said that he could go into many houses where there were only a few potatoes to be shared among an entire family, and they didn't know where the next meal would come from. Most of the 150 or so working children were offspring of the small masters in these trades; there were only about 40 apprentices. Despite the poverty, the adult population of Wednesfield appeared much healthier compared with that of Wolverhampton, adults being more upright, taller and less subject to asthmatic conditions. Traps counted as light smiths' work, undertaken at a small workshop containing a forge, a bench and a vice. Boys were not beaten cruelly, although this had been the case some years previously. The master of the National School may well have been the model for more enlightened behaviour for he told the Assistant Commissioner that, if a schoolmaster could not govern his boys without beating them, 'he is not fit for his office.'[19] As in other Black Country towns many men were much addicted to drink, indeed besotted, which for some, meant inadequate amounts of food and clothing, besides over-work to compensate for the time lost in drinking at the beginning of the week. A local vicar suggested that instead of publicans being prohibited from becoming a constable, it would be a good thing if they were allowed to, as there would then 'be authority on the very scene of danger.'[20] The parish clerk confirmed that boys were well treated except where the masters were excessive drinkers. And some of the masters behaved very well to their apprentices. While, in the past, there had been a neglect of Sunday school, a great number of boys were attending by 1840.

The main trades of Darlaston were gun-locks, hinges, stirrups and also, to a lesser extent, the manufacture of coach springs, nails, buckles and buttons. The hours worked by children were generally from 6 a.m. to 7 or 8 p.m. in summer and from 7 a.m. until 8 or 9 p.m. in winter. Night work was the exception. More boys worked in these trades than girls, although some girls made washers. One of the larger manufacturers attested that children from the age of ten were capable of working from 6 a.m. till 7 p.m. with proper time allowed for meals and that 'it would be better if no children should work till 10 ... because when they begin younger they have not strength to do the stint and their constitutions, as well as their minds, are injured by it irreparably.'[21] Girls worked both at forges and pit banks, working in pairs at the pit mouth from 6 a.m. till 6 p.m. They were 'perfectly independent' often entering beer shops, calling for a pint and smoking pipes like men. It could be said that there was little difference in their circumstances from those of men, except that many suffered by becoming pregnant and would bear three or four children each, while young.

Darlaston was said to have a bad reputation for abusive treatment of children and young persons employed in its trades and manufactures, a magistrate saying that many small masters (of Darlaston and Willenhall) were not fit to have apprentices. But the Assistant Commissioner believed that this reputation was, in most cases, undeserved, being based on abuses committed in earlier times. A local innkeeper agreed that apprentices used

Diagram of a small nail forge.

Girl nailor putting the point on a nail.

to be badly treated, but thought this was not the case by 1841. There was a lack of education provision, neither parents nor masters seeming to see any benefit in it.

One iron merchant reported in 1841 that he believed there was as much iron made in Bilston as in the whole of Sweden. Coal and iron mining and iron manufacture were 'carried on to a prodigious extent within the small circumference of eight or nine miles.'[22] There were about seventeen iron and brass founders in the town, as well as twenty to thirty japanners and tinplate workers. An eight-year-old girl worked at making hinges from 6 a.m. to 9 p.m. and said that she was very tired at night. She could read but the Commissioner noted her 'very ill-health ... not well-grown.'[23] He estimated that between 400 and 500 children were employed overall. There were reports of children as young as four, five or six being taken down to sit in the mine. Few accidents occurred in the above-ground industries but they were common in the pits and often fatal. The girls working in the screw factories were thought to be 'some degrees above' the pit-bank girls; while the girls working in japanning, as in other Black Country towns, were 'altogether superior.' A few years before the Commission, a boiler had burst at one of the screw factories and 106 people, mainly girls and women had been badly scalded; several had died, and some were buried in the blast. A boiler burst at an iron mill in 1841 and some people were dreadfully scalded.

The main manufactures of Dudley were glass making, glass cutting, the manufacture of fire-irons (shovels etc.), vices, nails and chains: 'The places where they work are generally very close, filthy and without sufficient ventilation.'[24] The Assistant Commissioner found no evidence of cruel beating 'except in isolated instances'. A Dudley Magistrate who was interviewed considered that, on the whole, children in Dudley were well-treated and were generally not sent to work until the age of ten. The larger employers took an interest in the children's education but, on the whole, parents did not. As a local vicar noted, 'being uneducated themselves, how should they?'[25] This priest started up a school for up to twenty girls at his own expense, insisting that they attend regularly from age eight to around fourteen, that they cut their hair (to keep lice away). But numbers fell within a year as parents wished to use their girls for childminding or other domestic tasks.

Mothers did not administer Godfrey's Cordial to pacify infants

Boys at a pots and pans workshop, the supervisor with a raised stick in the background.

(and sometimes their young carers) giving, instead, a mixture of chalk and laudanum, known as Atkinson's Infant Preservative and sometimes 'pain-easing drops' which were Laudanum in tincture. However it was commented that the use of these child sedation mixtures was not nearly so prevalent as in Wolverhampton.

Two large factories in Sedgley, one an iron-foundry, the other a screw manufactory, employed children and young persons of both sexes. With the exception of these works, most of the inhabitants were engaged in making forged nails, many of the forges being at the back of the hovels where they lived. The best little forges were about 15 ft long and 12 ft wide in which seven or eight people worked, but most of them were smaller – approximately 10 ft long and 9 ft wide, filthily dirty and looking like a dilapidated coal hole or little black den. They had, generally, sunk up to a foot below the level of the ground outside, and this contributed to their slushy condition, since they could not be properly cleaned, even if the owners had the inclination to do so. 'In this dirty den there are commonly at work a man and his wife and daughter, with a boy and girl hired by the year.'[26] The forge was in the centre of the room with hardly any standing room and each person had an anvil, hammers and other tools. A forged nail was made from a strip of iron, the red-hot end being put on the anvil and given a point by hammering. Depending on the length required, the tip was almost entirely cut from the rest of the rod and the point was placed in a vice on the bench. The rest of the rod was twisted off and the end was flattened to form the nail head by heavy blows from a hammer, known as an oliver, operated by a foot treadle. Olivers varied in size, depending on the job to be done and sometimes children jumped on and off the treadle together to work it. What was considered harmful – and morally degrading – was the situation where boys and girls worked at olivers in the same workshop and where, in the heat, they stripped off much of their clothing. A twelve-year-old boy said that he worked from 5 or 6 a.m., sometimes rising at 3 a.m., working until about 9 p.m. He was given a quota to make per week (a 'stint') and was required to put in however many hours were necessary to make it.

Casting steel ingots, a boy assisting in the process with molten metal.

An exceptional case was a fifteen-year-old who was allowed to fit schooling into his working day – he worked at nailing from 6 a.m. until 8.45 a.m., had his breakfast and then went to school until 12 noon, worked at nailing until 1 p.m., had dinner, went to school from 2 to 5 p.m., had tea and then worked again at nailing until 9 p.m. He admitted that he felt very tired sometimes, particularly when doing heavier work. He could read, write and do arithmetic. He was described by the Assistant Commissioner as healthy, strong, clean and well-clothed, although rather stunted in stature.

Children were treated with indifference by their parents, whether in food, clothing or over-work, while to those who were hired by the year, especially if orphans, there was often great cruelty practised. Boys were sometimes struck with a piece of red-hot iron; they were sometimes sent a 'flash of lightening' from a bar of white-hot iron swung by the man to shower fiery particles at the boy. Another punishment called 'winding-up' was sometimes practised in the warehouses, an iron hook used for winding up nail bags being fixed to the boy's trousers, the boy being wound up through a trap door to the room above with his head facing downwards. There was some disagreement about how common these practices were in 1840, although it was acknowledged that they were formerly common. A local innkeeper, formerly an Overseer of the Poor, said that in his time he had often hoped that there would be an inquiry on working children. While some masters treated the boys well, 'it used to be dreadful'. He related the story of an apprentice who was known to have been ill-treated by his master, suddenly going missing. And then in approximately 1839, when some dilapidated houses were pulled down, the skeleton of a boy was dug up. One witness thought that the children of Sedgley were worse off than in the cotton mills, for they were dealing with fire from 6 a.m. until night. More girls worked at nailing than boys: Sedgley might appropriately be termed the district of female blacksmiths.

Two manufacturing processes were particularly highlighted as being injurious. Fine glass dust was inhaled and got into the eyes and mouths of those who cut the edges of glasses to fit spectacle frames; the other was plating and tinning spurs and buckles, the article being rubbed in a box or pan on the ground containing sal-ammoniac which was harmful when inhaled.

Housing was given special mention for its wretchedness. The Assistant

Commissioner 'never saw one abode of a working family which had the least appearance of comfort or wholesomeness, while the immense majority were of the most wretched stye-like description.'[27] There was no underground drainage, nor even a gutter above ground, nor were there any privies, families tending to use a corner of an adjoining field, often shared with neighbours.

The main manufactures of Walsall were buckles, spurs and bits – 'in fact all kinds of horse-ironmongery.' There were also some spectacle and button factories, glass grinders and two very large factories making various articles in ivory and bone. Besides apprentices, few children were employed in these trades. A number of girls worked at stitching horse bridles; they were all paid piecework, those interviewed being clean, well clothed, but not particularly healthy looking.

Boys who worked at a spur-plating factory were well-treated, but some felt very tired at night. One boy 'going on 10', was described as being disagreeably dirty and in dirty rags, never washing himself before going home. He felt very tired and could neither read nor write, although his mother told him he would go to night school soon. A fifteen-year-old girl who worked at buckle-making, from 6 a.m. until 6 p.m., additionally had to mind the house on returning home as she had three younger siblings. She was described as being very thin with her shoulder blade bones a little displaced; and rather dirty and raggedly clothed. An eighteen- or nineteen-year-old (she didn't seem to know her age exactly) had been working at the bevelling hand press for six or seven years, acknowledging that it was very hard work. She did a twelve-hour day with two and a half hours for meals and lived by herself in lodgings, her father being dead. She had attended school for a few years, but left at the age of ten and was too tired after her week's work to consider attending Sunday school. She could read a little but had never learned to write. She often had a headache and her right side ached.

The Relieving Officer thought that the working children in Walsall were not unkindly treated by their employers 'They are worked hard, but well fed, and not improperly corrected.'[28] He alleged that indoor apprentices were mostly in a better state than those who lived with their parents and were hired out on a weekly basis, saying that those who lived with their parents could be identified in the streets by the rags they wore.

The most schooling children experienced was Sunday school, in which some of the teachers were 'quite uneducated', one not knowing where the River Thames was, another saying that Shakespeare was a soldier. A sixteen-year-old Sunday school teacher was scathing in his assessment of the competence of some of the other teachers – none of the teachers taught by any particular method. He gave up teaching in the boys' Sunday school because he was ashamed of the way his colleagues taught. A 35-year-old bit maker who superintended the church Sunday school reported that up to 1000 children attended the Sunday school regularly; there were ten such schools, some being open to teach writing as well for two nights a week. He confirmed that parents, on the whole, seemed indifferent to their children's schooling, wishing to get them off to work as early as possible.

The main small metals trades of Wednesbury were gas-pipes, coach-springs and axels, gun locks and screws. Most people worked a twelve hour day, with time allowed for meals – and no night work (except at the rolling mills and blast furnaces). In addition there two very large factories: an iron foundry and an edge-tool factory. Almost all of the work consisted of forging – gun-locks and other small articles of ironmongery – being light smith's work, whereas gas-pipes and coach spring and axle manufacture was very heavy, requiring great furnaces and heavy hammers.

Young people were, however, 'seldom tasked very much beyond their strength'[29] and few girls were employed in the town's industries. An eleven-year-old boy who worked at a coach-spring and axletree workshop was sometimes beaten with a rod when he didn't work as hard as usual on account of a bad headache and stomach ache. An eight -year-old boy was employed putting water on the iron being hammered at a foundry, he felt very tired at night since he worked so hard with large pieces of iron. Even so, he went to night school and could both read and write.

The workplaces were often dilapidated with rotten stairs and floors, while machinery was not boxed or fenced by even a single bar or rail. At one workshop the men and boys 'must watch their moment for a rush past a portion of dangerous machinery while in motion, or to evade the sudden egress of red-hot bars or pipes from the furnace.'[30] There had been a number of accidents in the previous year, although when measured against the yardstick of mining accidents, they were far fewer.

The numerous Wednesbury apprentices were not over-worked and their treatment and care was better than in other towns of the Black Country. Most children interviewed by the Assistant Commissioner were healthy, well-fed, clean and well clothed. There was relatively little severe chastisement, although one boy had had his arm broken by a blow with a piece of iron. His parents had seen it as a good opportunity to send him to school until his arm had healed. A fourteen-year-old boy acknowledged that he was sometimes beaten, but the man he worked under knew that if the beating increased, he would go and get a warrant against him. More employers provided encouragement to the children, sometimes books, or a 'feast of meat and puddings'. The Assistant Commissioner commented favourably on the church and chapel schools, remarking that they were better than those he had seen in other towns in the region and children tended to remain at school for longer.

The health of the inhabitants was generally good although many women suffered from hernia as a consequence of carrying enormous weights of coal on their heads, caused by the custom that each woman was allowed to take home as much coal as she could carry and greediness or need caused

Glass furnace with a boy blowing glass.

them to carry too much. Girls and boys of all sizes accompanied them, carrying smaller loads on their heads.

Stourbridge was noted for its glass, brick and fireclay works, besides 'great numbers of nailers and chain-makers' in and around Cradley. Chainmaking was much more localised than nail making in the Black Country. Its manufacture was introduced to the Black Country in the 1820s and the trade continued to grow through the nineteenth century and up until the First World War. The largest chain factory, making anchor and cable chains, was at the Lye and the children and young persons were well paid and well treated by the masters. Small chain was made in domestic workshops, being used for gardens, enclosures and horse bridles, amongst other uses. The small chains were commonly known as 'swimmers', on account of the regular demand for them in America. The outworker acquired bars of iron of between 3 and 8 feet long and of an appropriate thickness, depending on the size of chain to be made. The process involved forge and hammer with the help of a tool called a 'dolly'. This was a kind of hammer, the head of which was arched on the underside. When this was placed on the iron and the upper side of the head hit by hammers, the rounded shape of the chain link was formed. A man with a heavy hammer, holding the chain links with tongs in his other hand, was assisted by a boy with a lighter hammer in one hand, managing the dolly with his other hand. Heavy chain required greater heat, which necessitated bellows to provide a blast. A man would work with two boys and, when the chains were large, often three or four and sometimes as many as six. 'When the children are too little to be efficient, on account of their stature, blocks are placed half round the anvil, upon which the little creatures have to stand.'[31] Children were also employed in blowing the bellows. When a child was asked what he did, the answer was usually 'I dolly and blow'. Children began in this trade aged seven or eight. In the Cradley area girls were taught both nail and chain making so that when there was no demand for one they could make the other. Boys were put to nailing between the ages of five and seven, as soon as they could wield a hammer or blow the bellows, although the Assistant Commissioner met one boy who had been put to chainmaking at the age of four. Girls usually began aged eight or nine, having previously been looking after siblings from the age of five. A seventeen-year-old girl said that she could make one foot of chain, comprising seventeen links, in around ten to fifteen minutes.

Black Country chainmakers, depicted grotesquely to emphasise the hardship of the trade.

There were 2896 chainmakers in Staffordshire and Warwickshire in 1861 and 6,550 in 1911. While there were some large factory-like workshops for cast nails and a few for forged chains, there were many more backyard workshops for forged nails and chains. By the 1862 Commission on Children's Employment, conditions seemed to have changed remarkably little in these outworking trades, much of the evidence almost replicating that of the 1840s. By the 1870s 'more than 45%' of chain making was still undertaken in small workshops, most of it being undertaken by women and children. From the 1860s onwards the proportion of women to men as chain outworkers increased and, as the nail industry declined, ex-nailers moved into chainmaking and, by the 1880s the difference in earnings between a factory chainmaker and an outworker was considerable. A factory owner who also employed outworkers gave evidence to the Lords Committee on Sweating in 1889: young women outworkers earned 46p per week, while youths earned 62.5p, from which one eighth was deducted for workshop expenses, whereas the net earnings of his male factory employees was 135p.

Towards the end of the nineteenth century, while there were still numerous single-handed outworkers in the Black Country, many of the 'small masters' were subcontractors. From the 1830s onwards, the hand-made nail trade, which had engaged thousands of outworkers, began to meet competition from machine-made nails in Wolverhampton and Birmingham, and towards the end of the nineteenth century, also from Leeds and Warrington, besides overseas. Although there was some revival of the market for hand-made nails between 1870 and 1875, the production of nails did not fall at the same rate as the demand for them, with the result (as with hand loom weavers in woollen textiles) that the industry was characterised by overproduction, poverty, degradation and exploitation. Control of the trade fell into the hands of middle-men known as 'foggers' (factors), who supplied the raw materials and paid for the finished product. Many foggers also controlled the tommy (truck) shops. And, towards the end of the nineteenth century, as the nail trade became less and less secure, it was, for many, a supplementary source of family income which (with the exception of horse-nails which were a speciality of Dudley) depended increasingly on the labour of women and children. As the industry became more marginal to the Black Country economy, the location shifted to more remote villages on the Worcestershire border around Bromsgrove. By the 1870s the nail industry was in terminal decline, but it took a long time to die, 17,700 nailers being recorded in Staffordshire, Worcestershire and Warwickshire in the 1871 census. One of the last large nail and chain manufacturers employed between 1,800 and 2000 people in 1876, of whom 800 were young persons. At this date they were all outworkers but, by the late 1880s, the number had fallen and around 15 per cent of them were located in the firm's own large workshops. The owner of the firm, George Green, told a Lords Committee in 1889 that there were 42 'large nail-makers' in the trade – but he didn't define 'large' or say whether he included foggers in this total. The grip that foggers had on the industry was such that that some two-thirds of nail workers were reckoned, in 1871, to be paid entirely or partly in kind. Since the nail makers depended on the fogger for both raw materials and nail purchase, they had to contend with his sharp practices in fuel prices, provisions, and the 'cheating' scales in his warehouse.

Notwithstanding the large amount of information gathered in the Children's Employment Commissions of 1842 and 1862, outwork, including the so-called sweated trades of the Black Country, lacked reform. The

Royal Commission on Children's Employment of 1862 produced more evidence of the exploitation of children which resulted in The Factory Acts Extension Act (which covered all establishments employing more than 50 workers) and the Workshops Regulation Act, both of 1867 (which covered all workplaces, including domestic locations, employing 49 or fewer people). The Workshops Act prohibited the employment of children under the age of eight and set out the maximum hours per day older children, young persons and women could work. But, until the system of inspection was extended from factories to workshops (in 1871) there was no means of enforcement. Even then the regulations applied to factories were more stringent than those that applied to workshops. A Royal Commission of 1876 recommended a new definition but the resulting 1878 Act excluded home-workplaces. Outwork undertaken in the home context was less subject to regulation than subcontract work in a factory or public workshop. And, as was shown in successive enquiries in the nineteenth century, parents could be amongst the most exploitative of all when it came to the employment of children. As in other industrial sectors, it was to be the Education Acts which, perhaps, did more to regulate children's employment in the Black Country trades than legislation applied to the workplace.

ELEVEN

Outwork

Introduction

As THE TERM SUGGESTS, outwork was usually undertaken in the home or adjoining workshop of the worker, sometimes in premises owned by an employer. Some outworkers were independent, selling on their goods, while others worked for a single employer who supplied and owned the raw materials. Weaving, for example, was generally undertaken within the weaver's house, sometimes in a dedicated loomshop, often an upper room, or in a part of the family living space, as was framework knitting for hosiery, or gloving. Some outwork was an almost entirely rural activity – straw plaiting and pillow lace making, for example – while 'machine' lace and hosiery making in the East Midlands was undertaken both in towns in Nottinghamshire and Leicestershire, as well as in the surrounding villages. Some outwork trades were specific to particular localities, buttons in Birmingham, for example, and matchbox making in London.

Some outwork trades (eg. weaving, tailoring, boot and shoe making) provided occupations for the family, as did nail and chain making; others, such as pillow lace, gloving and straw plaiting engaged woman and children only throughout the nineteenth century. Later in the nineteenth century, with the advance of mechanisation and falling wage levels for outwork, many of the outwork trades that had previously occupied the whole family became jobs for women and children only. In outwork the hours worked by children were largely unseen and uncontrolled until the

Young people, mainly girls, in a London matchmaking workshop.

late nineteenth century and parents or other relatives could be amongst the most exploitative of child labour.

The apparent freedom of outwork was more imagined than real. If a child worked for a parent or parents, exploitation was a very real possibility. The flexibility of working hours could be a burden, adults being prepared to work late into the evening towards the end of the week, often being inclined to take things easier or not work at all on Mondays. Towards the end of the century the outworker was less likely to be their own master, depending on middlemen for raw materials and, possibly, tools. The phrase 'domestic system' sounds almost cosy; in reality it was anything but.

At the end of the eighteenth and early part of the nineteenth centuries it was believed that it was advantageous 'to place the children of the poor in trades or occupations' as early as possible. The advantages were thought to be twofold: the expense of maintaining the child was removed from parent or parish and the child was trained 'in habits of industry and virtue.'[1] At Greetham, Co., Durham, children were apprenticed to a wide range of trades and on differing terms. One boy was apprenticed for six years to a tailor, while another was apprenticed in the same trade until the age of 21. A boy was apprenticed for seven years to a comb-maker, another until the age of 21 to a farmer. A charity school at Stockton-on-Tees adopted a similar plan, it being claimed that there was better attendance and behaviour when there was an expectation of apprenticeships being taken up and the possibility of rescuing a particularly able child.

In 1803 the Foundling Hospital, London, issued a statement on the management of the children. Babies were put out to wet nurse, being returned to the hospital at the age of four. Children, it was claimed, remained there and were placed in the school until the age of thirteen or fourteen, at which stage they could be apprenticed. The Hospital defended its apparently very poor record of infant deaths when babies were placed out for nursing, while remaining silent but altering its practices, regarding the age and destinations of apprentices. Applications for apprentices were said to be far in excess of the children available for placement. Girls became skilled in needlework and were 'moderately instructed in household work',

A tailoring workshop

Bookbinding; the child on a stool.

while boys being 'sufficiently advanced in reading, writing and arithmetic', were useful apprentices to London shopkeepers; the governors favouring these apprenticeships over those in 'more opulent families'[2] with several servants, or those in the country farther away from oversight. (Many Foundling Hospital children were also sent away to mills in the Midlands and the north of England.)

Industry Hall was built near Hawkstone, Shropshire, in 1789, to provide schooling for ten boys and thirty girls, aged between five and ten, there being no employment for children in the vicinity, 'they (having) been permitted to run about all day, contracting habits of idleness.' The children were taught to read 'and work of various kinds so as ... to enable them to obtain their livelihood as mechanics, or to fit them for good and useful servants.' Several quotations from the Old Testament ('spare the rod ...') were placed in prominent positions 'so as to attract their attention and shew them the advantage of their being whipt.'[3] Fleeces were brought into the school and picked, spun and knitted into stockings which were offered for sale by a local haberdasher.

Birmingham Overseers decided to separate children from the 'depraved and incorrigible persons' who frequently occupied the workhouse, establishing a separate residential institution about a mile from the town. Girls undertook needlework and knitting for the asylum and workhouse and, in summer, boys were occasionally sent to farms and gardens in the vicinity. The earnings from these activities enabled a workshop to be built where 40 boys were employed in heading pins and sticking them in rows in paper. Another workshop was built for 40 girls who were engaged in straw plaiting for women's hats and bonnets. The children were well fed with meat three times a week, besides soup, puddings, rice, bread, cheese and beer. The children 'once the pest and dread of housekeepers and manufacturers, are now sought with avidity as orderly and useful servants.'[4] The Asylum Committee produced accounts which, between 1798 and 1804, demonstrated an annual saving of approximately £400 a year from the Asylum compared with putting individual children out to nurse. (Birmingham Workhouse, like others in the larger towns, also sent children to mines and mills.)

Knitting was something that men, women and children did in the Yorkshire Dales. The women had knitting schools where the children were (often minimally) taught and where they sang knitting songs which helped to maintain a regularity of action and reminded them how many rows they had to do. They knitted woollen caps, stockings, jackets and nightcaps which were sold in Kendal market.

Straw plaiting

Wheat was not only a valuable crop for grain and a source of straw for human and animal bedding; the long, straight, stems could be plaited into strips which were made up into hats, baskets and footwear. The straw plaiting industry was well established by the early eighteenth century in the south Midlands and South East and, since it required much dexterity but little strength, it became a predominantly female occupation, often for the poor in workhouses. English straw was relatively coarse and fashionable folk preferred hats made from Italian straw, but imports were restricted during the Napoleonic wars and, in the early nineteenth century, the invention of a tool for splitting English straw prompted increased demand for English straw plait.

In the severe winters of 1800 and 1801, many women and children in Avebury, Wiltshire, were in dire poverty and this led a local man to propose that the poor be taught to plait split straw, offering to find someone to instruct them. All females in the parish were invited to attend the class, the stipulation being that cleanliness was essential, no matter how ragged the clothing. The plaited straw was sold in London and Bath. Within a few months the plaiters could work in their own homes and nearly 100 women and children earned between 15p and 50p per week. 'The vermin with which the cottagers swarmed' became a thing of the past, cottages were clean and the people no longer dressed in rags. So successful was the scheme that the Society was dissolved, the people working from home, using their new skill. Concern was expressed that this might be a fickle industry that would last only a few years, for 'there are few manufactures in the kingdom in which so little capital is wanted, or the knowledge of the art so soon acquired.'[5] But those who raised the question were quick to point out that if it was a means of providing instruction to children in habits of 'order, cleanliness application and usefulness' it would have been justified. In Herefordshire, Bedfordshire and Buckinghamshire there were two clear branches of the trade: one making lengths of plaited straw, an industry widely carried on in the villages; and the other making straw plaits into hats and bonnets, particularly around Luton and Dunstable. As the trade developed, children were increasingly engaged in plaiting and, in 1818, it was said that a wife and children could earn more than her husband in straw plaiting families in Hertfordshire. A child plaiting for eight or nine hours a day in 1837 could earn 3.5p a week at the age of eight, increasing to 5p aged nine, and 10p by the age of twelve. In the 1851 census, 25 per cent of all Hertfordshire plaiters were under the age of fifteen.

A simple straw splitting machine was invented in about 1785, which speeded-up the production of lengths of straw ready for plaiting. Children were widely engaged in the industry, being often both taught the technique and subsequently supervised in 'plait schools' which ensured that each child met his/her daily quota, there being little claim to the provision of a wider education. A twelve-year-old boy described his work: he could neither read nor write; began work at the plait school at 9 a.m., finishing at 6 p.m., providing that his quota was achieved. And if it was not, the school mistress did not hesitate to use her stick. Children sat, tightly packed, on benches or stools in an ill-ventilated room. They were often pale from being cooped up in such tight spaces and it could be cold in winter as there was no room for a fire.

The tools of the trade were simple: just a hand-held splitter, a splint and simple plait mill (a small roller like a hand-held mangle) to flatten the straw. The harshest task mistresses were often mothers who insisted on their very young children going to a plaiting school, and the parents often set the plait target which had to be met each day. A seven-year-old girl told the 1864 Children's Employment Commission that she worked in a plait school from 8.30 a.m. till noon, from 1 p.m. until 4 p.m. and from 5 p.m. until 8 p.m., her mother set her five yards to do in each of the three school sessions, plus one yard at dinner and one yard at tea time. To help to remember the pattern sequences, as well as to relieve the boredom, the children often chanted rhymes as they worked:

> Under one and over two
> Put it tight and that will do.
> Or:
> Criss-cross patch and then a twirl
> Twist it back for an English pearl.[6]

A medical witness to the 1864 Children's Employment Commission commented that the crowded plait school rooms, the lack of exercise and long spells between meal times led to children becoming sickly and suffering from stomach and catarrhal diseases. One Hertfordshire plait school mistress commented that 'The fever took off a good many here a few months ago.'[7] The Workshops Act, by which attempts were made to limit the number of children allowed in each workplace, together with the introduction of compulsory schooling from the 1870s, sounded the death knell for plait schools. The schools could no longer be made to pay, although some continued as evening activities and hard-pressed parents continued to evade the law.

Boots and shoes

Outwork flourished in the older centres of boot and shoe production – London and Northampton – until the mid-nineteenth century. A 'standard' leather shoe consisted of an 'upper' of soft leather and 'bottom' or sole of something tougher. Both parts had to be cut out and then the pieces of the upper were stitched together and placed on a last and joined to the insole, before the sole and heel could be attached. Mechanisation of the industry depended on quite distinct technical developments, mechanisation of the lasting process proving the most difficult. This all took place over time so that some processes could be factory based whilst others remained as outwork. In the older centres of shoe manufacture outwork flourished, materials for uppers and bottoms being cut in the warehouses and workshops of the manufacturers and delivered to outworkers, who returned the goods virtually finished. Some outworkers were single-handed operators, others worked for subcontractors, known in some places as garret-masters, who controlled larger groups of workpeople. London garret-masters of the 1880s were alleged to engage in some of the worst types of sweated labour in the industry. In the domestic context children were extensively employed as part of the family production unit in preparing wax and thread and in stabbing holes in the leather ready for stitching. From the 1850s onwards, sewing machines were increasingly used and these could be used in the home. The 1862 Royal Commission on Children's Employment showed that some large manufacturers preferred this form of organisation; a Leicester manufacturer who rented out sewing machines at 1*s.* a week claimed to get, by this means, a better class of girls, whose parents would prefer them not to work in a factory. Boys could quickly earn as much as their fathers; William Arnold earned 65p a week before the age of twelve, making army boots during the 1870/71 Franco-Prussian War. Domestic outwork continued in many centres of the boot and shoe industry until almost the end of the nineteenth century; garret-masters were still putting-out work in Norwich in 1910.

Hosiery

In 1589 William Lee, a Nottinghamshire clergyman and inventor, devised a stocking frame knitting machine. He sought a patent from Elizabeth I and was declined on two occasions, allegedly because it was feared that the mechanisation of knitting would put many hand knitters out of work. Instead he moved to France with his brother and nine workmen and frames, where he was granted a patent. After William's death, his brother James returned to England, settling in London and this initially led to the establishment of two centres of the knitting industry – the East Midlands and London.

Lee's machine at first produced coarse woollen stockings but, by the early eighteenth century had been adapted for finer wool, cotton and silk. Later in the eighteenth century new meshes, including net, were made on knitting frames. Like handloom weaving, knitting generated a range of associated occupations. Yarn had to be wound onto bobbins before knitting began and much needlework was involved in mending, stitching, seaming and making-up. Winding and sewing were done by women and children. There were said to be around 150 stocking frames in the countryside in 1664 and by 1812 the number had risen to 25,000, with the migration of the London end of the industry to the East Midlands. By 1812 the domestic hosiery industry was widely dispersed through 82 small towns and villages in Leicestershire and Nottinghamshire. Leicester became the focus of the worsted hosiery trade, while the cotton hosiery industry was centred on Nottingham. While some hosiers were well-to-do and had a dozen or so knitting frames on their premises, artisan knitters had a frameshop within their house, containing between one and three knitting frames. Former knitters' cottages can be identified by the long windows, in contrast to the domestic scale of the other windows in cottages. A unique feature of framework knitting was that, unlike other outwork industries, the knitter usually rented the knitting frame. A complicating factor was that the man who supplied the frame was not necessarily the man who supplied the knitter with work.

In a number of East Midlands villages there were seaming 'schools' on the pattern of the pillow lace and straw plaiting schools of the south Midlands. By the time they had reached the age of six or seven, many children were working long hours. One seven-year-old boy, William, told the Children's Employment Commission that his four-year-old brother had begun winding that week, working for two hours in the morning 'and does the six bobbins which father sets him. Next week he will wind after dinner and leave off when it gets dark ... I shall seam till candlelight ... Emily is going on five ... She seams my father's (stocking) legs from breakfast till tea at 5 ... and does ten legs a day.'[8] William said that he was rarely in bed before 11 p.m.

The hosiery industry was susceptible to changes in fashion and these fluctuations contributed to difficulties in the industry between 1815 and the 1850s. By the 1840s framework knitters in the towns tried to avoid putting their children to the frame, if possible; with meagre wages and too many operatives, prospects in the hand-frame trade were bleak and there were other employment possibilities. But, in rural areas, alternative employment was unavailable and even when, later in the nineteenth century, steam-powered frames were installed in factories, winding and making-up frequently continued to be outwork for women and children. A female Nottinghamshire framework knitter told an Assistant Commissioner in 1862 that she had seen a twelve-year-old boy arrive home at about 8 or 9 p.m. then being required to stitch the fingers of three dozen pairs of coarse gloves. He also worked a (knitting) frame. It was hardly surprising that this exploited boy, with no real home, asked if he was big enough to be a sailor.

Children, it has been said, were the greatest sufferers from the persistence of outwork in the final processes of the framework knitting industry. In smaller communities there were 'seaming schools', rather like the straw plaiting and lace schools and one clergyman said in 1845 that parents in his village refused to keep their daughters at the National School because they were not allowed to take their seaming to school with them. A middleman who worked for the large hosiery manufacturer, Morleys, reported in 1854 that the fine goods were made by men 'and the coarse work is done by women and children to fill up their time and assist their families. If I let a fine (stocking) frame to a man, he applies for a coarse cotton frame for his family to work at ... and they will assist in doing the winding and seaming, which helps to make the family comfortable.'[9] An agent for another large hosiery firm, Thomas Corah of Leicester, managed 100 frames which created work for 32 men, 22 stocking-makers' children, 30 agricultural labourers' children and sixteen agricultural labourers' wives. Another agent employing 100 frames near Hinckley, at the same time, had 40 men, 26 women and 30 children working for him. Mechanisation finally put an end to all but the most determined older outworkers; hosiery factories containing steam-powered knitting frames being built in the 1850s and 1860s. But, as with other industries with a strong outwork component, determined stalwarts, or those resistant to change, could eke out some sort of a livelihood for many years more.

Pillow lace

Pillow lace, so-called because it was actually made by hand over a pillow, was chiefly produced in two areas of rural Britain. One was the Honiton district of Devon and the other the larger part of Buckinghamshire, Bedfordshire, Northamptonshire and adjacent parts of Oxfordshire. One of the features of the trade was that it had to be learned at as early an age as possible so that the child could be nimble-fingered while her hands were pliable. This meant beginning at five years old or even younger.

While some were taught the craft by their mothers, other girls attended 'lace schools' which, like straw plaiting schools, were little concerned with education. There were fifteen lace schools in Newport Pagnall (Bucks), teaching some 210 children in 1835. Hours were long, discipline strict and, to save fuel costs in heating, children were crammed into small airless rooms. This, in itself, was a health hazard with sealed windows and chimneys, but the task too was a health hazard. The bulky shape of the pillow and the small size of the child bent over it gave them permanently bowed chests. And, since the hours of work stretched beyond sunset in winter, children's eyesight was damaged. To save on the cost of candles, bottles were filled with water and placed around a central candle, acting as lenses to magnify the limited amount of light. Young children in lace schools tried to sustain concentration while relieving boredom, by singing counting songs, as in the straw-plaiting trade.

Parents in the lace manufacturing districts thought that they should send girls to a lace school as early as possible. A farm labourer in the 1860s considered it to be 'a matter of course that his daughters will be sent to a lace school at four or five years of age, and that from the time of their leaving the school to the time when they leave his house for good, it is his wife's business to see that they stick to their lace pillow and work at least as many hours as he does himself.'[10] As late as the 1870s an Assistant Factory Inspector in Devon reported that parents still thought that they had produced children 'for no purpose' unless they became wage earners in the pillow lace trade as soon as possible. Wages varied with the age and skill of the girls and the state of the trade. In the 1843 Royal Commission on Children's Employment it was claimed that, in the Midlands, a young woman must work hard for fourteen or fifteen hours a day to earn 17.5p a week; twenty years later children under ten were thought to be lucky if they made 5p a week. In the early 1860s a fairly skilled eight-year-old Buckinghamshire or Oxfordshire girl could earn between 7.5p and 12.5p a week and a moderately skilled thirteen-year-old could earn between 12.5p and 15p a week. At the 1851 census 1988 children aged between five and nine were recorded as working in the traditional areas of pillow lace making and this was probably an underestimate.

Children working in the pillow lace industry in 1851

County	Aged 5–9 years	Aged 10–14 years
Devon	259	968
Buckinghamshire	621	1424
Bedfordshire	354	893
Northamptonshire	754	2124
TOTAL	1988	5409

By the 1850s pillow lace was facing severe competition from machine lace but, because it was made at low cost by women and children, it continued as a cottage industry until the late nineteenth century. By this time the demand for pillow lace had fallen and the passing of the education acts had made it illegal to employ the very young.

Machine lace

Machine lace-making was a distinct and quite separate branch of the textile industries, using spun silk as the raw material, until 1804, when machine-spun cotton could be spun to a degree of fineness required in the manufacture of Nottingham lace. In 1773 a patent for 'point-net' (lace) was taken out for a silk-mesh that could be cut in any shape or form, without the web being damaged as the loops were cut. The technique was perfected in 1786, using an adaptation of the stocking frame and, three years later, the patent was cancelled, triggering rapid growth in the industry. Once cotton could be spun finely enough, lace manufacturers could produce a much cheaper and whiter net than that made of silk. Point-net production developed rapidly from there being approximately twenty frames in 1786 to 1,500 in 1810. In that year it was estimated that machine lace manufacture provided employment for between 10,000 and 15,000 people 'including women and children'. As in the hosiery industry, lace finishing processes were largely carried out by women and children, many being engaged as outworkers in hand-embroidering. The early developments in mechanisation took place in Nottingham, the centre of the cotton hosiery trade and machine lace soon acquired the name Nottingham lace. The early 1820s were boom years and lace machines were installed in factories, not because they were power driven, at first, but for reasons of cost. Lace was vulnerable to changes in fashion and smaller lace makers were driven out of business. By the 1860s it was a factory industry. But, in times of brisk trade great numbers of women and children were employed well into the evenings, sometimes until midnight, to wind thread onto bobbins which boys placed in the machines. These tasks could only be done when the machines were not working and, as finished goods came off the machines at different times, the bobbin winders had to be kept on the premises ready to do their work at any time of the day or evening. Fifteen-year-old youths were required to work night shifts with men, sometimes from 4 a.m. until midnight. Machine lace workers were not covered by factory legislation until 1861 and, until that date, exploitation went undetected. The final processes of mending, running, scalloping, and embroidery were done by hand, much of it continuing as outwork in people's homes. Women, to whom lace was given out to embroider, employed young women at home and these women hired children from the age of six, so that the lace might pass through three or more hands.

As with the hosiery industry, mechanisation of the major process led to a rise in the need for outwork. It was estimated that, in addition to the 38,000 lace factory workers in 1867, there were between 90,000 and 100,000 women and girl outworkers who were paid 25p a week. One Nottingham dealer commented in the 1860s 'there is no place where children work so hard for their parents, and parents live so much on their children, doing little or nothing, as here.'[11] Even with the introduction of compulsory schooling, children worked before and after school hours. By the early twentieth century, however, despite there being some 7000 outworkers in the Nottingham lace trade, very few were children.

Gloving

Gloving occupied children in fewer localities than weaving, pillow lace or straw plaiting and was sometimes done in conjunction with other outwork industries. In mid-Victorian times gloving was an outwork occupation near Yeovil in Somerset, at Woodstock in Oxfordshire and in parts of Worcestershire and Herefordshire. In 1851, 242 children aged between five and nine and 1,441 aged between ten and fourteen worked at glove-making in Somerset. Most children worked with their mothers – in the Worcester area an adult and two children could make six pairs of 'best men's gloves' a day, being paid about 17.5p for a dozen pairs. A fourteen-year-old girl from Evesham told an Assistant Commissioner in 1864 that she had begun gloving at the age of eight, working from 8 a.m. until dusk: 'We never work by candle light; that hurts the eyes very much.'[12] In Somerset, children either worked in the cottage of an agent or did gloving at home in the evenings after school and this was difficult to eradicate, even after the passing of the 1867 Workshops Act, for home working was virtually unseen.

Young children aged seven and eight in Somerset suffered particularly in winter when 'their feet are numbed by the cold and their hands rendered incapable of working from time to time by contact with the (cold) brass work of the gloving machines.'[13] This was 'a brass machine which holds the gloves in a vice, and has a row of little holes close together, through which the needle passes, and which keeps the stitches regular.' A girl from

Ilchester said that her eyes suffered and that, while she could see well at the beginning of the week, by the end of the week all the holes seemed to run into one and the supervisor would bang her on the head, thinking she was lazy. An eight-year-old began gloving at the age of five and was very clear that, when she was older, she would prefer to go into service. While later nineteenth-century factories at first put out stitching to workers at home, the development of machinery in the industry made this uneconomic – and child labour in the industry ceased.

BOYS EXERCISING AT TOTHILL FIELDS PRISON.

Boys exercising at a London prison.

TWELVE

Children of the streets

Most large towns were teeming with activity in the nineteenth century – many shops, street sellers, goods being moved by handcart; with newspaper sellers, porters, errand boys and much else besides. Some children worked specifically for one shopkeeper, usually being described as butcher's boy, baker's boy or draper's boy. These were probably the more fortunate ones, usually working in smaller towns. For many children in London and the large industrial towns there was no alternative to finding some sort of a livelihood on the streets. Charles Dickens wrote movingly about children in tragic circumstances such as Oliver Twist the orphan, and Jo the sweeper, in Bleak House. Working on the streets could be dangerous; street fights and violence, severe weather in winter for sparsely clad children, living hand to mouth wondering where the money for the next meal would come from, and where to sleep, all took their toll. There seems to have been a degree of camaraderie amongst children in certain street trades – if a lad failed to earn anything one day he might be given a coin or two by his mates. Many boys ended up in prison.

Street sellers

Child street sellers were numerous in the larger mid-nineteenth century towns, the greatest number being in London. Many were the offspring of street sellers, following parents in the same goods be it fruit, flowers, herring, whelks or matches. Henry Mayhew published his illustrated four-volume *London Labour and the London Poor* in 1861–2, the novelist W. M. Thackeray writing that Mayhew provided 'a picture so wonderful, so awful, so piteous and pathetic, so exciting and terrible that readers of romances own they never read anything like to it.'[1] Mayhew invented oral history a hundred years before the term was first used. He suggested that, while costermongering (selling fish, fruit, vegetables) seemed to be an hereditary pursuit, street selling, in all its forms, was the most precarious way of living. Wet weather could reduce a street seller almost to starvation in a matter of days and fruit and vegetable sellers were particularly hard-hit in the winter. Mayhew commented that 'the costermonger was almost always accompanied by a boy aged between ten and sixteen who helped to call out for trade, sometimes managing to appeal to the pity of passers-by. Boys hung around markets such as Covent Garden and Billingsgate, hoping to be hired. When they were hired they didn't appear to negotiate a wage but depended on the generosity of the costermonger. Boys were paid by the day – less than 0.5p, receiving meals and, sometimes, being allowed to take some fruit home in their pockets for their siblings. One old costermonger told Mayhew 'It is grievous to see the children, as soon as they are able to speak, thrust into the streets to sell and in many instances I am sorry to state, to support their parents.'[2]

Mayhew also investigated children connected in other ways with street life: children of street musicians, cabmen, besides those of the poorer class of labourers connected with the river. As soon as a boy or girl was strong enough to carry a basket and able to understand the relative value of money from a farthing to a shilling (0.1p–5p), he or she went to sell in the streets. One mother of three children sent them all out to sell matches and 'if they made 6*d.* (2.5p) a day among the three of them ... perhaps it saved their lives when things were at the worst.'[3] One nine-year-old girl sold bootlaces and had been a street seller on and off for two years. She started by selling nuts, encouraged by her mother who told her that if she only made 1*d.* (less than 0.5p) 'its a good piece of bread'.[4] The girl acknowledged that things were bad in winter and on some days she and her parents went to bed to save on fire and candles. Another girl, eleven or twelve years old, lived with her father, her mother having been dead for some years, and worked in the streets when there was nothing to eat at home. An orphan boy aged between fifteen and sixteen was taken in by a laundress who gave

Street children; a contrast between the barefooted girl and the small child behind her with the well-dressed adults.

him a start with an old basket and a few things to sell. Then he sold muffins but, as it was only a winter trade, he sold watercress and cherries in the summer, then apples, oranges, nuts and chestnuts, then garters. Another orphan was about to be taken to the parish overseers by others in the house where he had lived, so he ran away and want drove him to beg. One day he made nothing and towards evening of the following day, still having been given no coins and desperate from hunger, he went up to an elderly man walking in Hyde Park and said 'Sir, I've lived three weeks by begging, and I'm hungering now; give me sixpence (2.5p) or I'll go and steal.'[5] The man stopped and, without a word, gave the boy a shilling (5p) and this was enough to start him selling matches.

An orphan girl, whose dying mother made her promise to try to find a place in which to live without becoming a street seller, went about for three months, selling all the furniture and clothes until she had nothing to wear but what she stood up in and nobody knew her to give her 'a character' (a reference). In desperation, her money all gone, she met a young woman in the street and asked where she could get lodging. She was taken to a respectable lodging house for women and girls and became a flower seller. At first she felt too ashamed to ask people to buy her flowers but gradually she learned to sell although 'what I shall do in the winter I don't know ... I can't bear to think on it.'[6] Several hundred children, mostly girls, sold flowers on the streets of London in the mid to late nineteenth century, running along barefoot calling 'please gentleman, do buy my flowers, poor little girl.' Others were 'step girls' cleaning front doorsteps at houses which abutted the street or pavement. There were fewer opportunities for girls (without resorting to prostitution) than for boys, selling being the most usual occupation.

A London match girl in the mid-nineteenth century.

A London girl flower seller in the mid-nineteenth century.

There were many more opportunities for boys to earn in the streets. But many boys did sell in towns all over Britain; anything from matches, leather straps, firewood, fly-papers, cheap jewellery, nutmeg graters, shirt buttons, and boot-laces to ice-creams, hot peas – even flowers. But they also sharpened knives, were organ grinders, and perhaps, most common of all throughout Britain, they were self-appointed newspaper sellers. A boy would buy, say, three papers for one penny (0.42p) and sell them on at a halfpenny (0.21p) each at a local railway station morning and evening. Mayhew estimated that there were between 10–20,000 child street sellers in London in the mid-nineteenth century and that there was 'scarcely any age at which … money may not be earned.'[7] In East London, many greengrocers would have an errand boy, while in the better-off suburbs they might employ up to twenty boys; even small suburban sellers regarded it as a point of honour to have one. There were boys who hauled goods on barrows through the streets in the larger towns and there were 'van boys' whose task was to load and unload boxes and parcels from horse-drawn carts, sitting among them during delivery, to make sure none fell off or were stolen.

There was a large demand for boys' labour towards the end of the nineteenth century but there was also concern that boys moved from job to job, most of the work being unskilled. It was casual and lay-off was common. Youths in street trading, in particular, were thought to turn to crime when they did not earn enough to meet their needs.

Mud-larks

London mud-larks (despite their fun-sounding name) spent much of the working day soaking wet and covered in mud, for their work was river-finding, wading sometimes up to the waist, through mud left by the receding tide to look for bits of coal, chips of wood, bits of rope, and any pieces of metal, copper nails being particularly prized –in short, any sort of refuse washed up by the tide. 'These poor creatures (wrote Mayhew) are

A London mud-lark; working along the Thames at low tide – one of the most dangerous and strenuous tasks.

certainly about the most deplorable in their appearance of any I have met in the course of my inquiries.'[8] They would sell any coals found to the poor of the neighbourhood, while the iron, bones and copper nails were sold at the rag shops. Occasionally they would find a tool or saw which they would exchange for biscuits and meat with seamen. Henry Mayhew gathered a group of about twelve to speak to; some were as young as six and none was over twelve years old. One, whose mother was alive said that he had once had a pair of shoes, but a long time ago; he didn't mind in summer but it was very cold in winter. Many of them suffered badly from chilblains on feet and hands in the winter; both children and old people 'crawling among the barges at the various wharfs along the river'. They could hardly be said to be wearing rags and their bodies were 'grimed with the foul soil of the river'.[9] Mud-larks generally lived in courts or alleyways by the river but, when combing the river, they worked on their own, never speaking to others. They were either the children of the very poorest, perhaps with one parent alive, or they were orphans 'compelled from utter destitution to seek for the means of appeasing their hunger in the mud of the river.'[10] Mudlarking had its dangers, as barefoot children trod on broken glass, nails and other sharp materials buried in the mud, one boy telling Mayhew that if this happened he went to his lodging and dressed the wounds, returning straight away to the river 'for should the tide come up without my having found something, why I must starve till next low tide.'[11]

Crossing sweepers

This was a term which covered a range of jobs from, literally, sweeping a muddy road crossing (crossing sweepers welcomed rain as this distributed more mud), opening the doors of cabs, begging or, in the evening, 'tumbling' outside theatres in London, but only if there were no policemen about (they had a secret language by which to warn each other of a policeman coming by). 'A broom doesn't last us more than a week in wet weather, and they cost us twopence halfpenny each (*c*.1p); but in dry weather they are good for a fortnight.'[12] London crossing sweepers had pitches, often working in pairs with agreed 'house-rules'. If one saw two gentlemen approaching he would call out 'Two toffs' or if a man and a woman 'A toff and a doll' and,

London crossing sweepers in the mid-nineteenth century; both boys barefoot.

whoever called first, kept the money. One of their more lucrative activities was calling (and getting) a cab for people coming away from the opera, particularly if it was raining. In winter, they would stage snowballing outside Charing Cross Hotel and guests would toss coins to them. They paid around 1p a night for lodging and once or twice a week ate meat, tossing to see who would get the largest piece and sometimes, if they fell on hard times, they would sleep out all night but 'if any of us gets nothink [*sic*] then the others give him a penny or two'.[13] Mayhew interviewed several crossing sweepers including the 'captain' of the boy sweepers, a sixteen-year-old who appeared to put on a hangdog act for Mayhew but was rumbled by members of his gang. His father, a widower, turned him out of home at the age of nine and he developed a tumbling act 'I taught 'em all to tumble ... I was the fust to introduce tumbling backwards' but the 'king' of the tumblers was even better 'he could bend his little legs round till they curved like long German sausages ... and when he turned head over heels, he curled up his tiny body as closely as a wood-louse'.[14] An orphan, he lived with his grandmother and aunt and gave them all the money he made.

Girls were also crossing sweepers, although there were fewer of them. Mayhew interviewed a twelve-year-old girl crossing sweeper who didn't work in a gang but had her 'own' crossing in Oxford Street. She lived with her widowed father who earned very little. She was also minder for her five-year-old brother and three-year-old sister who sat on the steps close by her crossing. 'If it's wet I has to stop at home and take care of them.' She began to earn by singing songs in the streets when her father was out of

Street performers in London in the mid-nineteenth century.

STREET-PERFORMERS ON STILTS.

[From a Sketch.]

work and she was the only earner. But she only had a small repertoire and, as she couldn't read, she had no means of learning more songs. Working as a crossing sweeper from 9 a.m. until 4 p.m., she earned between 2.5p and 3.2p. In the winter she cleaned ladies' doors in the Lincoln's Inn area. A thirteen-year-old girl, her clothes in tatters, had worked as a servant/nursemaid for a couple who left England to go 'to a place called Italy – perhaps you've heard tell of it, Sir' and then she turned to begging, besides selling a few laces and matches. She first swept at a crossing with boys but they asked for some of her minimal earnings so she moved on to another mixed group 'I don't stop out at nights like the boys, but I gets home (her grandmother's) by ten at latest.'[15]

Prostitution

The journalist W. T. Stead undertook a campaign against child prostitution in the 1880s, demonstrating how easy it was to buy children for prostitution by purchasing a fourteen-year-old from her mother and then making public how he had both bought and rescued her. Josephine Butler wrote about child prostitutes in Brussels – English girls aged between ten and fourteen who had been abducted in English villages, sold and taken abroad. Butler sought to save girls and return them to England. Set in the context of dire poverty, particularly for women and girls, there may have been few perceived alternatives. Henry Mayhew found that female child mud-larks only remained at that job until 'such time as they were capable of adopting the more easy and more lucrative life of the prostitute' on Ratcliff Highway and other 'low neighbourhoods'[16] in the East of London.

Regulation of street children

By the late nineteenth century public opinion was growing against child street sellers; they were considered to be unsightly, to be too independent, likely to fall victim to petty crime and, in 1878, Manchester Corporation contacted the Home Secretary describing the evident evils resulting from child street sellers hawking newspapers, matches, and other articles at unreasonable hours. In 1880 the Corporation was unsuccessful in its attempt to obtain legislation governing street selling but, in 1882, it promoted its own Corporation Bill and a clause was inserted in this prohibiting under fourteen-year-olds from selling on the streets after 9 p.m. between April and October and after 7 p.m. during the rest of the year, unless they had attained a specified educational standard. In 1883, street trading rules were included in Birmingham and Sheffield's respective Corporation Acts, and later, Cardiff, Hastings and a number of other towns followed suit. Other towns, notably Newcastle-upon-Tyne, Bristol, Liverpool and Manchester passed bye-laws to regulate street trading under the 1882 Municipal Corporations Act. But they were not entirely effective – children claimed not to know that they were supposed to have a licence to trade, and parents turned a blind eye, or positively required their children to work in the streets.

In 1897 evidence on children's work was collected at 54 London schools by the Women's Industrial Council. Out of 26,000 pupils, 729 boys and 523 girls were working for wages. Of the boys, 313 worked in shops and 102 sold newspapers; while 135 girls were baby-minders and 115 were domestic cleaners. One eight-year-old boy delivered milk each morning for 7.5p a week, another child chopped lump sugar each evening for approximately 1p per day. Two years later the London Education Department surveyed schools on the question of children who worked for wages. Out of 147,349 working children identified, about a quarter were aged ten or under and about 130 were under seven years old. Nearly 30 per cent of working children worked for more than twenty hours per week, including a boy who placed skittles for 34½ hours a week, working after school from 6 p.m. to 11 p.m. each day and who often fell asleep in afternoon lessons. In 1901 a Government Committee on the Employment of School Children was set up; there being an estimated 300,000 school children undertaking waged work, including approximately 100,000 working in shops, 25,000 undertaking various forms of street selling and 50,000 (mainly girls)

Butcher's boy at the end of the nineteenth century, looking well dressed to attract custom. (Mary Evans Picture Library)

doing some form of domestic work. The Committee opposed a ban on child labour but, two years later, The Employment of Children Act (1903) was more effective in regulating child retail, street selling and other child labour by prohibiting boys of under fourteen and girls of under sixteen years of age from working between 9 p.m. and 6 a.m. Local authorities were empowered to make the regulations more stringent but most of them dragged their feet in drawing up the necessary bye-laws.

In 1905 the author of a publication entitled 'The Child Slaves of Britain' reported on conditions in London, Manchester, Birmingham, Liverpool, Glasgow and several other towns, in each of which he sought to lodge in comparable accommodation to the very poorest inhabitants. It was not so much that he brought new evidence to light, but that he could demonstrate how, despite endeavours of some corporations, and the passing of Factory and Workshops Acts, child exploitation continued. Boys engaged in milk delivery were usually up by 5 a.m. and arrived late to school. A twelve-year-old London boy worked in a coal yard 'and staggers into the classroom exhausted, fainting and covered in coal dust.'[17] Manchester's Corporation Act was passed in 1901, coming into effect the following year, in which nearly 2000 licenses were granted to children who were still required to attend school, but it was found that many children, including some clearly under the permissible age for street trading, were working the streets. When accosted at 10 p.m., one replied 'Mother told me to bring back a shilling tonight ... or to look out for a basting.'[18] In Birmingham outwork trades, one mother kept a girl away from school on a medical certificate (keeping vermin sores on the child's scalp open by rubbing sand into them), while another rubbed grease and sand on her daughter's scalp, having cut all her hair off, both of them in order to keep their girls sewing hooks and eyes onto cards; others hid their children when a School Inspector was doing the rounds, so as to keep them at work. In one Birmingham street a woman and a small girl were found 'who were dying of starvation in the hook and eye trade: 'Starting the two of us early on Saturday morning and working hard all day Saturday, and beginning again on Monday morning and on till dinner time, we earned 1*s.* 6*d.* (7.5p).'[19] When visited, neither had eaten anything all day. Boys worked for more than 40 hours a week at chopping firewood, wheeling coal, or in barbers' shops, the latter 'rarely get home on Saturday nights till past midnight and ... are expected to attend again with the lather-brush all Sunday morning.'[20] Both boys and girls worked in dangerous trades in Birmingham; girls in enamelling factories and boys in file-cutting, in both of which trades lead was present. In Edinburgh many children were barefoot, even in winter. Boys often worked for seventeen hours on Saturdays and twelve to fourteen hours was common.

In Glasgow, many children made paper bags, earning three farthings (less than 0.5p) an hour and young girls assisted their mothers in shawl-fringing. In Liverpool, children assisted in fish curing, while many boys were 'knockers-up' calling out to dock workers who had to be at the waterfront in the early hours: 'On bitter, dark wintry mornings you may see little shivering wraiths flitting from house to house, beating tattoo on the murky window-frames'.[21] It became clear that in not every case was it necessary for the child to work, or at least for such long hours; an example given was the London family in which the father earned £2 a week, the mother kept a prosperous laundry and 'whose children were forced to work every hour that they could stand on their legs. The father spends his wages "swaggering about in saloon-bars". The children are badly fed ... There is so much beer drunk in this home and the children always share in it.'[22] Until half-timing was abolished in 1918 child street work, in all its many forms, proved difficult to control.

THIRTEEN

Child protection and the regulation of child labour in Britain

LIBERAL REFORMERS alluded to children as slaves in three areas of work in Britain in the early nineteenth century: chimney sweeps from the 1770s, pauper apprentices at the beginning of the nineteenth century and other mill children in 1830. The term slaves was applied to working children more widely by mid-century. Public awareness of the plight of chimney sweeps was raised from the 1770s when Jonas Hanway, together with master-sweep David Porter, drew up ideas for regulating the work of chimney sweeps' boys. Hanway published *The State of Chimney Sweepers' Young Apprentices* in 1773, the year after a significant ruling concerning a negro slave, which came to be known as Somerset's case, was made by the Lord Chief Justice. The case concerned an African boy, James Somerset, brought to England by a man from Virginia, who wished to take him from England to sell him in Jamaica. The Lord Chief Justice ruled that this was unlawful and it was popularly interpreted to mean that slavery was illegal in England and Wales thereby, in principle, emancipating the remaining negro slaves, or potential slaves in England, who were mostly domestic servants. (In practice this was not enforced at the time.) In 1787 Josiah Wedgwood, a passionate anti-slavery advocate, made a medallion showing a kneeling negro in chains, his hands held up in supplication, together with the words 'Am I not a Man and a Brother'.

In 1785 Hanway brought together eighteen letters he had written on the subject of child sweeps under the title *Sentimental History of Chimney*

Wedgwood dish with the image of the medallion he first cast in 1787: 'Am I not a Man and a Brother?'

Sweeps in London and Westminster and in the following year the first Act to control the employment of child sweeps was passed. William Blake published *Songs of Innocence* in 1789, one poem, 'The Chimney Sweeper', beginning with the words:

> When my mother died I was very young,
> And my father sold me while yet my tongue
> Could scarcely cry ''weep! 'weep! 'weep! 'weep!'
> So your chimneys I sweep & in soot I sleep.

In the following twenty years or so a number of European countries abolished slavery and some American states began to pass laws for the gradual emancipation of slaves. A bill for the abolition of slavery was passed in the House of Commons, but rejected by the House of Lords in 1805; slave trading was abolished in the British Empire in 1807 and in 1834 The British Slavery Abolition Act came into force. Slavery was abolished in North America (although not the fall-out, by any means) before child chimney sweeps were outlawed in England. The allusion to slaves was certainly being made more widely in the early 1800s by campaigners for the abolition of child chimney sweeping and, later, a master sweep, giving evidence to the Children's Employment Commission of 1863, stated that apprenticeship 'is as bad as Negro slavery ... only it is not so known ... I had myself formerly boys as young as 5½ years, but I did not like them; they were too weak. I was afraid they might go off (die) ... They go off just as quietly as you might fall asleep in the chair by the fire.'[1]

A woman arrived in Bristol from the West Indies, in the nineteenth century, bringing with her a female negro servant. Shortly after their arrival in lodgings the landlady sent for someone to sweep the kitchen chimney. The servant was amazed at the sight of the little sooty black child and declared that she would sooner drown one of her own children than see him become a chimney sweep. Calling the sweep child over, she gave him a sixpenny piece, moistened her finger and began to rub the boy's cheek to ascertain whether he was really a white child beneath all the grime.

Given the similarity of a sweep's boy's apparent colour to that of an African Caribbean slave, together with the rising public concern over their conditions of work, the analogy with slavery was a powerful one.

Pauper apprentices in cotton and worsted textile mills were also likened to slaves in 1802, as were mill children in 1830. The analogies were not entirely fanciful, although there was no comparison with regard to scale, there being vastly more African slaves in America and the West Indies (some in England); and their ill-treatment was on a much larger scale. The African was taken by force, transported and sold into slavery thousands of miles from home; sweeps' apprentices were frequently 'bought' from desperately poor parents, while children were sometimes stolen, particularly in rural areas, and sold on. Some workhouses were known to paint a falsely positive picture of factory conditions in order to gain a child's acceptance of work in a cotton mill, for the child was required to agree. Press gangs, too, more or less captured youths to serve on ships. The American slave could be sold as the slave-owner's property; he/she and their children were owned for life; pauper apprentices, on the other hand, were tied until the age of 21 and could be 'passed on', before their time was up, if the owner of a mill became bankrupt. In 1784 a Manchester newspaper carried an advertisement to let the labour of 260 children with accommodation for carrying on the cotton business. If a slave in North America absconded, and many did, they were hunted down and brought back. Cotton mill apprentices, too, were known to run away and were brought back if caught. In both cases there was punishment, often of some cruelty. Female slaves were subject to sexual abuse by their owners, as were some female mill apprentices – either by supervisors or mill owners. The American slave wore a collar and might be chained. Some child apprentices in mills were tormented by being chained and flogged, either as punishment or for sport. The American slave was branded, child workers were not, although some who worked in furnace industries were occasionally punished with hot metal bars. While some American slaves rebelled as a gang, acts of protest by mill children or sweeps were made individually. In the case of the American slave, he/she was ripped from their culture; sweeps and pauper apprentices, being younger on the whole, knew less of what they were missing.

The plight of child workers in different occupations was highlighted by significant champions campaigning on their behalf. Some were individuals, others were groups that had formed around a common cause. Some champions were industry-specific, others campaigned on a wider industry front. Jonas Hanway, a champion for child sweeps, did not see effective regulatory legislation in his lifetime but, with others, he significantly raised public awareness and initiated the movement for reform. David Porter, a friend of Hanway's sent a petition to Parliament in 1788 and, in 1792, published a pamphlet on the plight of young sweeps. Dr Thomas Percival, a Manchester physician, was a pioneer in promoting sanitation and public health, making a connection between the diffusion of fever and the long hours worked by children in some cotton mills in 1784. His report impressed the county magistrates who directed that it should be printed and distributed and in 1795 the Manchester Board of Health was founded, the advice offered by this body being reprinted in the Report of Sir Robert Peel's Committee in 1816. Dr Ferrier of Manchester, an associate of Percival's wrote, in the 1790s on the subject of children engaged in night work in mills. Their work clearly strongly influenced Robert Peel who, from a cotton spinning family, initially dismissed the move to restrict the hours of child workers in cotton mills but, on becoming an MP, promoted the 1802 Health & Morals of Apprentices Act which was, in effect, an extension of the Poor Law. In 1815 Peel, prompted by the New Lanark cotton spinner Robert Owen, introduced a Bill to amend the 1802 Act. It was put off for three months and, in 1816 he moved for a committee to consider the state of children in factories. The Cotton Mills and Factory Act was passed in 1819.

Richard Oastler of Yorkshire, a supporter of William Wilberforce in the 1807 campaign for the abolition of slavery, sent a series of letters, headed 'Slavery in Yorkshire'[2] to the Leeds Mercury in 1830, having been alerted by a worsted spinner who agonised about the need to employ children in his mills in order to remain competitive. Oastler wrote 'In the worsted mills they are employed thirteen hours, with an interval of only half an hour, and in the woollen mills they work fifteen hours, with an interval of two hours for meals'; he termed this a state of slavery.[3] In 1833 he wrote 'It is notorious that the health of the negro slave, of the adult felon, of the horse, of the ass, of the hare, of the rabbit, of the partridge, of the pheasant, of the cabbage, and of the strawberry is protected by law, but at the same time, the Children of the Poor are unprotected by the law.'[4] Oastler campaigned for a ten hour day for all employees. George Smith of Coalville, Leicester, was the brickworks child champion. Recognising that brick works were not covered by existing factory legislation, he began to raise public awareness in 1869. For there to be a chance of achieving change, champions of specific industries needed the support of MPs and not drawn from only one party. Michael Sadler, who took the lead for factory legislation in 1831,was a Tory, as was Lord Ashley, who became 7th Earl of Shaftesbury in 1851, who was a tireless campaigner on several fronts. In 1833 Ashley campaigned to limit the working day of a child to no more than ten hours; in 1842 he introduced the Mines and Collieries Bill to Parliament; he supported numerous climbing boy bills and was a promoter of the Ragged School movement for the education of poor children.

Amongst the groups which were founded to campaign for the protection of child workers was the London Society for Superseding the Necessity for Employing Climbing Boys, founded in 1803, with the Bishop of Durham as President, William Wilberforce being a Vice-President. This Society had grown out of the Society for Bettering the Condition and Increasing the Comforts of the Poor, established in 1796. Other societies were founded to campaign for climbing boys including one in Sheffield, founded in 1807, being followed by others. The Society of Friends (Quakers) was also vocal in promoting the regulation of climbing boys, bringing sweeps to court for breaking the law, occasionally presenting a sweeping machine to a sweep on condition that he discharged his boy. And, later in the nineteenth century members of the Women's Industrial Council investigated child labour amongst school children in London.

The initiatives proposing and supporting legislation to control the exploitation of children in the workplace were taken by individuals and groups over a period of more than a century. In the case of legislation to protect child sweeps it took 87 years before an Act was passed which effectively controlled chimney sweeping. The 1788 Chimney Sweepers' Act set the minimum age for climbing apprentices to eight years, it limited the number of apprentices any master could have to six; apprentices were to wear a hat badge with the name of the master or mistress on it and no chimneys were to be climbed in which there was actually a fire.

But there was no provision for law enforcement and, between 1817 and 1819, Parliament received a number of petitions calling for the abolition of the climbing boy system. Indeed, while the subject was being debated, children under the lawful age of eight were still climbing the chimneys of Westminster. Between 1817 and 1819 Select Committees investigated the employment of climbing boys and in 1818 a bill to abolish climbing boy employment was passed in the Commons but was rejected by the House of Lords. The situation was repeated in the following year, the Earl of Lauderdale getting to his feet and, after saying that he would be in favour of the bill were machines sufficiently effective, told a 'wild goose' story of the alleged practice in parts of Ireland of tying a rope round the neck of a goose and dragging the bird up the chimney 'which was cleansed by the fluttering of its wings.'[5] The bill, amidst much laughter, was lost once more. In 1834, subsequent to the 1833 abolition of the slave trade in Britain and the passing of the Factory Act, The Chimney Sweep Act was passed, in which an apprentice had to be 'willing and desirous' of following the trade and the minimum age was raised to ten. But there was still no enforcement and the Act continued to be violated.

It was mainly through the active support of the future Lord Shaftesbury that a new Bill was introduced to Parliament in 1840. The Act was passed, banning the apprenticeship of boys under the age of sixteen and the climbing of chimneys by any person under the age of 21 but, in the absence of a means of enforcement, it was relatively meaningless. The House of Commons threw out the 1854 Chimney Sweepers Bill 'and said not a word of sympathy for the wretched children.'[6] In 1864 Lord Shaftesbury took up the cause of climbing boys once more; the mood of the country had changed, perhaps not a little influenced by the publication of Charles Kingsley's *Water Babies* the previous year. The Chimney Sweeps Regulation Act was passed, prohibiting the employment of children under sixteen as chimney sweeps. The licensing of master sweeps was not sanctioned, however. It took the death of eleven-year-old George Brewster at Fulbourn near Cambridge to activate Parliament to approve Shaftesbury's 1875 Chimney Sweepers' Bill, by which master sweeps were to be licensed each year, laying the duty of enforcement on chief constables of every district. The Bill was passed rapidly and unopposed by both houses. Child chimney sweeps from that year onwards were a thing of the past. Lord Shaftesbury is commemorated by the statue of Anteros in Piccadilly Circus, London and a picture, published after his death, shows ragged, barefoot children, including a sweep, laying wreaths at his memorial.

The condition of pauper apprentices in cotton mills came to the attention of medical practitioners in some northern industrial towns in 1784 when Dr Thomas Percival and colleagues, at the behest of Lancashire J.P.s, investigated an outbreak of typhus, then called 'low putrid fever', in cotton mills at Radcliffe, near Bury. The cause was identified as the overtaxing of children, together with the factory atmosphere. Recommendations included the need for ventilation, whitewashing factory walls and a reduction in the hours worked by children, together with the provision of schooling. This led to county J.P.s resolving, in 1784, to decline to allow apprentices to be bound in factories where they would be worked at night, or for more than ten hours a day. Dr Ferrier wrote that the continuance of night work deprived children of 'fresh air and exercise which nature points out as essential in childhood and youth'.[7] In 1795 Dr Percival and associates met to form the Manchester Board of Health, advising on legislation to regulate the hours and conditions of work in factories. In 1803, West Riding J.Ps passed a resolution that children should not be apprenticed to mills where they would be liable to work at night or for more than ten hours a day. These concerns spread to London and the parishes which regularly dispatched pauper apprentices to Lancashire, Derbyshire and elsewhere. As a consequence, a number of Poor Law Guardians began to undertake reasonably regular inspections of mills. The extent to which these visits resulted in improved management and supervisory practices is, however, debateable.

The first Factory Act, the Health and Morals of Apprentices Act, was brought in by Sir Robert Peel and passed in 1802, with little or no opposition. It only applied to pauper apprentices and is particularly associated with those employed in cotton and worsted mills. Its provisions were to regulate the hours and conditions of the work of pauper apprentices; working hours were to be limited to twelve a day, night work by apprentices was to cease by June 1804. Apprentices were to be taught the three 'R's and each was to receive a new suit of clothing once a year. Factories were to be whitewashed twice-yearly and properly ventilated. Apprentice accommodation was to be separate for boys and girls and no more than two children were to share a bed. Apprentices were to attend church at least once a month. J.P.s were to appoint two inspectors, from amongst their number, of which one should be a clergyman, to visit the factories and fines of from £2 to £5 were to be levied for neglecting these regulations (Appendix 2). It was, of course, an impossible task for the inspectors in areas with hundreds of mills and factories and the Act was ineffective. There was further legislation concerning parish apprentices in 1816 and, in 1819, the Cotton Mill and Factories Act banned the employment of children under the age of nine in textile mills, limiting the working day to twelve hours for those aged under sixteen. The 1833 Factory Act further reduced the hours of work to nine for those under the age of thirteen and, for the first time, established a factory inspectorate to enforce the law. There were, however, too few inspectors effectively to cover the most densely industrialised parts of the country. This Act only addressed the problems of children working in textile factories and significant exemptions were made for silk mills, which were dependent almost exclusively on child labour.

Child labour in non-factory industries remained unprotected for many years. And some poor law authorities paid little attention to the conditions under which children were apprenticed. The economic value of young children to their outworking parents as winders, stitchers, menders, bellows-blowers, and a host of other jobs, was taken for granted as a fact of life until legislation, which included workshops, together with compulsory schooling, in the last quarter of the nineteenth century, controlled the growth of child labour. Adult outworkers complained about the abuse of child labour, not only for ethical reasons but because children's wages led to the depression of adults' wage rates.

It has been suggested that one of the reasons why workshops and domestic workplaces were ignored by Parliament was because it was thought that the decline in parental control of children was more acute amongst children in larger factories and mines. Evidence brought to the Children's Employment Commission of 1842/3 contains a number of examples of children (including girls) working at night and, in locations such as mines and industries, where men were scantily dressed because of the high temperatures; young teenage pregnancies were a frequent occurrence. It took two Royal Commissions in the 1840s and the 1860s to address the widespread employment of children in the immense range of trades besides cotton and wool textiles. Both of the Commissions generated a huge amount of first-hand information from Assistant Commissioners who visited key manufacturing regions in England, Wales, Scotland and

Ireland, interviewing employers and children, besides seeking evidence on housing conditions, the provision of schooling and religious knowledge. A major Factory Act was passed in 1844 which lowered the age at which children could work in regulated trades to eight years, but required eight- to twelve-year-olds to attend three hours of schooling a day. This was the beginning of 'half-timing'. However, unless schooling was paid for by an employer or provided free by a charity, this provision was much abused or ignored. School log books contain plentiful evidence of how the system operated. Legislation often seemed to encourage innovative ways of avoiding the restrictions. Some manufacturers devised relay systems for children between the ages of nine and twelve, where one shift took over from another during the day. Some factory inspectors supported this and the practice seems to have been fairly widely adopted.

After the passing of the Ten Hours Act of 1847, which restricted the work of young persons and women to ten hours a day between 6 a.m. and 6 p.m., one industry after another was brought within this law: bleaching and dyeworks in 1860 and 1862 respectively, lace factories in 1861, calico calendering and finishing by Acts of 1863 and 1864; while bakehouses were partly regulated by an Act of 1863. The 1862 Commission worked in the context of growing unease about the absence of legal protection for children who worked outside the already regulated factories, together with a growing concern for their education, producing yet more descriptions of child labour in unregulated industries. The Factory Act of 1864 brought earthenware pottery, match making, percussion cap and cartridge making, paper staining, and fustian cutting (a coarse cloth of cotton, sometimes mixed with flax or cheap wool) partly within the scope of existing textile industry legislation. This Act, informed by expert medical and sanitary commissioners, for the first time required ventilation to be applied in industries where dangerous gases, dust or other by-products of manufacturing processes were involved. This was followed by the Factory Acts Extension Act of 1867 which brought all workplaces employing more than 50 persons in manufacturing industry under the Factory Acts.

The extension of state inspection to workshops – and their regulation – was instituted by the Workshops Regulations Act of 1867. This brought all workplaces employing fewer than 50 persons within factory legislation. It prohibited the employment of children under eight years of age, restricting those aged between eight and thirteen to half time working.

Child employees were to attend school for some time each week. This was followed by the Education Act of 1870. There were, however, still omissions, children working in brickyards not being protected by legislation, for example, until 1871. The minimum age at which a child could work half time in manufacturing was raised to nine in 1874, to eleven in 1891 (later reduced to ten by the Home Secretary) and twelve in 1901. This latter Act made no exceptions to the employment of any child under the age of twelve.

The passing of the Mines and Collieries Act of 1842 followed an intensive campaign and a parliamentary report containing shocking accounts of the working conditions of children in mines, together with, for the first time, graphic illustrations of young people hauling waggons, crawling on hands and knees, half naked children being hauled up a mine on a rope, girls with coal baskets on their backs climbing ladders, and little trapper children sitting by 'their' door to open it for waggons to pass through, closing it again to control the passage of potentially explosive gases. This 1842 Act prohibited underground working in collieries and mines for children under ten and for women; it also provided for the establishment of an inspectorate but, by their own admission, the first mines inspectors did not go into the mines. And in 1844 working hours were limited to enable children to attend school in the mornings or afternoons. The age limit for boys working underground did not change until 1861 when an Act prohibited the employment of boys under twelve (yet employment between the ages of ten and twelve was still permitted on production of a schoolmaster's certificate ascertaining that the boy concerned could read and write.) From 1872 boys under twelve were not permitted to be employed underground (save where the Secretary of State granted an exemption in mines working very thin seams).

The Agricultural Gangs Act of 1867 prohibited the employment of children under eight years of age and the mixing of the sexes in public gangs, but farmers sought to get around the Act by creating private gangs. The Agricultural Children's Act of 1873 prohibited children under eight from being employed in agriculture (with the exception of farmers' own children) and those between the ages of eight and ten were only to be employed if a parent could certify that the child had attended school on 250 occasions in the preceding twelve months (150 times if aged over ten). The Act proved ineffective and was subject to inconsistent interpretation.

In the late 1870s, child street workers in major towns and cities were coming under greater scrutiny. Manchester Corporation approached the Home Secretary about street trading in 1878 and in 1880 the Corporation sought legislation to have child street trading at unsocial hours banned. In 1882 a clause was inserted in Manchester's own Corporation Bill prohibiting children under fourteen years of age from selling on the streets after 9 p.m. in the summer and after 7 .p.m. in winter, unless they had reached a prescribed educational standard. In the following year slightly different clauses were included in the Sheffield and Birmingham Corporation Acts and subsequently in other towns. Bye-laws were passed in Bristol, Liverpool, Newcastle upon Tyne and elsewhere to regulate street trading but they were difficult to enforce and were invalidated in a High Court decision in 1887.

These attempts at regulation were endorsed by the anti-cruelty movement, the first English Society for the Prevention of Cruelty to Children being founded in Liverpool in the 1880s. Based on a model developed in New York, it was followed a year later by a similar society in London. While the principal aim of both societies was to protect children from physical ill-treatment by adults, they also had a concern for child slaves, the street sellers who sold and begged at night. The Prevention of Cruelty to Children Act was passed in 1889 prohibiting boys under fourteen and girls under sixteen from performing or offering goods for sale on the streets between 10 p.m. and 5 a.m. Children under ten were prohibited from undertaking these activities at any time.

By the 1890s child labour was coming under increasingly critical scrutiny. In 1891 Parliament amended the new Factory Act, raising the minimum age of all half-timers from ten to eleven years, contrary to the wishes of the Government. At the same time there was growing international concern over child employment and a congress was held in Berlin. The *Child's Guardian,* the journal of the NSPCC, listed the ages at which children in other European countries were allowed to commence factory work. The minimum age was ten in Britain, and twelve to fourteen in most other nations. Only Italy had a lower minimum age (nine).

The 1886 Shop Hours Regulation Act restricted the hours of work for children and young persons in retail to 74 hours per week, including meal times, but supervising its implementation was problematic. There were still gaps in legislation to protect child workers from exploitation, one sector being the myriad of street activities in which they could work, including running errands, taking messages, domestic work, selling newspapers, various sweated trades such as beadwork, artificial flower making, paper-bag making and boot sewing. The plight of the young people in these activities was highlighted by Mrs Edith Hogg in an article published in 1897. She quoted evidence collected by the Women's Industrial Council from 54 London schools with a total of 26,000 pupils. Of these 729 boys and 523 girls were working for pay; the figure excludes all those who worked at home for parents or other family members without pay. Without exception the rates of pay were low – about ¼p per hour for errand running, delivering newspapers for under 1p an hour. Probably the most exploited were girls who were expected to undertake domestic work for little or no pay. In November 1897 the Women's Industrial Council organised a conference on London home industries, details being passed to the Home Office and the Education Department. Soon afterwards the Education Department's Elementary Schools (Working for Wages) Return revealed that of the working children identified, around a quarter were aged ten or less and approximately 28 per cent of the children worked for more than twenty hours a week. Under pressure from the child protection lobby, the Interdepartmental Committee on the Employment of School Children was established in 1901. While it opposed a ban on child labour it acknowledged the need for further regulation. In 1903 the Employment of Children Act sought to safeguard the health of these children and to prevent employment from interfering with their education. However the Act was vague on some points and over-permissive on others which reduced its value.

The enforcement of the law regulating the employment of children as sweeps, in factories, mines, workshops, in agriculture and other sectors, was non-existent until the establishment of a factory inspectorate in 1833 and a mines inspectorate in 1842, but there were too few of either and, by their own admission, mines inspectors did not actually enter the mines. Moreover other sectors covered by the piecemeal nineteenth century legislation had no means of enforcement. Children lacked the legal status and presence to negotiate their own working conditions; they depended on others to do this for them and, while some trades had children's champions, others did not. Many children continued to work where work was available, on the insistence of their parents, sometimes to the annoyance of trades unions seeking to protect jobs for men.

From the mid-nineteenth century, the hours a child could work were, in principle, restricted to enable him/her to attend school and, toward the end of the nineteenth century, a changing climate of public opinion held that children should be attending school rather than being in waged work. Half-timing was a recurring problem for schools – children's absences being noted in school logbooks. A Gloucestershire school logbook from the 1860s noted that, when a premium for child labour was offered, impoverished parents accepted it and sacrificed the education of their children. An exasperated head teacher noted that formation of character was out of the question 'when children are compelled to go to work at such an early age and where the influences in mills are generally bad.'[8] Children's attendance could be sporadic: 'Half time scholars are still very irregular in their attendance owing to the stoppage of some of the works at the mill.'[9] Factory inspectors sought to enforce existing regulations, a teacher receiving a note from a local mill in 1871 'concerning the Factory Inspector's complaint of insufficiency of time in the afternoon attendance of half time children ... Mr Earnshaw must insist that the afternoon set attend school 2½ hours during the months of Nov, Dec, Jan and Feb and 3 hours in the afternoon of the other months ... This is decidedly an innovation in this district.'[10] But the head teacher had to continue to insist on regulations – in 1874 'During last week many of the half timers were absent from the usual school work. I therefore called the attention of the mill authorities to these irregularities and they intend all absentees make up school time before going to work next week.'[11]

In 1880, the requirement for compulsory attendance at school for all children between the ages of five and ten and, from 1891, the abolition of school fees, resulted in the proportion of children between the ages of five and fourteen in school rising from 24 per cent in 1870 to 70 per cent in 1900. It is clear, however, that there was regular truancy; around a quarter of those who should have been at school in the 1890s were non-attenders. In 1891, three Kent parishes had school enrolments of approximately 77 per cent and, while out of school, all girls worked at home, only half the boys did, the other half worked away from the home, probably on local farms. In rural areas there was still hostility to the requirement for compulsory education. And, in 1911, 39,000 boys were employed in agriculture, still over half the number of 30 years previously.

By the early twentieth century parents and families had less autonomy over children. The Children's Act of 1908 enabled the state, through local officers, to act against child neglect and abuse. All young people up to the age of sixteen were legally classified as children although, by 1910, 80 per cent of working class boys left school promptly when reaching the age of fourteen (or thirteen if they were given exemptions). It was the increase in prosecutions for non-attendance, as much as anything else, which led to 100 per cent primary school attendance in the early twentieth century. Boys aged thirteen, however, continued to be hired as farm servants well into the twentieth century.

None of the Factory, Mines or Workshops Acts addressed the non-paid employment of children in the domestic context. The Education Acts only legislated children out of the paid workplace. It is estimated that, in 1912, between 7 and 10 per cent of children aged over seven were still employed. More effective workshop legislation, the extension of the inspectorate to workshops, as well as the schooling requirement, failed fully to eradicate children's outwork, for children were still set to work after school. A report of 1899 stated that over 200,000 children were employed at home on a part-time basis. Evidence given to the Select Committee on Homework in 1907–8 described child work before and after school in lace finishing in Nottingham, gloving in Somerset, box making, sewing buttons onto cards and other outwork trades in Birmingham. The most difficult conditions to control were where children worked in scattered units in irregular employment. And, during the First World War, children helped out at harvest time in many parts of the country.

A milestone was reached in the 1918 Education Act which prohibited the employment of children during school hours, also restricting the hours a young person could work before and after school, as well as on Sundays. A child's place was finally acknowledged to be at school and in the home.

There is no single reason underlying the diminution of child labour through the nineteenth century. In some sectors, notably cotton and worsted textiles, and coal mining, technology reduced the need for very young children. The greater automation of spinning and weaving and, in mines with wide coal seams where more machinery could be used, tasks previously undertaken by young, low-paid children, were reduced in number. In the mid- to later nineteenth century there was some male opposition to women and children displacing men by undertaking work in mills at lower rates of pay. The introduction of legislation in the nineteenth century prohibiting or controlling the employment of young children in the workplace by no means received unanimous approval, to the great frustration of liberal reformers such as Lord Shaftesbury. Moreover, ideas about childhood gradually changed, working-class incomes rose, child mortality rates fell and families became smaller. By the 1870s some factory inspectors were more vigilant in checking up on school attendance. These factors, together with the means of enforcement of factory legislation becoming more effective, and with a focus on the rights of the child to education, were mutually re-enforcing in regulating child paid employment.

A 1901 Committee on the Employment of School Children specifically addressed the issue of children engaged in street trading, something that had increasingly vexed national and local politicians in the late nineteenth century. It recommended regulation, rather than prohibition, it being suggested that twenty hours of 'light work' each week could be 'beneficial'. But this recommendation was not accepted and, under the Employment of Children Act (1903), child street trading was prohibited. However, it was left to local authorities to regulate the enactment and, without considerable additional resource for the purpose, this was unlikely to happen.

By the time that the Children and Young Persons Act (1933) was passed the minimum school leaving age had been raised to fifteen. The Act specified that no child under twelve years of age was to work – but local authorities could permit younger children to work for their parents or in light agriculture or horticulture; and local authorities could raise the minimum age for child employment in particular occupations. The hours a child was permitted to work were also addressed; no child being permitted to work before 6 a.m. or after 8 p.m. on a school day, or for more than two hours on any school day, or a Sunday. There were other restrictions such as the weight of any load to be moved or lifted. And, street trading was prohibited, which suggests that little had changed since the beginning of the century.

The Employment of Children Act (1973) passed smoothly through Parliament, being approved by the three main political parties. At the time the bill was going through Parliament it was clear that there was variation between local authorities in the permitted age children could begin work. This option was removed, authority being vested, instead, in the Secretary of State. Local authorities were still, however, responsible for monitoring. But implementation of the Act was delayed, perhaps, because

Work in the home; two reasonably well-dressed girls undertaking unpaid work in the home. (Mary Evans Picture Library)

it transpired that around half the number of teenage schoolchildren had some form of regular work and implementation of the Act would require considerable resources. The Act remained on the statute book but was not implemented, consultations with local authorities in 1975 and 1977 leading to the conclusion that the resource implications could not be justified. Further questions were raised in Parliament in 1985 which led to a similar conclusion.

In 1991 an application was made to bring in a bill to amend the 1973 Act, in particular to the definition of the word 'child', it being commented that the then currently enacted laws dated from the 1920s and 1930s. It hardly needed to be pointed out that the world of the late twentieth century was a very different place from earlier in the century and also that new occupations, such as modelling, were 'wide open to abuse.' Meanwhile, Low Pay units in both Scotland and England showed the need for enforcement of the 1973 Act. Research showed that 43 per cent of children aged ten to sixteen had some kind of paid work but 74 per cent worked illegally (either in work prohibited for children, or without the requisite permit.) Children on milk rounds, for example, began work long before the legally permitted 7 a.m.; some children worked in market gardens or garden centres where they lifted loads that were far too heavy for them; others worked in kitchens in the proximity of boiling fat and water, and where there were often slippery floors. It is not surprising that weary children had accidents. Moreover, while earnings averaged £1.80 an hour, around 24 per cent of children earned less than £1 an hour and some as little as 50p. As was pointed out in a 1991 House of Commons speech 'Our children are our stake in the future and it is our duty to protect them from exploitation of all kinds.'

The European Union Directive on the Protection of Young People at Work was passed in 1994. This explicitly refers to the 'vulnerability of children' but it sets objectives rather than specific procedures. Work before 6 a.m. and after 8 p.m. should not be permitted; work should only be light, education being paramount. But, again, implementation was relatively ineffectual, local authorities continuing not to implement existing UK legislation.

Children in Britain and other countries of the Western world continue to work; indeed paid employment is undertaken by a majority of adolescents. While around 10–12 per cent of early teens undertake paid work, this figure rises to around 50 per cent at the age of sixteen and as much as 80 per cent by the time they leave school. Most countries have legislation which controls the minimum age for working while a child is still at school, as well as the kinds of work permissible. In Britain the minimum age for employment is thirteen and no young person below the minimum school leaving age (sixteen) may work during school hours or for more than two hours per day out of school time, no more than one hour of which can be in the morning. And the hours during which a young person may work are limited to between 7 a.m. and 7 p.m. Weekend and school holiday work is also restricted and anyone under sixteen must have a permit for employment. Young people often work in breach of these restrictions; sometimes deliberately, sometimes unknowingly in for example, baby-sitting, newspaper rounds, retail, agriculture and helping in small family businesses. Increasingly, older teenagers also seek organised work experience prior to going to university or undertaking further training on leaving school; while this, on the whole, is viewed positively it, too, has the potential for being exploitative.

FOURTEEN

Children at work in the world in the twentieth and twenty-first centuries

CHILD LABOUR IN THE WORLD in the twentieth and the beginning of the twenty-first centuries presents stark contrasts. In the developed world, from the second half of the twentieth century, children's work was regulated and school attendance had become the norm; children in the West who work, more usually (although not inevitably) do so from choice. In the developing world, on the other hand, many inherited patterns of child labour continue and, within the past twenty years or so, countries – and individuals – in the West have become more aware of this. Particular third-world factories have been headline news when it has become known that they exploit child and female labour to supply Western firms with shoes and clothing for retail sale. The emotive term 'slaves' has been applied to a number of different contemporary situations. International agencies have played a key role in raising consciousness and conscience. But, as this chapter shows, to translate Western legislation to other parts of the world, without acknowledging differences between societies, can be problematic and may not necessarily be viewed in a wholly positive light by those it is intended to protect. There is now a huge gulf between developing countries and the developed in terms of the kinds of work children do and what is viewed as unavoidable, or even acceptable, child labour. It is clear that children in many parts of the world today face adversity through poverty, ill health and violence. Adversity can be described in terms of contexts, situations or events which do not meet the needs of children, which violate their rights and threaten their well-being. But a situation which threatens a child's well-being in one situation may not in another. Context is all-important.

Early twentieth-century South Africa

Through most of the twentieth century, until the dismantling of South African Apartheid began in 1990, white repression of the black South African adult population was passed onto children and in the years of segregation African children were differently viewed from their European counterparts. In Natal most of the domestic servants were African male youths aged between twelve and twenty. There was demand for child workers at Durban docks in the early 1920s, some children as young as twelve running up gangplanks with baskets of coal, the 'grimy imps of the Wharfside'.

In rural areas a rigid labour discipline was imposed by the ruling of the Department of Justice to keep African juveniles in farm labour and The Native Service Contract Act of 1932 legalised the whipping of African boys under the age of eighteen for perceived offences against the repressive Master and Servant laws. Cross-border labour transfers took place, recruiters crossing from Southern Rhodesia (Zimbabwe) to Bechuanaland (Botswana) to 'pick up local youths' to work on Western Transvaal (South Africa) mines and farms. Recruiting agencies often illegally recruited child workers known as 'umfaans', while the Farmers' Labour Agency began to bring in thousands of foreign migrants from North Transvaal – mostly male children known as 'picannins'.

Underage child labour was poorly regulated between the two world wars, even when attempts were made to do so. It continued either because employers regarded it as cheap, or it was the only labour to be found, or because children were thought to do some jobs better. Women and children were capable of hoeing, weeding, herding and leading oxen used in ploughing, or odd jobs around the compound. The employment of children was a characteristic of both slave and non-slave systems on farms in herding, hoeing and weeding, while domestic service was often performed by children under sixteen as part of a contract for the whole family.

In the Second World War there was significant migration to the cities, particularly Durban and, while youth migration was still widespread, a new practice emerged, that of young people working in the sugar fields between the ages of sixteen and twenty, then moving on to work in industries in the towns. But unregulated migrancy, while diminishing in the sugar fields by the 1950s, was alive and well later in other agricultural sectors.

Wherever sugar cane was grown on a large scale there was a high demand for labour, for the cane loses its sucrose content quickly and requires processing as soon as possible after being cut. Sugar planters turned to youths and children, besides adults who had been declared unfit to work in the mines. Whenever attempts were made to regulate labour in the plantations, the planters' opposition won the day. A number of incidents were reported of young boys leaving various sugar estates in such a state of collapse that they died before arriving at their intended destination. When the Native Farm Labour Committee reported in 1940, it recommended what reformers had been advocating for two decades, namely the extension of the 1911 Mines and Works Act to sugar estates and sugar mills.

In the cotton growing area of South Africa there were many stories of white farmers kidnapping young African boys to work on the farms. As a result, it was said that if travellers stopped their cars in remote areas, the herd boys would 'scurry off in terror and hide in the grass.'

During the years of apartheid (1948–94) the situation for labouring children changed relatively little and, since 1994, despite a high proportion of the national budget being spent on education, the fact that so many people are inadequately educated is a large obstacle to economic development.

Boy soldiers and sailors worldwide

Boy soldiers and sailors were recruited at a young age in Western countries in the nineteenth century – Horatio Nelson was in the Navy by the age of twelve, surveying the Arctic by fifteen and a commissioned officer by eighteen. Robert Baden-Powell recruited twelve-year-old boys to deliver messages under fire at the siege of Mafeking in 1900. And the American Civil War has been termed the 'boys' war' since between a tenth and a third of all troops were under age – often incredibly young. John Joseph

Clem, a drummer boy, was all of ten years of age. It came to be realised that war on this scale was no place for a child and perceptions changed. By the First World War recruiters were ordered to keep all under eighteen-year-olds from the front but, somehow, around a quarter of a million under-age volunteers were accepted – a fourteen-year-old died at Gallipoli. Hitler's youth, mostly schoolboys, died in large numbers when sent to defend Berlin towards the end of the Second World War. It came to be recognised that war had become a professional business. Britain is now the only European country to recruit sixteen-year-olds into the regular army.

In the developing world, however, many boys particularly in Africa, were conscripted into national and rebel armies in the 1990s and the early twenty-first century. A ten-year-old soldier in Sudan in the 1990s could sleep with an eye open, throw a grenade, fire an AK47 gun, hack an enemy with a machete. A child soldier from Sierra Leone said that for five years 'my life was characterised by cutting limbs, killing, raping, and drug abuse ... I cannot now trace my relatives ... Even if I find my relatives who will want to take a child like me? My innocence was exploited, my development was violently suppressed ... my parents and anything that gave me a sense of safety was annihilated.'[1] Many boys were conscripted into the Syrian army in the 1980s and 1990s in the war with Eritrea; they had made the transition to manhood in all but years. Some went through the initiation

Boy soldiers in Africa.

ceremony emphasising their manhood but, after the war, they experienced greater difficulty in integrating back into civilian life than those who had not been initiated, who still thought of themselves as children.

Amnesty International claimed, in 1999, that at least 300,000 children under the age of eighteen were involved in armed conflict in Sierra Leone, Liberia, Congo, Sudan, Uganda, Sri Lanka and Myanmar, and the use of smaller and lighter weapons meant that they could fight alongside adults. Those not actually fighting were used in reconnaissance, or to plant or clear mines, a highly dangerous task. Pictures of child soldiers in Sierra Leone in the 1990s appeared in papers worldwide, the story usually suggesting that they had been taken from settlements against their will and intimidated and indoctrinated, possibly with doses of alcohol and drugs. Child soldiers were often brutalised, having seen family members killed, and there seems to be little doubt that they could be extremely cruel; young boys committing rape, torture and amputation. Both boys and girls were abducted in Uganda, a sixteen-year-old girl, who had been abducted, told of how a boy tried to escape from the rebels but was caught and his hands tied before the other child captives were made to kill him with sticks. He was known to the girl in question – they were from the same village – she still dreams about him asking her why she did it. Congo still has the highest number of child soldiers, a warlord being committed to fourteen years in prison for recruiting children between 2002 and 2003. It has been estimated that 200,000 children were recruited against their will in Somalia between 1991 and 2004.

In Cambodia, under the Khmer Rouge regime (1975–79), children were indoctrinated and forced to denounce and kill suspect adults. 'Comrade Child' was lauded as being unpolluted by the corrupt past. Even a twelve-year-old could be in charge of a work camp; children became notorious for the cruelty they inflicted and, even today, there is a certain anxiety about children on the part of some adults whose memories of committed atrocities linger.

Palestinian children have been brought up surrounded by evidence of the conflict with Israel. Rioting and stone throwing have become a military art, graded according to age. In the violence of the 1990s the older children orchestrated proceedings: the seven- to ten-year-olds were tyre rollers – the tyres being set alight in the middle of the road – the eleven- to fourteen-year-olds attacked passing cars with slings and the 'veteran stone throwers'[2] used rocks to attack specific vehicles. Were these young people acting as much as anything out of boredom, or were they seeking to attract notice, or had they become sufficiently politicised to know exactly why they were doing this?

Estimates of the number of children currently fighting worldwide suggest a total figure of around 300,000 in Central Africa, Afghanistan, India, Sri Lanka, The Philippines and Myanmar. And the rehabilitation of child soldiers causes concern. Should they bear responsibility for their past actions? They are, after all, children. This begs the question of when a young person can be deemed to be responsible for his/her actions. Some of those who suffered at their hands believe they should be punished. There have been rehabilitation programmes in both Uganda and Sierra Leone, but the number of children who have been through them is still small, compared with the total number of former soldier children. And what are the most effective programmes? Some have argued that therapy and counselling are the most appropriate; others have questioned this, putting forward models of healing and forgiveness. Amnesty International has played a significant role both in drawing attention to the scale of the problem and in seeking solutions.

The United Nations Convention on the Rights of the Child was agreed in 1989, coming into force in 1990. Article 38 states that no child under fifteen should take a direct part in hostilities or be recruited to a country's armed forces. In 1998 the International Criminal Court ruled that enlisting children under the age of fifteen was a war crime. Later international treaties state that children under eighteen should not be involved as combatants in armed conflict. Such regulation can only be effective where governments recognise the rights of the child and have the means of enforcing them.

The developing world in the twenty-first century

Children's work in rural areas of developing countries generally begins with child care and some household work such as floor sweeping from the age of four or five, progressing to clothes washing, cooking and feeding animals at the age of six, to work outside the homestead such as caring for animals in the fields, ploughing and harvesting by the age of eleven and, by the age of thirteen, perhaps, working for a wage. The urban child might begin with domestic chores in the home at the age of five or six, undertaking a simple home-based piecework task by the age of seven or eight, moving to more complicated work by the age of eight or nine. By their early teens the young person would very probably be employed in a workshop or small factory.

Street children in African and South and Central American states do not generally choose to be there; they become street children through force of circumstances. Governments at local and national levels often regard street children as a degrading nuisance who might deter foreign tourists. And different governments deal with the problem in different ways, most of which involve elimination from view, including murder by vigilante squads. While some children may go to the streets in search of excitement, the majority see there to be no other option; abuse at home and hunger drive many there. But street living is frequently violent and abusive; finding somewhere to sleep, clothes to wear, somewhere to wash, and sufficient food, besides warmth in winter, all contribute to making street living a daily problem for millions of young people in the developing world.

Shack/shanty towns in different parts of the world share many common characteristics. They are defined by grinding poverty. A fourteen-year-old Angolan girl fled from the fighting taking place between the government and rebels to a shack in the port of Lobito. When interviewed in 2001 she was wearing filthy rags for clothes, drinking polluted water, 'we have to lay out pieces of paper on the ground and lie on them' and most of her time was spent cooking, cleaning the shack and caring for her six siblings. With no opportunities for study or for reasonably well-paid work 'you can't afford clothes or shoes because they cost too much.'[3] A thirteen-year-old Thai girl lived with her mother and siblings in a squatter settlement near a tourist resort. They scavenged for scrap metal on a local rubbish tip, working among filth, rats and the ever-present threat of infection. When children are not scavenging, they beg from tourists, an activity that runs the risk of being caught and fined by the police. Rubbish tip scavenging is also prevalent in South America.

In a society characterised by sharp social contrasts, such as Brazil, childhood is something experienced by the rich and virtually non-existent for the poor. In the towns, middle and upper class families employ domestic help from lower-class neighbourhoods. In the latter, children are

Cambodian child scavenging on a waste tip.

expected to contribute to the family from as young an age as five or six in cleaning, washing clothes and dishes, and taking care of younger siblings. The mother from a poor district knows that, to survive, her children must be tough, obedient, subservient and street-wise.

Child labour, much of it unpaid, is a characteristic of Third World countries. In El Salvador, a nine-year-old girl lived in dire poverty with her family; she ran the house as both parents worked and she looked after her younger brother. When there was not enough food in the house she and her little sister didn't eat, although her young brother did. Girls who work at home begin work at a younger age than their brothers and work between four and sixteen hours a day. Age and gender affect a child's experience of poverty in Nepal; while older children may be sent away to work in carpet factories, their younger siblings remain at home working in agriculture and girls take on a large share of the domestic duties. While Pakistan law forbids a child of under the age of fourteen to work, many parents who live in poverty illegally place their children in sweatshops or carpet factories, where working conditions are often worse than in recognised legal places of work. In Rwanda, after the genocide when so many adults were killed, children created households together, the burden of responsibility particularly falling on the oldest girl.

Children work full-time for pay in factories, mines, brickyards or other

Older girl scavenging.

Child carrying building stones
on a still-soft scalp.

Children making bricks.

sources of work and this is generally thought of as 'child labour'. The reasons children work vary between societies, cultures, specific situations, families and individuals yet, all too frequently, children's work is stereotyped by a set of assumptions which may only apply to some situations. This can lead to well-intentioned judgements, laws and policies that result in interventions which can be insensitive – and may be disastrous. The child worker exploited in an Indian silk mill; the African girl married off and expected to assist in a family business at the age of fourteen when she wished to continue schooling; the Scottish girl, also aged fourteen, who hadn't attended full-time school for three years on account of caring for her chronically ill father and her epileptic mother, have little in common except their age and the fact that they work. A study of working children aged between five and fourteen in 36 developing countries, undertaken in 2000, suggested that 68 per cent undertook some kind of work, the vast majority being in unpaid domestic work, mainly part-time. And, while some of the work may have an element of play, at least to begin with, leading and herding cattle, or street trading, for example, it soon becomes exploitative.

Just as children's work in the mid- to later nineteenth century was sometimes viewed as competing with that of adults so, in the twentieth and twenty-first centuries, children's main advantage is their competitiveness – the low price of their labour, added to which they are more exploitable. A child may assist an adult on piecework rates, being subcontracted at a lower rate despite, perhaps, being equally productive. Some employers deliberately seek out part-time child workers in order to cut costs.

Young children in Indonesia are known to have been working from the age of five or six in agricultural and household work. The Indonesian equivalent of half-timing has been in existence for over a century and now, their Government having ratified the UN Convention on the Rights of the Child and being one of the first four countries to join the ILO's Programme for the Elimination of Child Labour, a schedule has been set for the elimination of the most exploitative forms of child labour.

There is still a long way to go in regulation, inspection and monitoring against standards in the developing world in the twenty first century. Ravi was sold by his parents to work in an Indian carpet factory. He received no pay, worked for twelve to fifteen hours a day, seven days a week, beaten, tortured, half-clad and inadequately fed. He, amongst others, was fortunate in being liberated in 2004/5. He had considered trying to run away but recognised that, if caught, he would have been beaten mercilessly. In Bangladesh there have been a series of clothing factory collapses and fires; girls of thirteen years and upwards being forced to work for eleven hours

Children clearing the street in India.

a day in appalling conditions in some locations, while making clothing for well-known high street stores. Workers were said to be verbally and physically abused, male managers targeting younger females who, they allege, are not working sufficiently fast. One fourteen-year-old girl acknowledged that they had to work in order to eat. In 2015 up to 1.7 million children of five years and upwards worked in illegal brick factories in Pakistan. In one newspaper report a seven-year-old worked six days per week from first light until midnight. Nike became the focus of accusations of subcontracted child labour in Pakistan and Cambodia in a magazine article published in 1996. Half of the world's soccer balls are made in Pakistan, a country which has laws against child labour and slavery, but which takes little action to combat the widespread practice. In 1997 Nike asked a diplomat to examine its subcontracting practice abroad, but the resulting report (inevitably used by the company to suggest that things were not so bad as previously thought) was widely criticised for being too favourable. The good name of the company was severely at risk and in 1998 the CEO acknowledged that 'The Nike product has become synonymous with slave wages, forced overtime, and arbitrary abuse.'[4] The following year the company, in partnership with other concerned companies, created the Fair Labor Organisation, a non-profit monitoring body. While Nike admitted that it 'blew it' in respect of child labour, the Chairman recognised that 'of all the issues facing Nike in workplace standards child labor is the most vexing.'[5]

USA child migrant workers

Some three to five million migrant and seasonal farmhands were working in the USA in the late 1990s, of which 250,000 were children travelling with their families, three quarters of whom (187,500) were estimated to be below the age of fourteen and living in poverty. In addition many under the age of eighteen travelled alone. In total, estimates of child migrant workers in the late 1990s varied from 300,000 to 800,000. Most young farmworkers were Mexican, others arriving from Guatemala, El Salvador and Haiti. Migrant families did not travel merely to one location during the year but, often, to two or more and in different states. By the age of twelve, a migrant child might be working between sixteen and eighteen hours per week, a Guatemalan youth saying that this was essential in order to eat.

Prior to 1966 no USA federal child labour laws covered agriculture. Children under sixteen were not permitted to work during school hours, but before and after school and during school holidays, they performed and continue to perform a wide range of tasks on the farm. Children over fourteen may undertake most agricultural tasks and those under twelve can work under certain conditions with parental permission or work alongside their parents as many migrant children do. Schooling was – and is – a problem both for the migrant students and the schools; there are language problems, besides different curricula, textbooks, standards and policies, let alone cultural issues, each time the family moves. School enrolment for migrant children is lower than of any other population group in the USA and the high school drop-out rate is twice the national average. In 1966 The Migrant Education Program (MEP) was enacted by Congress, becoming law in that year. This required all states receiving funds to coordinate with other states in educating migrant children and, since then, the school participation rate for migrant children has greatly increased. Michigan, in the north, and California in the west receive large numbers of migrant children. Living accommodation might be a shared apartment or trailer in which children have no space for study – and sometimes little parental support to do so, the mother calling for help in heating the tortillas, clearing the table or doing the dishes. Not surprisingly students who worked more than twenty hours a week were less likely to do homework or earn high marks. The poverty of so many migrant families could mean that many had too little to eat: even when farmworker children attended school, they were often tired, irritable, or unable to concentrate due to hunger, illness or fatigue.

The domestic life of a migrant child revolves around a more or less permanent home and one or more migrant camps. Migrant families who follow the harvest might journey through the Carolinas to Virginia and Maryland and thence to Pennsylvania and New York, then on to Michigan, Ohio, Illinois and Indiana. And they also move within states to different farms. Some families move around for different crops within a relatively small area, while others travel in a northward progression as crops ripen, before returning to Texas, Florida or Mexico. Then they have to find whatever work they can before beginning the northward migration in the following year. Migrant families in the US are perceived and view themselves as strangers wherever they are. Texas and Florida are net exporters of human labour, approximately 40,000 students from Texas schools leaving with their families for agricultural work further north; around half that number leaving Florida schools for agricultural work on the eastern seaboard and the Midwest.

Not surprisingly migrant children find socialisation in schools harder; they may have language difficulties, they will not know fellow classmates' names, will not understand playground culture and, moreover, may look and dress sufficiently differently to cause a degree of alienation. However, great strides have been made in migrant education through cultural sensitivity in the classroom, activities that can be engaged in for a range of classroom subjects, such as using art for story-telling. New programmes have been introduced to provide a bridge between school and college, with additional help in coaching and counselling. The results have been highly encouraging. Nevertheless, in 2000, Human Rights Watch published 'Fingers to the Bone' highlighting the USA failure to protect child farmworkers. If accompanied by a parent, a child can still begin work at the age of twelve (the minimum age for non-agricultural workers being fourteen) and they can work for unlimited hours before and after school. Approximately 50 per cent of migrant children do not finish high school, many averaging 30 hours of labour a week. The term 'guest workers' for migrant labour is an interesting euphemism in the circumstances; on the one hand immigrant labour is required; on the other there is national concern at high rates of illegal immigration. This is a circle that will be hard to square.

Work and school in the late twentieth/twenty-first centuries

In 1995 a British TV company investigated a clothing factory in Morocco and found girls aged between twelve and fifteen working there. The film director's assumption was that factory work was bad for these girls who should have been at home or in school. As a consequence of this, Marks & Spencer, which retailed the clothes in the UK, sent some staff to investigate.

They visited the factory and found no young people employed there. What had happened was that the younger children were asked to hide, some subsequently being required to sign resignation papers. On the face of it the outcome seemed right. But when young girls working in the factory were asked for their views, the issue became more complex. They worked from 7.30 a.m., often until 8 p.m., with no overtime pay and an hour for lunch; and their supervisors used to insult them. Girls explained why the work was important to them; it enabled them to buy school supplies, including books. Until the 1990s, Moroccan girls had only worked in the home and for no pay, being expected to take on household tasks from around five years old. Paid work outside the home gave them some degree of freedom and boosted their self-esteem, improving their status within the family, besides offering the hope of education and entry to the labour market, as well as delaying marriage. The Moroccan government had passed laws which allowed young people aged between twelve and eighteen to take two-year apprenticeships; the employer being required to offer training and the apprentices being allowed to attend professional classes. While the clothing factory investigated by the TV company and M&S had abused the law, the girls had all reached the minimum age for apprenticeship in Morocco and the age for employment in light work permitted by the International Labour Office (ILO). Moreover they believed that they had been given opportunities that would otherwise have been denied them. On subsequently being denied work in the clothing factory, they could not go to school if they had not previously attended and, for those who had, it was difficult to re-enter. In Zimbabwe, on the other hand, children at 'earn and learn' schools in the early twenty-first century were paid at the same rate as adults, receiving, in addition, their schooling.

In multi-cultural contemporary Britain children and young people continue to be employed part-time in a range of family businesses. Chinese take-aways, for example, are small-scale but intensive family businesses with a need for a minimum of two people on duty at any one time – one person at the counter and another in the kitchen, over long and unsocial hours. Children and young people in the family are expected to take their turns. Many young people, while recognising that the family well-being depends on the relative success of the business, see a conflict with their desire for higher education and feel the need to break away. This, while not necessarily engendering a sense of guilt, is an acknowledgment of the needs of the young person in question. Allied to this is the parents' sense of their child becoming more 'English' and less an integrated member of the Chinese community.

Besides paid employment, some 50,000 children, mainly girls, undertake significant day-to-day caring responsibilities for others; for parents, siblings, grandparents. A sixteen-year-old who gave significant amounts of time in caring for a disabled brother said 'some people do the things they want because they choose to. Young carers don't always get the choice but what we want is not sympathy ... but recognition and encouragement for what we do.'[6] Children in contemporary Britain work in retail, small businesses, cafés and restaurants, as well as on the land, and this has been regarded as acceptable in not undermining the concept of childhood. Under appropriate conditions it is regarded as beneficial. Not only do many children and young people wish to earn additional 'pocket money' but work experience enhances their abilities to gain employment upon leaving school, or gaining a place at college or university. Probably a majority of young undergraduates in North America have part-time work to assist with college fees and living costs and this is, increasingly becoming a pattern in Britain too. While many undergraduates work in bars and retail, purely in order to raise funds, unpaid 'work experience' is increasingly important. In this, the young person seeks a placement for a relatively short period of time in a specific business or sector with the intention of enhancing professional career opportunities – the would-be doctor is more likely to be accepted in medical school if he/she has had direct experience of working in a hospital, for example.

There has been a growth in the number of young people engaging in start-up businesses while still at school. Invention by children, leading to a business, is often the result of a perceived need not recognised by adults. In the USA, Connor's Kits for Kids – experiment kits – were invented by a junior school lad who felt frustrated at not always getting answers to his many science-based questions. He began his business in 2004 with the intention of showing that science is fun. Nine-year-old Chris Haas invented a basketball that teaches players where to place their hands when shooting and it has sold around the world. Thirteen-year-old Shubham Banerjee, having played with Lego since the age of two, designed a low-cost braille printer at the family kitchen table in Santa Clara, California. It all began when he asked his parents how blind people could read; they replied, 'Google it'. His idea, devised as a school science fair project, is to be able to print braille reading materials from a personal computer or electronic device on paper, using raised dots instead of ink. He has a start-up company which has already received investment from backers. Google Sciences Fair is a competition to find the best research and/or invention by a young person aged between thirteen and eighteen years of age. 'All that is needed to win is curiosity, interest, patience and hard work, and never (to)be afraid of failing.'[7]

Invention by young people in the UK is encouraged by various sponsors, with awards and encouragement to develop. In 2011, eight-year-old Kylie had a sore throat. Within three years she had been diagnosed with cancer, undergone chemotherapy, survived and invented a backpack for young people similarly afflicted. Patented in 2014, it has internal rods, a pump, a controller and coil to hold the medicine bag. Kylie won the UCONN Invention Convention Patent award. Twin girls Ameeta and Aneeta Kumar, Young Scientists of the year in 2014, designed a project to develop an early diagnostic tool for cancer; while Fred Turner, Young Engineer of the year in 2014, built a PCR machine (a DNA amplifier) in his basement to test why his brother was red-headed and he wasn't. The worlds of IT and virtual reality know no age limits, some able inventors being just into their teens. BrainBox Range organises a Young Games Inventor, the 2016 winner of which, Sebastien Fleming-Smith, created a memory-based game called Shaperise. Every year there is a Big Bang UK Young Scientists and Engineers Fair to select the UK Young Scientist and UK Young Engineer of the Year. There is a large number of entrants and, amongst the over 200 finalists for 2017 were inventors of a robotic car, a portable wind power generator, a litter picking robot, tectonic tiles, and banking for microbusinesses.

The James Dyson Foundation encourages young inventors to develop engineering products. Dan Watson invented the SafetyNet to allow fish which are too small to sell to escape and won a Dyson Award. And the youngest person in the UK to be awarded a patent was five-year-old Sam Houghton who, inspired by Wallace and Gromit, invented a double-headed broom to help his father to sweep up leaves in the garden.

Malala Yousafzai is an international role model for the rights of girls to education. In October 2012, at the age of fifteen, she was called for by name on a school bus in Pakistan and shot three times by a member of the Taliban because she had fearlessly spoken-out promoting education for girls. She was flown, in a critical condition, to Birmingham and, over time, has made a courageous and amazing recovery. She could not speak at first and, after coming out of a coma, communicated with doctors by writing in a notebook. She now lives in Birmingham with her parents and two younger brothers and has travelled the world campaigning for universal education, while studying for her GCSEs. On her 16th birthday she made a speech to the United Nations, urging world leaders to campaign against terrorism, illiteracy and poverty: 'They thought that the bullet would silence us. But they failed ... weakness, fear and hopelessness died. Strength, power and courage was born.'[8] Malala's ambition is to become prime minister of Pakistan – her hero is Benazir Bhutto, twice prime minister of Pakistan, assassinated in December 2007. Bhutto's children visited Malala in hospital and gave her two of their mother's shawls, one of which Malala wore when addressing the United Nations. In 2014 she was awarded the Nobel Prize for Peace, the youngest-ever recipient.

Malala was interviewed for The Guardian by a young London political activist, Inez Sardee-Adoo, since at University, with a clutch of internships behind her. Inez was deeply shocked when the street riots in Tottenham occurred only yards away from her family-run restaurant. Her leadership potential was spotted at the age of sixteen by a teacher who suggested she went on a leadership course run by the University of the First Age (UFA). She came to prominence in the lead-up to the London Olympics when she addressed over 1000 young East Londoners to ask Lord Coe that the Olympics be a London Living Wage Olympics. One month later the Olympic bosses agreed to support the demand and, for this, Inez was named Community Leader of the Month.

Education in Japan has a different slant – namely long hours of study, learning by repetition, while not protected by labour laws, such that children in some schools have been described as labourers. Adversity in this case is not due to poverty but the social pressure exerted by relatively affluent parents who decide what is 'best' for their children. Japanese media highlighted the growing incidence of 'adult' health issues such as high cholesterol, high blood pressure, ulcers, diabetes and stress-related baldness, attributable to attendance at cramming schools, in addition to regular school, long hours of study and high parental expectations. Musical and sporting prodigies may experience unremitting study and practice and no labour laws protect them. While Article 28 of the United Nations Convention on the Rights of the Child state that education should be compulsory, some children may experience this differently; less as a right, more a burden.

Sometimes rights can seem to be mutually exclusive; the right to protection may be contrary to the freedom to participate; in developed countries a child's right to education does not conflict with the right to have a childhood; whereas in developing countries the right to education may conflict with the right to be adequately fed and clothed, and yet one is likely to be dependent on the other.

'Appropriate' action

The International Labour Organisation (ILO) was established in 1919, being commissioned to work towards the abolition of child labour, limits being placed on young people's work to enable them to continue their education. A series of minimum age conventions on working children were created between 1919 and 1931, first on industrial employment, then employment at sea, large-scale agricultural work, and different kinds of non-industrial work. But the employment of children in and by their own families was exempt. In 1973 a general Minimum Age Convention was established aiming to eradicate child labour below fifteen years of age. From 1998 onwards it has become one of the ILO's 'core conventions' and all member states are required to respect, promote and achieve it, whether they have ratified it or not. In the widespread consultation leading up to this there was a remarkable absence of children's voices or adults speaking on their behalf, the United Nations International Children's Emergency Fund – UNICEF – and United Nations Educational Scientific and Cultural Organisation – UNESCO – sent one representative each. Subsequent evidence showed that about one third of children in developing countries, especially those aged between eleven and fourteen, those in rural areas, and girls, did not attend school on a regular basis; it was pointed out that enforcement would be well-nigh impossible and that, without work, there might well be no school opportunities. In 1999 the ILO's 'Worst Forms' Convention and the subsequent United Nations Millennium Development

Goals, followed by the United Nations International Children's Emergency Fund (UNICEF), the World Bank and a number of international non-governmental organisations' (NGOs) pronouncements on the struggle against child labour, led to a shift from objecting to all child labour, to a consideration of the effect of particular activities on the life of children. Factory and sweat-shop work, in particular, is regarded as physically, socially and psychologically harmful.

The United Nations Convention on the Rights of the Child (UNCRC), of 1989, laid down the right of the child to be protected from exploitation and harmful work activity. In 2001 the UN called for a study to be undertaken of Children and Violence. Each of these initiatives, undertaken in the interests of children, was founded on assumptions which have been challenged, not least by children themselves. For example, a group representing working children in India, in its submission to the UN, reported that the government in seeking to eradicate child labour, undertook raids on workplaces and rounded up the children like stray dogs. They complained that they were not consulted; no one asked before the raids if they needed to be rescued. In 2004 the ILO produced the figure of 218 million children being engaged in labour of one form or another, of which 126 million were doing work described as dangerous. The European Union unequivocally supports the abolition of all forms of child labour, a stance echoed by many non-European governments.

Working allows children to resist with dignity the economic, political and suppressing model that criminalises and excludes them. The alternative to work was not necessarily the education espoused by governments, but grinding poverty in villages. 'Working may help build children's sense of efficacy – an extremely important developmental factor reflecting the combination of self-esteem and competence.'[9] The voices of working children are increasingly being heard in international debates and what they make clear is that they do not feel consulted or listened-to by the very agencies seeking to support them.

A world child labour map published, in 2014,[10] classified countries according to levels of risk from extreme, to high, medium and low. Much of central Africa, besides Mexico, India, Pakistan, Cambodia and China were classified as extreme risk, Russia as high, some parts of Europe as medium, Britain and North America as low risk. The purpose was to show businesses where 'they might be hurting themselves' by using child labour in terms of reputational damage, consumer boycott, investor alienation. A senior human rights analyst pointed out that child labour was not a problem unique to developing countries, for example children work on small farms in the USA. And, while there has been some decrease in the amount of child labour worldwide, in its worse forms such as sexual trafficking, forced military participation and dangerous mine work, little progress has been made. There is clearly much still to be done and the answers are not necessarily straightforward.

To be effective, policy worldwide will need be built on a set of clearly articulated principles which acknowledge children's human rights as expounded in the UN Convention on the Rights of the Child; but that children's well-being and development should be evaluated in context. What is appropriate in one situation may well be inappropriate in another. Children worldwide have the right to education and to be protected from exploitation or abuse in work and from work that is dangerous. What is also abundantly clear is that children have the right to be heard and that their best interests in context should be paramount.

Appendix One

Factory and other legislation directly affecting working children in Britain

1802: The Health and Morals of Apprentices Act: Applied to orphan apprentices in textile industry. No child under nine to be apprenticed; working day limited to twelve hours; no night work. No means of enforcement.

1819: The Cotton Mills and Factories Act: No child under nine to be apprenticed. Working week for those aged nine to sixteen limited to 72 hours. No means of enforcement.

1825: Cotton Mills Regulation Act: Addressed evasion of 1819 Act by mill owners; magistrates allowed to act. Permission for water powered mill owners to make up for time lost between 11 a.m. and 3 p.m. No means of enforcement.

1829: Act to Amend the Laws Relative to the employment of children in Cotton Mills & Manufactories: Relaxed formal requirements re specifying all partners in a mill.

1831: Labour in Cotton Mills Act (Hobhouse's Act): Working hours of under eighteen-year-olds restricted to twelve. Night work forbidden for those aged under 21. No means of enforcement.

1833: Factory Act: No children under nine to be employed; silk mills excepted. Those aged nine to thirteen restricted to nine hours a day, 48 hours a week; with two hours of school a day. Children and young persons not to work before 5.30 a.m. and after 8.30 p.m. Factory inspectors appointed.

1842 Mines Act: Children under nine and women prohibited from working underground.

1844: Factories Act (Graham's Factory Act): Applied only to textile industry, limiting work of children aged eight to nine years to 6.5 hours a day, thus instituting half-timing. Maximum hours for nine- to thirteen-year-olds, nine hours. Women and children not to clean machinery while it was moving. Dangerous machinery to be fenced.

1845: Calico Print Works Act: Limited to factories printing design onto cotton fabrics. No children under eight to be employed. Eight- to thirteen-year-olds and women not to work before 6 a.m. or after 10 p.m. Children under thirteen should attend school for 30 days per six months.

1847: Factory Act ('Ten Hours Act'): Women and young persons limited to ten hours a day or ten and a half if Saturday a half-day.

1850: Factory Act: (Acts of 1845 and 1847 had reduced hours per day in which women and children could work, but not the hours of the day in which they could do this.) Work times limited to between 6 a.m. and 6 p.m. in summer and 7 a.m. and 7 p.m. in winter. Children eight to thirteen not covered by the Act.

1853: Factory Act: Children aged between nine and thirteen working in mills not permitted to work before 6 a.m. or after 6 p.m. in summer, and in winter before 7 a.m. and after 7 p.m.

1860: Bleach and Dye Works Act: Bleach and dye works brought within same legislation as textile mills. Not applied to open air bleach fields but 1862 Act prevented night work at these.

1861 Lace Work Act: Lace making brought under textile mill legislation.

1863: Calendering Act: Calender works brought under textile mill legislation

1864: Textile Finishing Act: Finishing works brought under textile mill legislation.

1864 Factory Act: Pottery, match making, paper manufacture, fustian cutting brought within existing factory legislation.

1867: Factories Act Extension Act: Any workplace employing more than 50 persons in manufacturing industry brought within the Factory Acts; specifically potteries, lucifer match making, percussion cap and cartridge making, paper staining and fustian cutting.

1867: Workshops' Regulations Act: Workplaces employing under 50 persons prevented from employing children under eight years old. Children eight to thirteen restricted to half-time work. Young persons and women restricted to twelve hours (incl 1.5 hrs meal breaks). None of aforementioned to work after 2 p.m. on Saturdays in workshops with more than five employees. Children to attend ten hours of school a week.

1870 Education Act: Legislated for school attendance but neither compulsory nor free.

1871 Amending Factory Act: Supervision of workshops given to Factory Inspectorate.

1871 Factory Acts (Brick and Tile-Yards) Extension: No female, or any child under ten to be employed at a brick or tile works.

1874 Factory Act: No children under nine to be employed in textile mills. In 1875 this raised to age ten. Children aged eight could still be employed in non-textile factories and workshops.

1876 Education Act: School attendance compulsory for under ten-year-olds. Those over ten could leave, having attained the school leaving certificate.

1878 Factory and Workshop Act: Covered all mechanically powered textile and non-textile mills. Workshops treated as non-textile works. In relation to the employment of women and children, domestic workshops treated as the equivalent of non-textile factories. No child under ten to be employed. Those aged ten to fourteen half days maximum working permitted.

1891: Education Act: Age limit for half-timing raised to eleven (half-timing continued to be legal until 1918). Elementary education free.

1891: Factory Act: Minimum age for half-timers raised to eleven.

1893: Half Time Act: A child was permitted to spend half the week in school and half at work.

1901: Factory and Workshop Act: Minimum age for working raised to twelve. Also clauses re. education, meal times.

1908: Children and Young Persons Act ('Children's Charter'): Severe punishment for cruel or neglectful treatment of children; child employment in dangerous trades prohibited.

1909: Trade Boards Act: Introduced minimum wage legislation to cover men's tailoring, cardboard-box manufacture, lace finishing, chain making, under pressure from the Anti-Sweating League.

1918 Education Act: School leaving age raised to fourteen; half timing abolished.

1933: Children and Young Persons Act: Minimum age at which a child could work raised to twelve; no more than two hours on any school day. School leaving age fifteen.

1973: Children Act: Authority for permissible age to work vested in Secretary of State, not local government.

Appendix Two

Main requirements of the 1802 Health and Morals of Apprentices Act

Work Environment: Mill/factory internal walls and ceilings to be washed with quicklime twice a year. Windows and openings to provide ventilation.

Hours of work: No more than twelve hours (excluding meals) between 6 a.m. and 9 p.m. from 1 June 1803. Exceptions granted for mills with between 1,000–1,500 spindles – clause to come into force on 25 December 1803 and mills of more than 1500 spindles by 25th June 1804.

Apprentices' clothing: two complete suits of clothing to be constantly available, plus stockings, shoes, hats. At least one new suit a year.

Education: Some instruction in reading, writing, arithmetic each day for at least first four years of apprenticeship; to be undertaken in a dedicated room.

Religious instruction: For at least one hour on Sundays. Church of England apprentices to be examined once a year by a clergyman. Between the ages of fourteen and eighteen apprentices to be prepared for confirmation. All apprentices to attend church at least once a month or, if the mill is too remote, a service to be held near the mill.

Sleeping: Separate accommodation for male and female apprentices; no more than two to a bed.

Visitors: JPs, at Midsummer sessions following passing of the Act and annually thereafter, to appoint two persons 'not interested in ... or connected with' the mills/factories as Visitors. One to be a JP, the other a clergyman. They had full authority to inspect at any time of the day or during hours of work and to present a written report to the Quarter Sessions. If there were more than six mills/factories in the area, JPs to divide it up into districts.

Opposition to visits: If any Visitor opposed or molested, a fine of £5–£10 be to be levied.

Infections: Upon any evidence of an infection being found, the master/mistress to call a physician.

Penalties: A fine of £2–£6 for any wilful contravention of the Act. Half to be paid to the informer, the other half to the Overseers of the Poor.

Mills to be entered annually: At every Epiphany Quarter Sessions the master/mistress shall cause an entry to be made for such mills occupied by three or more apprentices or twenty others. 2*s.* to be paid for each entry.

Offences: All offences to be heard before two or more JPs. If fines not paid, power to commit offenders to gaol. No factory inspectors and no means of enforcement

Notes

Notes on chapter 1: Agriculture

1 J. Humphries, *Childhood and Child Labour in the British Industrial Revolution* (Cambridge: Cambridge University Press, 2010), p. 219.
2 *The Reports of The Society for Bettering the Condition and Increasing the Comforts of the Poor*, vol. 1, 3rd edn (London: pr. W. Bulmer, 1802), p. 28.
3 *Ibid.* p. 25.
4 W. Howitt, *Rural Life in England*, 1 (London: Longman, Orme, Brown, Green & Longmans, 1838), p. 157.
5 P. Horn, *The Victorian Country Child* (Stroud: Alan Sutton publishing, repr. 1985), p. 85.
6 E. Wallace, *Children of the Labouring Poor; The Working Lives of Children in nineteenth-century Hertfordshire* (Hatfield: Hertfordshire Publications, 1988), p. 34.
7 P. Horn, *Labouring Life in the Victorian Countryside* (Stroud: Alan Sutton publishing, repr. 1987), p. 62.
8 Humphries, *Childhood and Child Labour*, p. 248.
9 *Ibid.*, p. 29 quoting Arch, 1898.
10 Horn, *Labouring life*, p. 67.
11 *Ibid.*
12 Howitt, *Rural Life in England*, p. 157.
13 Humphries, *Childhood and Child Labour*, p. 240.
14 *Ibid.*, p. 240.
15 Horn, *Labouring life*, p. 81.
16 *Ibid.*, p. 81.
17 *Ibid.*, p. 84.
18 Horn, *The Victorian Country Child*, p. 90.

Notes on chapter 2: Climbing boys

1 Quoted in K. H. Strange, *The Climbing Boys, A Study of Sweeps' Apprentices 1773–1875* (London: Allison and Busby, 1982), p. 14.
2 *Ibid.*, p. 29.
3 *Ibid.* p. 19.
4 H. Mayhew, *London Labour and the London Poor,* vol. 2 (1861–2, repr. New York: Dover Publications, 1968), p. 348.
5 Elizabeth Turner, *The Daisy,* 1806, quoted in Strange, *The Climbing Boys,* p. 101.
6 Mayhew, *London Labour,* p. 368.
7 Strange, *The Climbing Boys,* p. 14.
8 *Ibid.*, p. 42.
9 *Ibid.*, p. 16.
10 William Blake, *Songs of Innocence* (London: William Blake, 1789).
11 Mayhew, *London Labour,* p. 355.
12 Benita Cullingford, *British Chimney Sweeps: Five Centuries of Chimney Sweeping* (Chicago: New Amsterdam, 2000), p. 120.
13 Strange, *The Climbing Boys,* p. 83.

Notes on chapter 3: Cotton

1 R. S. Fitton, *The Arkwrights, Spinners of Fortune* (Manchester: Manchester University Press, 1989), p. 152.
2 Jennifer Tann, *Children at Work* (London: Batsford, 1981), p. 31.
3 *Ibid.*, p. 31.
4 *The Reports of The Society for Bettering the Condition and Increasing the Comforts of the Poor,* vol. 2, 3rd edn (London: W. Bulmer and Co., 1800), p. 251.
5 *The Reports of the Society for Bettering the Condition and Increasing the Comforts of the Poor,* vol. 4 (London: W. Bulmer and Co., 1801), Appendix 1, p. 3
6 *Ibid.*, p. 2.
7 *Ibid.*, p. 3.
8 Quoted in Jennifer Tann, *Children at Work,* p. 32.
9 *Ibid.*, p. 34.
10 SPBC, *Society for Bettering,* vol. 2 (1800), Appendix 4, p. 271.

Notes on chapter 4: Bleaching and printing

1 *Report of the Children's Employment Commission* (1842), *Appendix* I. p. 6.
2 *Ibid.*, 11, p. 25.
3 *Ibid.*, p. 30.
4 *Ibid.*, p. 27.
5 *Ibid.*, G, 15.
6 *Ibid.*, G, 6.
7 *Ibid.*, G, p. 1.
8 *Ibid.*, G, i p. 12.

Notes on chapter 5: Silk

1 Katrina Honeyman, *Child Workers in England, 1780–1820* (Aldershot: Ashgate, 2007), p. 257.
2 Eileen Wallace, *Children of the Labouring Poor, The Working Lives of Children in Nineteenth-Century Hertfordshire* (Hatfield: Hertfordshire Publications, 2010), p. 77.
3 Peter Kirby, *Child Labour in Britain 1750–1870* (Basingstoke: Palgrave, 2003), p. 104.
4 Wallace, *op. cit.* p. 76.
5 *Ibid.* p. 77.
6 Anthony Calladine & Jean Fricker, *East Cheshire Textile Mills* (London: Royal Commission on Historical Monuments, 1993), p. 19.

Notes on chapter 6: Wool and worsted

1 Arthur Young, *A Six Weeks Tour through the Southern Counties of England and Wales* (London: Strahan and Nicholl, 1769), p. 68.
2 *Ibid.* p. 131.
3 Daniel Defoe, *A Tour through the Whole Island of Great Britain*, vol. 2 (Letchworth: Dent and Sons, repr. 1962), p. 195.
4 SPBC, *The Reports of the Society for Bettering the Conditions and Increasing the Comforts of the Poor*, vol. 1 (1802), pp. 31–3.
5 *Ibid.* p. 153.
6 *Royal Commission of Inquiry into the Condition of the Hand-Loom Weavers in England and Wales, Gloucestershire*, 1841–2, p. 409.
7 *Ibid.*, p. 424.
8 *Ibid.*, p. 424.
9 William Dodd, *The Factory System Illustrated in a Series of Letters to the Right Hon. Lord Ashley* (London: Frank Cass, 1842, repr. 1968), p. 53.
10 *Ibid.*, p. 53.

Notes on chapter 7: Coal mines

1 Quoted in Jennifer Tann, *Children at Work*, p. 42.
2 *Ibid.*, p. 46.
3 *Ibid.*, p. 46.

Notes on chapter 8: Tin, copper, lead

1 A. K. Hamilton Jenkin, *The Cornish Miner* (1927, repr. Newton Abbot: David & Charles, 1972), p. 24.
2 *Ibid.*, p. 105.
3 *Ibid.*, p. 223.
4 *Ibid.*, p. 223.
5 *Ibid.*, p. 224.
6 *Ibid.*, p. 224.
7 Quoted in Lynne Mayers, *A Dangerous Place to Work! Women & Children of the Devon & Cornwall Mining Industries 1300–1970* (Blaize Bailey Books, 2008), p. 22.
8 *Ibid.*, p. 237.
9 Children's Employment Commission, *Report by James Mitchell on the Employment of Children in the Lead Mines ... in Durham, Northumberland and Cumbria* (1842), p. 3.
10 *Ibid.*, p. 20.
11 C. J. Hunt, *The Lead Miners of the Northern Pennines in the eighteenth and nineteenth centuries* (Manchester: Manchester University Press, 1970), p. 45.
12 'Four pence a day', https://www.youtube.com/watch?v=d3A-8FB6Kpm, accessed 8 December 2017.
13 Winstanley, *op. cit.*, p. 56.
14 *Ibid.*, pp. 22–3.

Notes on chapter 9: Pottery and bricks

1 *Children in the Potteries Part 1* (a reprint of the *Commission on Employment of Children and Young Persons*, written 1841, published 1843) (Staffordshire CC, 1973), p. 13.
2 *Ibid.*, p. 13.
3 *Ibid.*, p. 46.
4 Charles Shaw, *When I was a Child* (1903, repr. Caliban Books, 1977), p.55.
5 *Ibid.*, p. 84.
6 *Ibid.*, p. 2.
7 *Ibid.*, p. 13.
8 *Ibid.*, p. 54.

9 *Ibid.*, p. 28.
10 *Ibid.*, p. 15.
11 *Ibid.*, p. 46.
12 *Ibid.*, p. 47.
13 George Smith, *The Cry of the Children From the Brickyards of England and how the Cry has been heard, with Observations upon the carrying out of the Act* (London: Haughton and Co., 1879; repr. Kessinger, 2015), p.31.
14 *Ibid.*, p. 31.
15 *Ibid.*, p. 33.
16 *Ibid.*, p. 75.
17 *Ibid.*, p. 145.
18 *Ibid.*, p. 146.

Notes on chapter 10: Black Country trades

1 Peter T. Marsh, 'Elihu Burritt (1810–1879) Peace Campaigner and American Consul', in *Oxford Dictionary of National Biography* (Oxford: Oxford University Press, 2012).
2 Samuel Sidney, Rides on Railways (London: Philimore, 1973).
3 *Ibid.*
4 R. H. Horne, reports for the *Royal Commission of Inquiry into Children's Employment* (London: William Strange, 1842), Q1, Q2.
5 *Ibid.*, Q3.
6 *Ibid.*
7 *Ibid.*, Q8.
8 *Ibid.*, Q8–9.
9 *Ibid.*, Q10.
10 *Ibid.*, Q11.
11 *Ibid.*, Q11.
12 *Ibid.*, Q12.
13 *Ibid.*, Q22.
14 *Ibid.*, Q39.
15 *Ibid.*, Q46.
16 *Ibid.*, Q31.
17 *Ibid.*, Q30.
18 *Ibid.*, Q40.
19 *Ibid.*, Q59.
20 *Ibid.*, Q59.
21 *Ibid.*, Q62.
22 *Ibid.*, Q64.
23 *Ibid.*, Q47.

24 *Ibid.*, Q73.
25 *Ibid.*, Q74.
26 *Ibid.*, Q75.
27 *Ibid.*, Q75.
28 *Ibid.*, Q82.
29 *Ibid.*, Q84.
30 *Ibid.*, Q84.
31 *Ibid.*, Q88.

Notes on chapter 11: Outwork

1 SPBC, *The Reports of The Society for Bettering the Condition and Increasing the Comforts of the Poor*, vol. 2 (London: W. Bulmer and Co., 1802), p. 116.
2 *Ibid.*, vol 4, p. 49.
3 *Ibid.*, pp. 188–92.
4 *Ibid.*, p. 203.
5 *Ibid.*, pp. 76–89.
6 Eileen Wallace, *Children of the Labouring Poor, The working lives of children in nineteenth-century Hertfordshire* (Hatfield: University of Hertfordshire Press, 2010), p. 60.
7 *Ibid.*, p. 57.
8 Duncan Bythell, *The Sweated Trades, Outwork in Nineteenth Century Britain* (London: Batsford Academic, 1978), p. 83.
9 *Ibid.*, p. 83.
10 Pamela Horn, *The Victorian Country Child* (Kineton: Roundwood Press, 1974), p. 101.
11 Duncan Bythell, *op. cit.*, p. 101.
12 Pamela Horn, *op. cit.*, p. 109.
13 *Ibid.*, p. 111.

Notes on chapter 12: Children of the streets

1 Henry Mayhew, *London Labour and the London Poor*, vol. 1 (1851, repr. New York: Dover Publications, 1968), p. vi.
2 Quoted in Tann, *Children at Work*, p. 52.
3 Henry Mayhew, *op. cit.*, vol. 1, p. 480.
4 *Ibid.*, vol. 1, p. 480.
5 *Ibid.*, vol. 1, p. 482.
6 *Ibid.*, vol. 1, p. 483.
7 *Ibid.*, vol. 1, p. 483.
8 *Ibid.*, vol. 2, p. 155.

9 *Ibid.*, vol. 2, p. 155.
10 *Ibid.*, vol. 2, p. 155.
11 *Ibid.*, vol. 1, p. vi.
12 *Ibid.*, vol. 2, p. 498.
13 *Ibid.*, vol 2, p. 497.
14 *Ibid.*, vol. 2, pp. 499–500.
15 *Ibid.*, vol. 2, p. 506.
16 *Ibid.*, vol. 2, p. 156.
17 Robert Harborough Sherard, *The Child-Slaves of Britain* (London: Hurst and Blackett, 1905; repr. General Books, 2009), p. 11.
18 *Ibid.*, p. 32.
19 *Ibid.*, p. 45.
20 *Ibid.*, p. 41.
21 *Ibid.*, p. 66.
22 *Ibid.*, p. 11.

Notes on chapter 13: Child protection and regulation

1 K. H. Strange, *The Climbing Boys: A Study of Sweeps' Apprentices, 1773–1873* (London: Allison & Busby, 1982), p. 15.
2 B. L. Hutchins and A. Harrison, *A History of Factory Legislation* (London: P. S. King, 1903), p. 46.
3 *Ibid.*, p. 44.
4 Hugh Cunningham, *Children and Childhood in Western Society since 1500* (Harlow: Pearson, 2005), p. 142.
5 Benita Cullingford, *British Chimney Sweeps: Five Centuries of Chimney Sweeping* (Chicago: New Amsterdam Books, 2000), p. 108.
6 Strange, *op.cit.*, pp. 82–3.
7 Marjorie Cruickshank, *Children and Industry: child health and welfare in North-west textile towns during the nineteenth century* (Manchester: Manchester University Press, 1981), p. 22.
8 Chalford, Glos, Half Timers' Log Book, 1873–96, Gloucestershire Archives S235/1/1 (I am indebted to Mr J. Loosley for this reference).
9 France Lynch, Glos, Half Timers' Log Book, 1873–96, Gloucestershire Archives S235/1/1.
10 *Ibid.*
11 *Ibid.*

Notes on chapter 14: Children in twentieth and twenty-first centuries

1 Heather Montgomery, Rachel Burr, Martin Woodhead (eds), *Changing Childhoods, local and global* (New Jersey and Milton Keynes: Wiley and the Open University, 2003), p. 170.
2 *Ibid.*, p. 162.
3 *Ibid.*, p. 58.
4 Digitalliterature.eu/Erasmus/projects/concrete-news/Pages/Treinador/suffer.html, accessed 16 February 2017; *The Independent,* 20 October 2001.
5 *Ibid.*
6 Montgomery et al. *op.cit.*, p. 27.
7 http://www.gogglesciencefair.com/en, accessed 16 February 2017.
8 http://www.google.co.uksearch?=malala, accessed 16 February 2017.
9 Michael Bourdillon, Deborah Levison, William Myers, Ben White, *Rights and Wrongs of Children's Work* (New Jersey: Rutgers University Press, 2010), p. 97.
10 *The Global Crisis of Child Labor in 1 Map,* https://maplecroft.com/portfolio/new-analysis/2013/10/15/child-labour-risks-increase-china-and-russia-most-progress-shown-south-america-maplecroft-index/

Further Reading

General

Ashby, M. K., *Joseph Ashby of Tysoe 1859–1919, A Study of English Village Life* (London: Merlin Press, 1974).

Aspinall, A. and E. Anthony Smith (eds), *English Historical Documents, XI, 1783–1832* (New York: Oxford University Press, 1959).

Berg, Torsted and Peter (transl.), *R. R. Angerstein's Illustrated Travel Diary 1753–1755* (London: Science Museum, 2001).

British Parliamentary Papers:

1833 (450)XX.i, *Royal Commission on the Employment of Children in Factories.*

1842 *Children's Employment Commission, Mines,* Picks Publishing.

1843 (430)X111.307, *Children's Employment Commission.*

1843 (431)X1V.i, *Children's Employment Commission.*

1864 (3414)XX11i, *Children's Employment Commission* (1862).

1866 (3678)XX1V.i, *Children's Employment Commission* (1862).

Burnett, John, *Useful Toil: Autobiographies of Working People from the 1820s to the 1920s* (London: Allen Lane, 1994).

Chapman, Stanley D., *The Early Factory Masters* (Michigan: David & Charles, 1967).

Court, W. H. B., *The Rise of the Midland Industries 1600–1838* (Oxford: Oxford University Press, 1938).

Cunningham, Hugh, *The Children of the Poor: Representations of Childhood since the Seventeenth Century* (Cambridge, Mass.: Blackwell, 1991).

Cunningham, Hugh, *Children and Childhood in Western Society since 1500* (Harlow: Pearson, 2005).

Cunningham, Hugh, *The Invention of Childhood* (London: BBC Books, 2006).
Defoe, Daniel, *A Tour Through the Whole Island of Great Britain*, 2 vols (Letchworth: Dent and Sons, 1724–6, repr. 1962).
Dodd, George, *British Manufactures* (London: Charles Knight, 1845).
Gomersall, Meg, *Working-Class Girls in Nineteenth Century England: Life, Work and Schooling* (Basingstoke: Macmillan Press Ltd, 1997).
Gray, Robert, *The Factory Question and Industrial England, 1830–1860* (Cambridge: Cambridge University Press, 1996).
Hendrick, Harry, *Children, Childhood and English Society 1880–1990* (Cambridge: Cambridge University Press, 1997).
Hopkins, Eric, *Childhood transformed, Working Class Children in Nineteenth Century England* (Manchester: Manchester University Press, 1994).
Horn, Pamela, *Labouring Life in the Victorian Countryside* (Stroud: Alan Sutton publishing, repr. 1987).
Horn, Pamela, *The Victorian Country Child* (Stroud: Alan Sutton publishing, 1990).
Horn, Pamela, *The Victorian Town Child* (Stroud: Alan Sutton publishing, 1997).
Humphries, Jane, *Childhood and Child Labour in the British Industrial Revolution* (Cambridge: Cambridge Univeristy Press, 2010).
Kirby, Peter, *Child Labour in Britain, 1750–1870* (Basingstoke: Palgrave, 2003).
Lavalette, Michael (ed.), *A Thing of the Past? Child Labour in Britain in the Nineteenth and Twentieth Centuries* (Liverpool: Liverpool University Press, 1999).
Montgomery, Heather, Rachel Burr and Martin Woodhead (eds), *Changing Childhoods, Local and Global* (New Jersey and Milton Keynes: Wiley and the Open University, 2003).
Nardinelli, Clark, *Child Labor in the Industrial Revolution* (Indiana: Indiana University Press, 1990).
Pinchbeck, Ivy, and Margaret Hewitt, *Children in English Society, From the Eighteenth Century to the Children Act 1948* (London and Toronto: Routledge and Kegan Paul and University of Toronto Press, 1973).
Rahikainen, Marjatta, *Centuries of Child Labour* (Farnham: Ashgate, 2004).
Raybould, T. J., *The Economic Emergence of the Black Country: A Study of the Dudley Estate* (Newton Abbot: David & Charles, 1973).
Tann, Jennifer, *Children at Work* (London: Batsford, 1981).
Ure, Andrew, *A Dictionary of Arts, Manufactures and Mines* (London: Longmans, Green, 1839).
Wallace, Eileen, *Children of the Labouring Poor, The Working Lives of Children in Nineteenth Century Hertfordshire* (Hertfordshire: Hertfordshire University Press, 2010).

Winstanley, Michael (ed.), *Working Children in Nineteenth Century Lancashire* (Preston: Lancashire County Books, 1995).

Agriculture

Agricultural Student's Gazette (Cirencester: Royal Agricultural College, 1875).
Howitt, William, *The Rural Life of England*, 2 vols (London: Longman, Orme, Brown, Green & Longmans, 1838, repr. General Books, 2011).
Jeeves, Alan H. and Jonathan Crush (eds), *White Farms, Black Labor: the state and agrarian change in Southern Africa, 1910–50* (Portsmouth, NH: Heinemann; Pietermaritzburg: University of Natal Press; Oxford: James Currey, 1997).
Patrick, John, 'Agricultural Gangs', *History Today*, 36.3, 1986.
Thompson, Charles D. jr, and Melinda F. Wiggins (eds) *The Human Cost of Food, Farmworkers' Lives, Labor and Advocacy* (Austin: University of Texas Press, 2002).

Climbing boys

Strange, K. H., *The Climbing Boys, A study of sweeps' apprentices 1773–1875*, Allison & Busby, 1982 (London: Allison and Bushby, 1982).
Cullingford, Benita, *British Chimney Sweeps: Five Centuries of Chimney Sweeping* (Chicago: New Amsterdam Books, 2000).

Cotton, bleaching and printing, silk, wool and worsted

Brown, John, *A Memoir of Robert Blincoe, An Orphan Boy: sent from the Workhouse of St Pancras, London, at Seven Years of Age, to endure the Horrors of a Cotton Mill...* (Manchester: *c.* 1832, repr. Sussex: Caliban Books, 1977).
Bythell, Duncan, *The Handloom Weavers: A Study in the English Cotton Industry during the Industrial Revolution* (Cambridge: Cambridge University Press, 1969).
Chapman, Stanley D., *The Early Factory Masters* (Michigan: David & Charles, 1967).
Collier, Frances, ed. R. S. Fitton, *The Family Economy of the Working Classes in the Cotton Industry 1784–1833* (Manchester: Manchester University Press, 1965).
Cruickshank, Marjorie, *Children and Industry: child health and welfare in North-west textile towns during the nineteenth century* (Manchester: Manchester University Press, 1981).

Fitton, R. S., *The Arkwrights: Spinners of Fortune* (Manchester: Manchester University Press, 1989).
Hargreaves, John and Haigh, Hilary, *Slavery in Yorkshire: Richard Oastler and the Campaign against Child Labour in the Industrial Revolution* (Huddersfield: University of Huddersfield, 2012).
Honeyman, Katrina, *Child Workers in England 1780–1820: Parish Apprentices and the Making of the Industrial Labour Force* (Aldershot: Ashgate, 2007).
Heaton, Herbert, *The Yorkshire woollen and worsted industries from the earliest times to the Industrial Revolution* (Oxford: Clarendon Press, 1965).
Jenkins, J. Geraint, *The Welsh Woollen Industry* (Cardiff: National Museum of Wales, 1969).
Plummer, Alfred, *The Witney Blanket Industry* (London: Routledge, 1934).
Plummer, Alfred and Richard E. Early, *The Blanket Makers 1669–1969, A History of Charles Early & Marriott (Witney) Ltd* (London: Routledge and Kegan Paul, 1969).
Ponting, K. G. (ed.), *Baines Account of the Woollen Manufacture of England* (1858, repr. Newton Abbot: David and Charles, 1970).
Prest, John, *The Industrial Revolution in Coventry* (Oxford: Oxford University Press, 1960).
Rose, Mary B. (ed.), *The Lancashire Cotton Industry, A History since 1700* (Preston: Lancashire County Books, 1996).
Rose, Mary B., *The Gregs of Quarry Bank Mill: the Rise and Decline of a Family Firm* (Cambridge: Cambridge University Press, 1986).
Trollope, Frances, *The Life and Adventures of Michael Armstrong, the Factory Boy* (London: Henry Colburn, 1840).
Waller, John, *The Real Oliver Twist. Robert Blincoe: a life that illuminates an age* (London: Icon Books, 2003).

Coal mines

Children's Employment Commission, 1842: Mines, https://web.archive.org/web/20160304121259/http://www.cmhrc.co.uk/site/home/index.html.
J.C., *The Compleat Collier: or the Whole Art of Sinking, Getting and Working Coal Mines etc…in…Sunderland and New-Castle* (London: G. Conyers, 1708).

Tin, copper, lead

Hunt, C. J., *The Lead Miners of the Northern Pennines, in the eighteenth and nineteenth centuries* (Manchester: Manchester University Press, 1970).

Hamilton Jenkin, A. K., *The Cornish Miner* (1927, repr. Newton Abbot: David and Charles, 1972).

Mayers, Lynne, *A Dangerous Place to Work! Women and Children of the Devon and Cornwall Mining Industries 1300–1970* (Blaize Bailey, 2008).

Rowe, D. J., *Lead Manufacturing in Britain, A History* (London: Croom Helm, 1983).

Rowe, Iain, 'When the Kids are United...Child Labour and Collective Action in Cornwall's Mines', Undergraduate Dissertation (Plymouth: Plymouth University, 2009).

Willies, Lynn, 'Derbyshire Lead Mining in the 18th and 19th Centuries', *Mining History*, 14 (1999).

Pottery and bricks

Baker, Diane, *Potworks and the Industrial Architecture of the Staffordshire Potteries* (London: Royal Commission on Historical Monuments, 1991).

Owen, Harold, *The Staffordshire Potter* (1901, repr. Bath: Kingsmead, 1970).

Shaw, C., *When I was a Child* (1903, repr. Firle: Caliban, 1977).

Smith, George, *The Cry of the Children from the Brickyards of England and How the Cry has been Heard...* (London: Haughton 1879, repr Kessinger 2015).

Staffordshire County Council, 'Children in the Potteries', pts I & 2, *Staffordshire Study Book* (Stafford: Staffordshire County Council, 1975).

Whipp, Richard, *Patterns of Labour; Work and Social Change in the Pottery Industry* (London: Routledge, 1990).

Williams, Mary, *The Pottery that Began Middlesbrough* (Redcar: C.Bks, 1985).

Black Country trades

Ashton, T. S., *Iron & Steel in the Industrial Revolution* (Manchester: Manchester University Press, 1924).

Bythell, Duncan, *The Sweated Trades, Outwork in Nineteenth Century Britain* (London: Batsford Academic, 1978).

Outwork

Felkin, William, *History of the Machine Wrought Hosiery and Lace Manufactures* (London: Longmans, Green and Co,. 1867).

Millington J. T. and Stanley Chapman, eds, *Four Centuries of Machine Knitting: Commemorating William Lee's Invention of the Stocking Frame in 1589* (Leicester: Knitting International, 1989).

Children of the streets

Sherard, Robert Harborough, *The Child-Slaves of Britain* (London: Hurst and Blackett, 1905; repr. General Books, 2009).

Mayhew, Henry, *London Labour and the London Poor*, 4 vols (1861, repr. New York: Dover Publications, 1968).

Song, Miri, *Helping Out: Children's Labor in Ethnic Businesses* (Philadelphia: Temple University Press, 1999).

Children at work in the twentieth and twenty first centuries

Bourdillon, Michael, Deborah Levison, William Myers and Ben White, *Rights and Wrongs of Children's Work* (New Jersey: Rutgers University Press, 2010).

Fyfe, Alec, *The Worldwide Movement against Child Labour* (Washington, DC: Brookings Institution Press, 2007).

Hutchins, B. L. and A. Harrison, *A History of Factory Legislation* (London: P. S. King & Son, 1903).

Montgomery, Heather, Rachel Burr and Martin Woodhead (eds), *Changing Childhoods: local and global* (New Jersey and Milton Keynes: Wiley and the Open University, 2003).

International Labour Organisation (ILO), 'Child Labour', http://www.ilo.org/global/topics/child-labour/lang--en/index.htm/.

ILO, 'Position Paper on Child & Work', 2006, https://www.pronats.de/assets/Uploads/position-paper-on-child-and-work.pdf.

Ruck, M. D., M. Peterson-Badali and M. Freeman (eds), *Handbook of Children's Rights: Global and Multidisciplinary Perspectives* (New York: Routledge, 2017).

Silan, Edelweiss, 'Working Children – Hopes and Realities', *SGI Quarterly* (April 2000).

Singer, Audrey, 'Immigrant Workers in the US Labor Force', *Brookings Paper* (2012).

Carroll, Rory, 'Lego-Silicon Valley Entrepreneur's Building Block to Technical Innovation', *The Guardian*, 25 January 2015.

Pinheiro, Paulo Sérgio, 'United Nations Study on Violence against Children' (United Nations, Expert apt. 2003, Rept 2006).

UNICEF, *Summary of the rights under the Convention on the Rights of the Child* (1989).

Index

While an undergraduate Carl Chinn recalls a lecturer postulating that working-class women were downtrodden and brow-beaten by their men: 'I remember thinking, "They're not in my family" ...I lacked the confidence to disagree, and to tell him that I knew many working-class women who were at least the equals of their men and who could fight physically. Indeed the first fight I had seen was when I was ten. My Nan had taken me and my brother down the Villa. An away fan had pinched Our Kid's scarf and Our Nan, just four foot eleven tall, turned round and laid the chap out with one punch. A tough woman whose fore-finger had been torn off by a machine at work, Our Nan was the daughter, mother and grandmother of strong, working-class women.' Often strong physically, women of the urban poor worked from when they were toddlers until they died. They worked inside and outside the house, cooking, washing, cleaning and planning how to get by; they worked as domestics in the houses of a middle class often arrogant and condescending in their attitudes towards them; they worked in factories, shops, mills and workshops; they worked in their neighbourhoods in providing vital services for their neighbours. Often earning her own income and receiving the earnings of her children, it was the mother who was in charge of the daily battle against hunger and hardships. Such supreme dedication and true grit earned these women the central role in the family and fostered the devotion of their children, who recognised a mother's command of the household finances, her ability to maintain a family's self-sufficiency through careful housekeeping and creative cooking, and her valiant efforts to stay clean and respectable. Married daughters chose to live close to their mothers, forming extended families in settled neighbourhoods and furthering cementing strong kinship ties. Older married women who were grannies and aunts held sway over large familial networks, and from this position of importance many of them achieved status in their neighbourhoods as layers-out, unofficial midwives, wise women, custodians of the moral code and guardians of the group consciousness. The women of the urban poor worked all their lives for their families and neighbours: they deserve our respect and admiration.

176 pages, illustrated, a classic £8.95

The upper and middle classes of Victorian England were marked out by their confidence they boasted that the sun never set on their Empire; they believed they were destined to lead other nations; and they bragged that their civilisation was pre-eminent.Their self-belief was assured because they lived in a country that had become rich through industrialisation.

But amidst great prosperity there was also much poverty. Deprivation and distress were widespread and obvious. In towns and cities, grand public and civic buildings were surrounded by poor dwellings later known as 'slums'. The poor crowded into these insanitary districts; they rented badly built dwellings with inadequate facilities; they did the dirtiest, hardest and most dangerous jobs; they ate the worst food; they suffered ill health and early deaths. Poverty blighted their lives. Many observers asserted that many of the poor were thriftless and feckless.

They stated that the muckiness of the poor districts was caused by dirty people who did not wish to raise themselves out of the mire. Gradually, however, social investigators began to question these scathing generalisations, arguing that poverty was usually the result of economic conditions over which individuals and families had no control.

Poverty Amidst Prosperity focuses on the urban poor themselves, and explains their way of life from within. Using working-class autobiographies and other evidence from working-class people themselves, Carl Chinn shows how people reacted to poverty, and brings to the fore their strategies for coping with their situation. He asserts that the urban poor were not passive victims of their circumstances, but that they fought against poverty with the support of neighbours and kin, and that they formed thriving villages in a dreadful urban environment. This book provides the ideal introduction to those seeking to understand poverty from the grassroots. Its wide range of evidence, clear analysis and strong argument stress the importance of communities, and give a voice to those whom traditional history has marginalised.

176 pages, £8.95